George Macaulay Trevelyan

George Macaulay Trevelyan

A Memoir

by

his daughter

Mary Moorman

HAMISH HAMILTON: LONDON

First published in Great Britain 1980
by Hamish Hamilton Ltd
Garden House 57-59 Long Acre London WC2E 9JZ

Published in the United States of America by
Hamish Hamilton in association with
David & Charles Inc, North Pomfret, Vermont 05053, USA

British Library Cataloguing in Publication Data

Moorman, Mary
　George Macaulay Trevelyan.
　1. Trevelyan, George Macaulay
　2. Historians – England – Biography
　942' .007'2024　　DA3.T7

　ISBN 0–241–10358–4

Printed in Great Britain by
Bristol Typesetting Co. Ltd,
Barton Manor, St Philips, Bristol

Contents

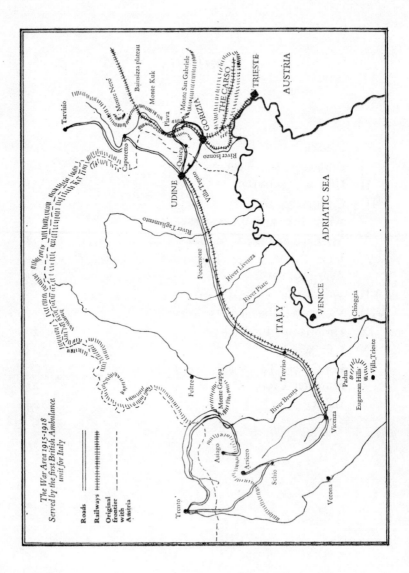

The War Area 1915-1918
Served by the first British Ambulance
unit for Italy

Roads
Railways
Original
frontier
with
Austria

AUSTRIA

TRIESTE

THE CARSO

GORIZIA

Monte San Gabriele

Plava

Quisca

River Isonzo

Monte Kuk

Bainsizza plateau

Monte Nerò

Tarvisio

Caporetto

Monte Kat

UDINE

Villa Trento

River Tagliamento

Pordenone

River Livenza

River Piave

ADRIATIC SEA

ITALY

VENICE

Chioggia

Treviso

River Brenta

Padua
or
Euganean Hills

Villa Trieste

Vicenza

Feltre

Monte Grappa

Asiago

Arsiero

Schio

Verona

Trento

Illustrations

Acknowledgements

Plate 1a is reproduced by kind permission of the National Trust, Wallington.
Plate 6 is reproduced by kind permission of the British Academy and appeared in the *Proceedings* of the Academy for the year 1963.
Plates 7a and 7b are reproduced by kind permission of Julian Trevelyan.

Preface

George Macaulay Trevelyan sternly forbade anyone to write his biography. His *Autobiography*, published in 1949, was, he said, quite enough. But the world in which he grew up has passed away so completely that it is as much a part of 'history' as the age of Napoleon or of the Stuarts. My decision to disobey his injunction is grounded on this consideration and also on a prolonged study of his personal letters from boyhood onwards—to his parents, his brothers and to myself—which convinced me that they are of both historical and literary importance, covering as they do two world wars, and therefore that some use should be made of them by someone who remembers him and shared closely his interests and tastes. A long and detailed biography would obviously be out of place, and I eventually determined to write a memoir of him based on such letters (there are several hundred) as I had access to. I am deeply indebted to his niece and my cousin, Pauline Dower, for allowing me to use the letters to his brother Charles (the late Sir Charles Philips Trevelyan) which are now in the University Library of Newcastle upon Tyne, to whose Assistant Librarian, Mr Alistair Elliot, I am very grateful for his constant courtesy and help.

I am also greatly obliged to Jocelin Young for the loan of letters from George Trevelyan to Geoffrey Winthrop Young who was his most intimate friend; to Lord Kennet for allowing me to quote from the letters to his father Hilton Young, the first Lord Kennet; to Dr Robson of Trinity for helping me with matters dealing with that College, and to Lord Noel-Baker for letting me use his memories of my father during the First World War. Miss Roma Bonar has allowed me to make use of her records of the 'Unit' in those strenuous days.

I

I thank the *Contemporary Review* for letting me make use of some articles I wrote for it in 1974, the BBC for their help in tracing broadcast talks; the *Spectator* for the use of an article called 'June 10th, 1940'; the Trustees of the Passfield Papers for permission to quote from a letter from George Trevelyan to Sidney Webb, and Margaret Cropper for allowing me to quote 'For George Trevelyan's Eightieth Birthday'. The London Library has shown me again its ready help. Finally to my old friend Helen Dutton I offer warmest thanks for typing the greater part of the book with such accuracy and care.

Durham 1978.

I

Welcombe and Wallington

George Macaulay Trevelyan was the best-known and the best-loved historian of England in the first half of the twentieth century. He could scarcely have belonged to a family more capable of nourishing him for such a calling, or been provided with homes and home-landscapes more rich in the beauty, the associations, the romance and the delight fitted to inspire it.

He was the youngest of the three sons of Macaulay's nephew, George Otto Trevelyan, who at the time of George's birth was Liberal MP for the 'Border Boroughs', Hawick, Selkirk and Galashiels. George was born on 16 February 1876 in the heart of rural Warwickshire, within two miles of Stratford-on-Avon, at Welcombe, the home of his mother's father, Robert Needham Philips, a wealthy Lancashire merchant and Liberal MP for Bury. Thus both George's father and his maternal grandfather were Liberal MPs. His mother, Caroline, was the eldest of three sisters and had no brothers. Mr Philips had inherited Welcombe, and with it an estate of some 4,000 acres, from his much older brother Mark, who died in 1873. Mark Philips, who built Welcombe, was one of the first two MPs for the newly-enfranchised Manchester after the Reform Bill of 1832.

The Philips family mansion was The Park, near Prestwich, in the countryside just north of Manchester. It had been built in about 1800 by Robert Philips, the father of Mark and Robert Needham, in an Italianate classical style; its wide lawns were well protected by shrubberies and the natural woodland of Prestwich Clough. A fine conservatory, a lily-pond and a great bank of azaleas and other flowering trees adorned it on the northern side. After Robert Needham Philips's death in 1891 it continued for more than fifty years to be the home of his unmarried daughter,

3

Anna Maria Philips, who became a most beloved and honoured friend to all that busy Lancashire district.

Robert Needham inherited The Park from his father. After he had inherited the Welcombe estate as well (from Mark), he used to address his Warwickshire tenants in terms of bluff north-country equality without a trace of feudal superiority. Mark had desired to entertain his friends in style, and so in the 1860s he had built Welcombe (now an hotel belonging to British Rail), in a fold of the rising ground just east of Stratford, first pulling down a curious house in the 'gothic' style of the late eighteenth century.[1] The new house was Elizabethan in design, as befitted the neighbourhood of Stratford, and was built of substantial red brick with mullioned plate-glass windows, Dutch gables and a forest of tall chimneys. Mark Philips had many of the details copied from the prints of Elizabethan houses in Nash's *Mansions of England in the Olden Time*. Two relics of the earlier property remained—a pond in the garden with an island in the middle, and on the top of a hill on the south side a small eight-sided and crenellated 'temple', commanding a most lovely view of the Avon valley as far as Bredon Hill and the Cotswolds. Inside it was a bust of Shakespeare. Both the pond and the temple have now unfortunately ceased to exist.

The house was built on a slope, facing south-east towards the Avon and Edge Hill. The church-tower of Hampton Lucy on the edge of Charlecote Park, where the young Shakespeare is said to have poached deer, could be seen from the windows, so that little George as he grew older could feel himself a sharer in the legendary adventures of Shakespeare's boyhood as well as in the tremendous realities of England's Civil War, of which in later years he was to write with eloquence and power. There were other houses in the neighbourhood whose stories made them part of the fabric of English history for ever—such as Compton Wynyates, the lovely mansion under Edge Hill, the home of the royalist Earl of Northampton, killed at Hopton Heath.

The Trevelyans spent many holidays with 'Pater' Philips at Welcombe. George cherished some delightful and greedy memories of dinners there cooked by Mrs Whale, 'a very great person',

[1] Before he built Welcombe, Mark Philips lived in the neighbouring village of Snitterfield, in an old house which he enlarged and which still stands. There are memorials to him and R. N. Philips in Snitterfield Church. A tall obelisk on the hill behind Welcombe also commemorates them.

who served a dish of whipped cream with every sweet. The jam roly-poly, which his grandfather called 'Dolly-in-a-blanket', accompanied by the cream, he never forgot. Welcombe passed to Robert Needham's eldest daughter, George's mother Caroline, Lady Trevelyan, on the death of her father in 1891.

Although his parents always spent the winter months at Welcombe, George had another and more wonderful home. Far to the north, where the wild moorlands of central Northumberland slope gradually down towards the farmlands and woods of the Wansbeck valley, stood a much older mansion, Wallington, soon to come by inheritance to George's father. It was built in the reign of William III, of the lovely grey-gold local stone, by Sir William Blackett of Newcastle, who bought the estates of the bankrupt baronet Sir John Fenwick, soon afterwards executed for his part in Jacobite plots. Its cellars were the basement of a fourteenth-century castle, the scene of the grim ballad, *Fair Mary of Wallington*. The wealth and enterprise of the mid-eighteenth-century owner, Sir Walter Calverley Blackett, gave it the shelter of beech woods to the north, east and west—they had just come to their glorious maturity in George's boyhood—and a kitchen garden east of the house with a long terrace walk adorned with lifelike lead figures. Inside, the house was made beautiful with the best Italian plasterwork, with portraits of the owner and of his niece, Susan Trevelyan, by Sir Joshua Reynolds and Gainsborough, and with embroidered panels and screens wrought by his mother, a daughter of the first builder.

A century later it received further adornment. By this time it had come by inheritance into the hands of the Trevelyans, a family of remote Cornish origin, long settled in Somerset, who, for three generations, had managed two estates three hundred miles apart, Wallington in Northumberland and Nettlecombe in Somerset.[2] Sir Walter Calverley Trevelyan, the third Trevelyan baronet of Wallington, married Pauline Jermyn, an artist and friend of artists, especially of that group who called themselves the Pre-Raphaelite Brotherhood.[3] Some of these came on long visits to Wallington and they left outstanding memorials behind them. Wallington had been built as a hollow square, with the

[2] Sir George Trevelyan, Bart., of Nettlecombe, married in 1733 Julia, only sister of Sir Walter Calverley Blackett. Sir Walter had no children and so Wallington passed to his sister's family.
[3] See *A Pre-Raphaelite Circle*, by Raleigh Trevelyan, 1978.

corridor windows looking into a gloomy court. The Trevelyans made the court into a magnificent great hall, carried up to the full height of the house, and lit by round skylights. The upper corridors now looked into this hall over Venetian balustrades, designed by Ruskin, between arches in whose spandrels William Bell Scott painted the whole story of 'Chevy Chase'—the great encounter between Percy and Douglas—from the gay morning hunt to the evening tragedy when the slain were borne from the field on biers of 'birch and hazel grey'.

> Over the Ottercaps Hills they came,
> And down by Rodeley Crag:
> At Greenleighton they lighted down,
> Stirring many a stag,

says the ballad of the Douglas and his men. This was all familiar country to the dwellers at Wallington, Rodeley (now Rothley) being only three miles away. Below, at floor level, the spaces between the pillars on the north and south sides of the Hall were filled by Scott with eight large canvases illustrating Northumbrian history. from the Romans building the Wall to the sturdy Tynesiders showing the world 'what can be done with iron and steel'. The hall thus became a remarkable 'pleasure-dome', colourful and gay and, as the Victorians loved to have things, instructive as well.

Sir Walter had no children, and he left Wallington in 1879 to his cousin, Sir Charles Edward Trevelyan, the Indian administrator and, as Head of the Treasury, reformer of the Civil Service. Sir Charles died in 1886, and thus his son, George's father, Sir George Otto Trevelyan, became the owner of the wonderful place. George Otto's mother had been Hannah More Macaulay, the sister of Thomas Babington Macaulay, the historian, poet and Edinburgh Reviewer, so that by that inheritance, and even more by the close association between the uncle and nephew in George Otto's boyhood and youth, the passion for history and literature entered the family. George Otto remembered as a little boy his uncle telling him that he was 'collecting materials' for writing his *History of England,* and how he thought he meant he was laying in vast stores of paper, pens and ink. George Otto's devotion to Macaulay was unbounded, and he celebrated it by writing a glowing and very popular biography, which was published in 1876, the year of the young George's birth.

As Macaulay's nephew and disciple, Sir George had been drawn to both politics and literature from his early years and longed to enter Parliament. His father eagerly promoted his wishes and in 1865 he was returned, as a Liberal, for the small, hitherto Tory borough of Tynemouth. In the House of Commons he learnt radical politics at the feet of John Bright, then at the height of his great battle for more democratic Parliamentary Reform. But from the 'Reform Bill' election of 1867 onwards, George Otto was for eighteen years member for the 'Border Boroughs' in Scotland, a constituency he greatly loved, with its memories of Sir Walter Scott and the Border ballads, Montrose's wars, and the Jacobite rebellions. It was a peaceful farming community now, and as it was only forty miles from Wallington—where the young member often stayed with his cousin Sir Walter Trevelyan and which his father inherited in 1879—it was almost home ground.

He had first met his wife, Caroline Philips, the eldest of Robert Needham's three daughters, when he was assisting her father in Lancashire at the election of 1865. The story of their engagement and its difficulties was told by their son George in after years in *Sir George Otto Trevelyan, A Memoir* (1932). They were married in September 1869, and set up house in London at 40 Ennismore Gardens. Their eldest son Charles Philips Trevelyan was born in 1870—the year of the first postcards. His mother's delightful sister, Anna Maria Philips, who became the beloved and ever-welcome aunt and great-aunt of the next two generations of Trevelyans, sent him a postcard—'Glad to hear of your safe arrival'. Charles, the Liberal politician and eventually Labour Minister of Education, became, although six years older, the confidant and spiritual companion of George, from George's Harrow days onwards, even more than the middle brother, Robert Calverley, the classical scholar and poet. But there was a strong comradeship between all three. Their favourite indoor pastime at Wallington was an extraordinarily elaborate war-game, played with armies of small lead soldiers representing many nationalities. It is thus described by Robert:

A large space of bare floor boards in my bedroom and afterwards in the museum (a spacious attic in which many early natural history collections were housed), was kept for military purposes, and there many hours would be spent in arranging

7

the English and French armies (each nearly 2,000 men strong), and manipulating their conflicts. The battles were Napoleonic in character . . . As there were three of us, two would command the armies of Wellington or Napoleon, while the third could act the part of impartial Destiny, receiving from time to time secret instructions from the opposing generals . . . and deciding how many and which soldiers should be killed and wounded, and knocking them over one by one with his finger . . . A battle would often take weeks of hard work and had sometimes to be left unfinished at the end of the holidays. But it was a wonderful game, and we continued playing it right down to our undergraduate days and even for some years later.[4]

George had been earlier taught the elements of this game by his father, when, as a little boy of six, too young as yet to go to school, he was living with his parents in the Chief Secretary's Lodge in the Phoenix Park, Dublin. Sir George had been appointed Chief Secretary in succession to the murdered Lord Frederick Cavendish in 1882. When he could spare an hour from the cares of office, he sometimes came up to George's nursery, and together they played with the little lead soldiers. Sir George wrote to his sister, Mrs Dugdale:

I have just contrived to set George playing at a 'City' instead of those eternal battles . . . His games are one continual revolution, in which the roughs, the police, the students of the University, the tradesmen and the 'gents' form different combinations, and always end by killing the whole of each other. He has no idea of the quiet flow of civil life.[5]

Perhaps George while at the Lodge unconsciously sensed the disturbed state of nearby Dublin, where even the Royal Irish Constabulary had mutinied. Certainly the Phoenix Park presented

[4] From *Windfalls*, by R. C. Trevelyan (1944). Quoted by permission of Julian Trevelyan. A letter from George to Charles written during his undergraduate days describes a walk over the moors to Elsdon and beyond in August 1895, in which he traces 'the scene of the fighting of August 14 and 15, 1817.' This imaginary battle, fought during an imaginary invasion of England after Napoleon and not Wellington had won Waterloo, was apparently being fought out with the lead soldiers at Wallington. The description is as serious as though he were exploring a real battlefield.
[5] G. M. Trevelyan, *Sir George Trevelyan. A Memoir*, p. 114.

almost daily before his delighted young eyes the spectacle of frequent reviews and 'sham fights' by real soldiers, 'who fired at each other and advanced and retreated with entrancing jangle and rattle across the open Phoenix'. And so, as he wrote long afterwards, 'unconsciously a sense of the drama of English and Irish history was purveyed' to him, with his father acting as 'commentator and bard'.[6] His own special detective, Mr Dunne, with whom he walked and played, was a real friend, though it was startling to discover, as George did one day, that 'he took the opposite side about the Battle of the Boyne'.

The seven-year-old George himself thus describes a review in the Phoenix in a letter to his mother: 'We came in time for the last review and there wer the R.H.A. the Stoc[7] the Rifles the Devons the Gaurds the Huzzars and Larnsers and we saw His Highness behind the Stock and the Huzzars charged at a full gallop swaining (swinging?) their swords as they went.' And he added a note about his own nursery field of battle: 'I have got the Knights to play with till the soldiers are unpacked.' 'The Knights' were some very splendid, large lead figures of mediaeval knights in full tournament armour who survived to be played with by George's own children.

Perhaps out of this rather exciting episode in his young life arose, a year or two later, George's first book, ' "Brave Men of Britain", by G. M. Trevelyan', written in an exercise book, and describing, in quite competent military language, various battles in the Napoleonic wars—the defence of Acre, the battle of Alexandria and finally Maida. He cannot have been more than eight when he wrote it and there are not many spelling mistakes, though the hand-writing leaves much to be desired.

When she married, Caroline Philips brought with her to her new home, as her personal maid, a Lancashire woman, Mary Prestwich. Very soon she changed her position in the household to become nurse to the boys, and she remained with the family as housekeeper until her death in 1923. Tall, and with a tender dignity, she was the embodiment of all that was best in the Victorian ideal of service to a family. She was a devout churchwoman of the Evangelical school, but her strongly-held creed did not in the least disturb her relationship with her more free-thinking employers. Lady Trevelyan had been brought up a Unitarian

[6] G. M. Trevelyan, *An Autobiography and Other Essays*, 1939.
[7] A stock was a gun-carriage.

and Sir George had not continued in the evangelical religion of his parents. Booa, as the boys called her always, imparted something of her gospel of salvation to George, who quietly deduced from it that his parents must be destined to a very uncomfortable existence in the life to come. This, however, did not seriously worry him, until at the age of thirteen, he privately rejected the doctrine of eternal punishment, and likewise that of the literal truth of every word of the Bible, and thenceforward contented himself with a non-theistic 'religion', strongly influenced of course by Christian ethics. The Bible as a whole, particularly the the Psalms, the historical books of the Old Testament and the Book of Job became the groundwork of his love both of poetry and history.[8] To Booa he always remained devoted, regarding her with a reverence he felt for no one else. He often said that she showed him what the Christian religion could mean and do in a personality. She in her turn loved all her three boys, but perhaps her strongest bond was with George.

She cared for the comfort of the body as well as the welfare of the soul. Her especial genius was in the making of 'parkin'—a Lancashire gingerbread made with oatmeal and black treacle. Many a tin of this delectable and yet sustaining cake was despatched by her to her boys in their school-days, at college and right on into their married lives, when it became equally acceptable to their children.

George's early education from the age of four was undertaken by Miss Martin, a lady whom he certainly liked (in spite of the rather puzzling fact that she was a Tory), and who equipped him well in such studies as were necessary before he began, at the age of nine, the days of exile, required then of almost all little boys of the upper and upper middle classes, to a private or preparatory school. The school was Wixenford, on the northern borders of Hampshire; both his brothers had been there before him, and Bobbie was still there when George arrived at the beginning of the summer term of 1885. He was a not unwilling pupil: the only subject that bothered him was mathematics, and even that was not disastrous, for at the end of his

---

[8] In his *Autobiography*, p. 23, he tells how, just before going to Harrow, he became aware that Darwin's teaching had destroyed the historicity of the early chapters of Genesis. This discovery caused him great agony of mind. 'It was the only violent religious crisis I ever passed through,' he says. He does not seem to have spoken of it to anyone.

second year he was given as a prize a richly bound copy of Percy's *Reliques of Ancient Poetry* (which contained *Chevy Chase* and other ballads of his own Northumberland), inscribed as being awarded for 'Industry' in 'Greek, History, French and Mathematics'.

Probably before he went to Wixenford at all, he had begun to make the acquaintance of Macaulay's *History*. It was at Wallington, and his mother read aloud to him the famous 'Third Chapter'—the description of the state of England in 1685. Many years afterwards, in the summer of 1917, when he was serving in Italy as Commandant of the First British Ambulance Unit there, I was having the same experience at twelve years old, and at Wallington. From the Italian front he wrote to me on 16 July: 'I shall be curious to hear how you like Macauley's 3rd Chapter. I remember so well Mama reading it to me for the first time when I was a little boy; it was in the library, and I used to lie with my head on the woolly rug against the fire and look up at the marble head carved on the mantelpiece, while she read. I was littler than you then. And Mama and the carved face are still there.'

At about this time he began writing ballad-poetry on his own account. There was a poem about a Cavalier being chased by some Roundheads, which he remembered many years afterwards, again in Italy in the middle of the First World War. 'I remember,' he said, in a letter to me of October 1915, 'the place where I repeated it to some boys at my school out on a Sunday walk. It went like this:

> Down Banbury Road a gay Cavalier
> Is galloping hard with the Saints in his rear.
> He's galloping hard and he's galloping fast,
> O can he reach Oxford and safety at last?
>
> For there his own true love is waiting in vain—
> She'll ne'er see his coat and fine feathers again!
> And never again his faith will he swear,
> For dabbled in blood is his long golden hair!

Thus this convinced Parliamentarian early expressed his sympathy with the Royalists—as he continued to do in later years when writing in earnest the history of those tragic times.

'Dear Papa, The history—Bowen—examination is on the 22nd of this month. Are you going to make me stop history, after the examination? I heard you say something about it last holidays. It seems to me you might let me go on till next year; because *then* there would be more than a year for me to do extra classics in before I went up to Harrow. If I do go on with history I shall know a good lot next Easter but I don't much mind, and I dare say it would be a very good thing to stop.'

This somewhat anxious letter was written from Wixenford in February 1887 by George, then not quite eleven years old. The 'history—Bowen—examination' consisted of three papers set by Edward Bowen, that most unusual of schoolmasters, into whose house, The Grove, at Harrow, George would go in the autumn of 1889.[9] Paternal authority took the hint, so gracefully given, and history was not stopped. In the following year, 1888, he got 97½ out of 100 in the examination and gained the prize—recording, however, in his diary: 'I don't think nearly so much of it now as I did before'. In fact he was almost bored with history by this time, writing to his mother before the examination that he did not want to go in for the prize a third time, as it was for 'English History which I am now quite sick of'. It would be better to enter Harrow on a more mixed diet of ancient history and extra classics.

At this time his father, after resigning as Secretary for Scotland in Gladstone's second administration, in March 1886, because he disagreed in part with Gladstone's Home Rule Bill, had lost his seat for the 'Border Boroughs' at the General Election in July. It was the election in which the Liberal Party was split over Home Rule, the 'Liberal Unionists' being obliged to side with the Conservatives. But Sir George could not stand this alliance, and soon reverted to Gladstone, Home Rule notwithstanding. In the following year, 1887, he was elected for the Bridgeton division of Glasgow. While the Home Rule Bill was being fought over in Parliament in the summer of 1886, young George wrote to his father: 'I cannot hardly realise what a historical crisis we are now in; I will be frightfully excited on Monday and Tuesday, and on Wednesday we shall *get the news.*' The news was the defeat of the Bill.

9 Bowen had been a friend and contemporary of George Otto Trevelyan's at Cambridge.

Wixenford was a conservative school; 'all the masters are bigotted Conservatives,' wrote George. 'Everybody is dead against Mr Gladstone and I have to hold my own against masters and boys alike'. George upheld the Liberal cause, as he said, 'with vigour' and more vigorously as the years went on. 'I see the *Daily News* about five minutes every day,' he wrote in 1888, 'but that is not very much, so please keep me well informed, so that I shall not exhaust my arguments.' His mother sent him press cuttings of his father's speeches and he pasted them into an album. He discovered that a boy called Tomkinson was a strong liberal: 'his father stood unsuccessfully more than once. He is in my bedroom and knows a good deal about it, so we have it all our own way and have great discussions.' When the Irish members were imprisoned he wrote: 'What a comfort and consolation it must be to those poor members in their cells, to know that they are suffering in a good cause, and that so many sympathise with them. One of the psalms today was *Why boastest thou thyself thou tyrant.* I am sure such tyranny cannot last for long, for no tyranny ever did last, much less in a civilised Christian country like Great Britain. Oh! how delightful it was to see that cartoon in *Punch* of *The Times* doing penance,[10] I laughed over it tremendously; how ashamed, and crushed, and humbled they must feel, if indeed they are sensible to shame! I am thinking,' he also wrote at this time, 'of a design for the "Intended cupola to Fox"; in the centre there should be a bust of Fox, and underneath should be written in letters of gold "Intrepid Fox". On the wall should be a representation of Parnell triumphing over *The Times* with the sword of justice, while the spirits of forgery and pergery fly in confusion, and Sir C. Russell[11] crowns him with a crown of shamrocks.'

His schoolfellows perhaps found the Liberal evangelist somewhat overwhelming. 'Had political discussion with Finlay[12] on the way down to school in the train,' wrote George in his diary.

---

[10] *The Times* had published articles containing what afterwards proved to be forged letters from Parnell condoning the murder of Lord Frederick Cavendish in 1882. The exposure of the fraud by a Special Commission took place in March 1889.
[11] Sir Charles Russell, later Lord Russell of Killowen, was counsel for Parnell in the enquiry by the Special Commission.
[12] William Finlay became a High Court Judge. He and George met again later at Trinity. His father, R. Bannatyne Finlay, was for a short time Lord Chancellor.

'He seems much more persuadable than last term. I suppose he is shocked at the way in which they are governing Ireland.' This was in January 1888. The longsuffering Finlay was 'made' to read 'Papa's speech'. And shortly afterwards George wrote: 'I have given Finlay a serious lecture, which seems to have done him good: he seems ashamed of the government and its infamous proceedings.' George continued in his diary for February: 'I am triumphant over the Tories now, after the election.[13] We had a great political discussion in the bedroom; came off victorious as usual.' Finlay, only a week after this, showed his sympathies by presenting George with 'a picture of the Liberal cabinet of 1878 in a frame; I shall have it hung in my bedroom; it contains Joe and Hartington! Ah!' (Joe Chamberlain had by now joined the Liberal Unionists, and Lord Hartington also.) George also recorded that he was 'making a heroic poem on the Edinburgh election—not yet completed.'

But it was not all politics. He read Macaulay's *History* during the rather wet summer of 1888: 'It was very wet on Thursday and Friday, but it was not at all dull, for I was reading Macaulay; I have read a great deal now and am very interested in it; . . . how I do wish he had lived long enough to write Anne's reign but perhaps if there was more of it, the last part would not be so good, but it was impossible for Macaulay to write anything uninteresting.' Forty years later he was himself writing 'Anne's reign'.

He went on to read his father's life of Macaulay. 'I wonder I never read it before,' he said. Finlay, 'a great admirer of Macaulay', had not yet read it, but Sir George conceived the idea of giving it him as a consolation for just missing Bowen's history prize. George took this proposal with extreme seriousness. 'I have been thinking,' he wrote to his father 'of your proposal about Finlay; . . . he is a great admirer of Macaulay, and I am making him admire him still more; he has read the Essays and *History*, but *not the Life*, which he certainly would be interested in; but his father has given him an old edition of the essays and *History*, which is a very good one and which is one of the earliest publications. There is no hurry, so think about it and please either write again about it, or tell Mamma what to say; I know he would value such a present and would be very pleased with

[13] The by-election at Edinburgh, where a Liberal was returned.

14

it; and I think it would console him for not getting the prize.'

George's lighter reading seems to have consisted of the ordinary run of boys' stories, some Waverley novels and Charles Lever's *Tom Burke of Ours* which, he says 'I liked more than I can say.' Then during the Easter holidays of 1888 at Welcombe he said, 'I have got a fit of Shakespeare now,' and read *Henry V*, *King John* and *Henry IV*, Part I.

His history master lent him a book called *Makers of Florence*, which interested him greatly. To his father he wrote: 'It is in a lovely binding, and with beautiful illustrations. It is all about the painters and sculptors and cathedral architects of Florence . . . I should like you to tell me about anything you saw in it—about the Palazzo and so on.' And in January 1888 he told his mother, 'I have invested myself in the works of Keats, for 6/-.'

Though liking Wixenford, and sending his parents careful accounts of cricket-matches and of his progress in lessons, he naturally kept an eager eye on the holidays. 'How nice it will be,' he wrote to his father at the end of one summer term, 'to travel up with you on Friday, for I generally travel alone; still, journeys to Wallington are always nice, and I would a thousand times rather travel alone *to* Wallington, than travel *from* it with all of us.' It was indeed a paradisal journey's end.

In the spring of 1889, just before George went on to Harrow, John Bright died. 'What a brave man he was,' wrote Bright's future biographer, 'to uphold the peace policy almost alone, in the face of nearly all England; but now it is evident to all how right he was . . . How different Mr Bright is from the liar whom all men will crowd . . .' (sentence unfinished.) The 'liar' must be Disraeli, who however had died seven years before, for in the same letter George remarked: 'Tomorrow is first April fool's day, and the second April fool's day falls on April 19'—Primrose Day, sacred among conservatives to Disraeli's memory.

Wixenford was in the parish of Eversley where Charles Kingsley had been Rector, and the school attended church there. George at this time was something of a sermon-taster. The sermons were apt to be long, for once, during the holidays, he records a 'short sermon which is rather a treat after the long ones at school! They were both long and, according to his diary, sometimes 'bad'. But on one Sunday the Rector 'preached one of

Kingsley's sermons instead of his own'. This was a great success. 'I don't think I have ever heard a better one before.' George was, by his Trevelyan descent, a 'Low Church' Anglican; his mother was a Manchester Unitarian and his father confessed no personal ecclesiastical allegiance. He had therefore an inherited dislike of elaborate ritual and a Puritan attitude to religious practices. When in London, he and Booa usually attended All Saints', Ennismore Gardens, which was then 'evangelical', and was close to the Trevelyans' home. But he records in his diary in April 1888: 'Yes! It's *Low* Sunday, but I went to an uncommonly *High* Church with which I was disgusted.'

At Welcombe he sometimes accompanied Grandpapa Philips to church at the old Guild Chapel in Stratford. Mr Philips, although a Unitarian, always attended Morning Prayer when there was no Unitarian Chapel at hand. When it came to the Apostles' Creed he used to proclaim the first article of belief—'I believe in God the Father Almighty, Maker of Heaven and Earth'—but went no further. One Sunday at Welcombe George wrote to his mother in London: 'I have now returned from church: we have had a splendid sermon, and a very broad-minded one; he is the Stopford Brooke of Stratford.' (Stopford Brooke was a well-known ex-Anglican clergyman of liberal views with a large following in London.) 'It's getting near luncheon,' he went on, 'so I must not write too long a letter, as I want to get done before luncheon. (My pen,' he added, 'has vastly improved since I was at church; perhaps it's been to church, and heard a good sermon too).'

During these years at Wixenford George discovered that he was short-sighted—he could no longer tell the time on the clock in his bedroom while lying in bed. So ever after that his blue eyes with their dark lashes were partially obscured by glasses.. Fortunately his eyes gave him no further trouble until the last half-dozen years of his life, when his sight gradually failed.

The headmaster of Wixenford was E. P. Arnold, a very tall, bearded man, formidable and not always just, but he clearly allowed his boys a good deal of individual freedom, in reading and going for walks, though his temper was uncertain and could cause both amusement and distress. 'Mr A. in fearful bate,' wrote George in his diary. 'It is a great pity he has such a bad temper as it makes everybody so miserable.' During the summer

16

term of 1888, George conceived the idea of recording Mr Arnold's moods in a barometric manner. He drew a line in his diary down the margin of each page (it was a Lett's Rough Diary with a week in an opening, and interleaved blotting paper, 1s. 6d.), and made his records in the spaces thus provided:

Monday: Sunny with occasional storms.
Tuesday: Set fair.
Wednesday: Changeable in morning: set fair in afternoon.
Thursday: Changeable, but very sunny on the whole.
Friday: Bright.
Saturday: Rising rapidly.
Sunday: Stormy.

Arnold was an exceptionally brilliant teacher of Latin Prose. He coached George and one other boy in it rigidly for a year, an experience which, George said many years later, had 'a beneficial effect on my English prose composition in after life.' But no amount of proficiency in Latin Prose could turn George's heart away from history to classics. Mr Wilkins's history lessons, as decribed by George, sound to modern ears uninspiring, but George seems to have taken them without complaint. 'I have to be working harder this term than I ever did before,' he wrote in his second year, 'and have not much time for reading but I am quite happy . . . Mr Wilkins, who takes us, tells us at the end of every lesson what we will have to prepare before the next lesson, it is always an old chapter that we have done before, then we prepare that in our own time whenever we like but we all do always prepare it and that's what takes up such a lot of my time; then Mr Wilkins asks us questions on it first thing next lesson, and then we read on some new aloud and he then gives us a few minutes to look it over and then asks us questions on that; so we thus look over the old and do the new.'

Wixenford lay in the heathy, sandy part of Hampshire not far from Sandhurst. Before he left, George was allowed to enjoy the pleasure of walking and rambling in this countryside. 'I am now a walker-alone,"[14] he wrote to his mother in his last term there.'I

14 An old Wixenfordian told me that being a 'walker-alone' did not mean solitary walking, but walking with a chosen companion without the supervision of a master.

saw a fox running over the heather.' Besides his prizes, he carried away from Wixenford a noble present—Matthew Arnold's poems in the new three-volume edition, inscribed: 'G. M. Trevelyan from W. Finlay, 6th July, 1889.'

II

Harrow, 1889–1893

George entered Harrow in September 1889 and was there until the end of the summer term, 1893.[1] Charles was now at Trinity College, Cambridge. George joined his brother Robert at The Grove, the house of which Edward Bowen was the brilliant and unusual master.

Harrow at this time was a school of about 600 boys, not quite as aristocratic as Eton, much favoured not only by country gentlemen but by the wealthy Victorian business class. Many of the boys when they left became almost at once directors of their family businesses. The school also had an Army tradition; my father used to say that the boys in the 'Army Class' were almost the only ones who did much work as they had to pass the entrance examination to Sandhurst. About a third went on to Oxford or Cambridge, where some did brilliantly enough, but intellectual interests among the boys were uncommon. Most were conservatives in politics; they cared for little but games or athletics, and, outside school, for racing. George wrote to his parents early in his second year: 'I am taking in the *Speaker* and find it a very good investment (only 5/- a term) as not only do I never see any other liberal paper, but I never get anything readable of any sort or kind that is connected with current events except the occasional cuttings and speeches you send me.' In another letter he wrote: 'I keep the flame of my liberalism bright in this dark corner by taking in *Daily News* and *Speaker*, and conversing with them for want of more articulate liberal friends.'

But his housemaster, Edward Bowen, was a Liberal, and once

[1] George Otto Trevelyan had been at Harrow from 1851–7, and was Head of the School and Gregory Prizeman. His three cousins, Walter Calverley, Arthur and Spencer Trevelyan had all been there, but his father Charles Edward, went to Haileybury in preparation for an Indian career.

(before he was housemaster) had stood for Parliament at the general election of 1880. Bowen's liberalism was an affair of the heart and conscience, rather than of the platform and the committee room. He hated the fashionable militarism of the day, preached 'Defence', not 'Defiance', and discouraged his boys from joining the rifle corps; he longed for an England, as he said in one of his speeches when a candidate, 'with equal laws, with class privileges abolished, with perfected education, with peace secured, with pauperism diminished, with Church quarrels set at rest'.[2] A housemaster with such political views—although it is clear he never pressed them on his boys in any proselytising way and although on the burning question of Home Rule he was a Liberal Unionist not a Home Ruler—must have been acceptable to the two Trevelyan brothers, especially to the fiery George, while his qualities of heart and mind endeared him to them for ever.

Bowen had made many reforms when he became housemaster; a single room for each boy; a cooked breakfast instead of bread-and-scrape. But, as he was himself totally without habits of self-indulgence, he was perhaps too anxious to discourage any kind of luxury among the boys. 'Fires in our rooms,' wrote George Trevelyan after Bowen's death, 'were not allowed until late in the year; too late we often thought, and we used to march to his study to petition him for warmth, wrapped up in rugs and other Siberian disguises, to his intense delight and amusement.' And once, says George, 'finding that I was in the habit of taking two hot baths a week, he remarked with pathetic displeasure, "O boy, that's like the later Romans, boy!"'

Although himself a Classic, Bowen's vision and energy had created the 'Modern Side' at Harrow in the late 1860s, with 'lots of history, modern languages, science, etc.', some Latin but no Greek. He delighted in all sorts of unusual and quaint methods of teaching and of exacting penalties. He believed that everyone should possess at least one piece of absolutely useless information, for instance, to know the names of the seven mouths of the Nile. If people failed this test, he would say, 'O boy, do a map of the Nile in five paints, boy!' 'Once,' says George Trevelyan, 'for ignorance of the whereabouts of the Cocytus (which I think I placed in Asia Minor) I did "a map of hell in five paints, boy!"'

[2] *Edward Bowen, A Memoir,* by the Rev. W. E. Bowen, 1902. A tribute to Bowen by G. M. Trevelyan, appeared in *The Harrovian* after Bowen's death in 1901. It was reprinted in *Edward Bowen, A Memoir.*

Bowen's most famous legacy to Harrow was the Harrow Songs —written by himself and set to music by John Farmer, the organist. Vigorous and sometimes moving, often rollickingly funny, some of them ranged beyond the immediate world of school or house, taking the singers in imagination back to Elizabethan days when John Lyon founded the school, or to the youth of Harrovians who had become famous men, like Byron and Peel.

> Byron lay, lazily lay,
> Hid from grammar and games away,
> Dreaming poetry all alone
> Up on the top of Peachey Stone.

(The Peachey Stone was a flat tombstone in Harrow churchyard.) The last verse touched something greater:

> Byron lay, solemnly lay,
> Dying for freedom far away:
> Peel stood up on the famous floor,
> Ruled the people and fed the poor.

Bowen's liberalism included religious attitudes which were at that time considered unorthodox. This meant in fact that he placed more emphasis on ethical than on doctrinal or mystical Christianity. Confirmation was then an event whose desirability few boys questioned. The preparation for it was undertaken partly by the housemasters, partly by the Head, who was in those days always in Holy Orders. Edward Bowen left all doctrinal teaching to the Head—who at that time was the physically gigantic J. E. C. Welldon, subsequently Bishop of Calcutta and ultimately Dean of Durham—and himself concentrated on moral issues and on some questions of general practical interest. He set a paper of questions to the candidates, among which were the following:

What is the Church, and why have one?

Will you say what you really think about swearing?

Re-write according to modern ideas any parts of the Catechism which seem antiquated.

'Confession': what do Protestants generally think about it, and why?

What he most cared about, and what he constantly impressed on his boys, was the duty of unselfish conduct and thoughtfulness for others. 'Never take a corner seat in a railway carriage when other people are in the compartment.' 'If you are going by train to play cricket, always travel third class; there may be men in the eleven to whom the difference in cost is of importance.'

In his Scripture lessons to the older boys on Sunday afternoons, Bowen taught the elements of Biblical criticism and analysis, showing for instance, the relation of the prophets to the Book of Kings, and how the Book of Genesis has more than one source. An old pupil afterwards wrote: 'It was all new to me, and took my breath away at first. But the lesson, once learnt, remained for ever, and to have begun scientific Biblical study under a teacher always fearless and always reverent has been to me an experience for which I cannot be too thankful!' To George Trevelyan, brought up in the undogmatic faith of his parents, but well-read in the Bible, with the strong Christian doctrines of Booa not very long ago rejected, and with his own scholar's mind, this approach to the Bible must have been welcome. He was not confirmed. Afterwards he used to tell how, on the day of the Confirmation, when the other boys had departed to the Chapel, he was sitting alone in the schoolroom, reading. Bowen put his head round the door. 'Going to be confirmed, boy?' 'No, Sir.' 'That's right, boy.'

George's political faith and fervour, his devotion to history and literature, and his lack of distinction in games (although he enjoyed 'footer'),[3] separated him from most of the other boys at Harrow almost from the beginning. As at Wixenford, he was an active campaigner for the Liberal cause, and during the General Election of 1892, he wrote to Charles: 'While you are fighting the good fight in the far North [Charles was assisting his father at Glasgow], I am forced to be contented with tearing down red placards in the House yard, and putting up blue ones, destined to a still more speedy doom.' 'In a school of 600 boys,' he wrote, ' I have found just two people capable of talking sensibly about politics.' Oddly enough, neither of these two was a Liberal. Philip Wilbraham Baker, afterwards a distinguished ecclesiastical lawyer, and a Conservative, of an old Cheshire family, was one[4]: the other was Roderick Geikie, son of Sir Archibald Geikie the geologist, a brilliant boy, Head of the School and Gregory Prizeman, who took a first in the Cambridge History Tripos in 1896

[3] In November 1892 he received his house 'fez', for which he said he had been 'working hard' all the term.
[4] He afterwards changed his name to Baker Wilbraham.

(the same year as George) and after a few years in the Civil service, became a fellow of King's.[5]

'I try hard,' wrote George, 'to convert these two friends, with amusement if not success for a result. I might just as well talk Greek politics to the rest of my acquaintance.'

Nevertheless, Harrow did much for George, and before he left he could say he was glad to have been there. 'I have after all learnt much—very much here,' he wrote to his brother Charles in his last term, 'more perhaps than if I had been at a school more to my taste. To have had one good deep draught of the waters of bitterness is well, provided the period of 'taking the water' has not lasted long enough to produce misanthropy.' The greatest boon was the almost unlimited opportunity it gave him, at any rate in his last year, for reading history and literature, and so discovering his true vocation. He always maintained that the masters in his time at Harrow were excellent—it was the prevailing character among the boys that bored and disgusted him. Bowen apart, the master to whom he owed most was George Townsend Warner, an old Harrovian who was an early 'Senior' in the History Tripos at Cambridge, and came to Harrow in time to ground George in Stubbs's *Constitutional History* and Cunningham's *Growth of English Industry and Commerce* before he left for Cambridge. 'He [Warner] is a great admirer and friend of Cunningham and enjoys expounding him,' wrote George. In the autumn of 1892 George won the Bourchier History Prize, which not only enabled him to buy '£9 worth of books', but 'proves I can do history, and that it is not a mere fad of mine wanting to do it at Cambridge.' In the spring of 1893 (his last year) he wrote:

I am putting my back into Stubbs in a way I was never able to do with Classics. I do three hours a week private lessons with Warner, who is very kind and spends his time quite willingly over me, and do about five hours a week in my own time at reading and analysing Stubbs. . . . I have abandoned the Greek iambic writing on Saturday evenings in favour of an historical essay for Warner. I proposed it and Welldon consented at once.

[5] His real love was for the stage, but his father would not allow him to make it his profession. Shortly after he went back to King's, his fiancée perished through her dress catching fire, and Geikie, deprived both of private happiness and of following his chosen calling, took his own life.

There were two other masters to whom he felt gratitude: one for his political and social ideas, the other for valuable help in learning to write good English. The first was W. E. Hine, the art master, whom George got to know simply as a friend, having himself no artistic talent. The Hines were Liberals and George went with relief to their house to talk without frustration about political affairs. Mr Hine's sister, Maud King, wrote poetry; Mr King was a dedicated radical who gave all his possessions to the poor and lived a simple life, 'working for the people' and studying social problems. 'It is very nice for me,' wrote George, 'in this sad world, to have the entrée on Sundays of at least one literary and liberal family, like the Hines.'

The other master was Robert Gilson, a classic and former Fellow of Trinity, afterwards headmaster of King Edward's School, Birmingham. Years afterwards George said that 'Mr Gilson was the man who "taught my mind" most at Harrow, and drilled me into less loose ways of thinking by personal intercourse and conversational criticism in connection with English essays. This happened to be particularly helpful to me and I am always very grateful to him for it; he was at once encouraging and critical.'

By the spring of 1893 George was longing for change and for a less uncongenial atmosphere. 'I live in literature and politics and history,' he wrote, 'and am *burning* for the world (be it only Cambridge).' He was inclined to look down on his school-fellows from somewhat Olympian heights. 'You aristocratic curs,' he said to himself, 'wait till I grow up and I'll show you whether I and my brain and pen which you despise so, or you and your horses and cricket-bats will win in the battle of life.'

In May of that year he wrote to his mother: 'I find that the only way to get along here is to be engaged vigorously all day at some literary, political or historical study. I am throwing myself into history with a vigour that I never knew myself capable of before; I study the *Daily Chronicle* daily, and the *Weekly Sun* weekly.' He spent every half holiday in the Vaughan Library (of which he was given a key) and rapidly developed from his reading a kind of social and political faith which had, as he admitted, the fervour of a religion. The newly-founded *Westminster Gazette* was added to the other liberal papers. In literature *Don*

Juan was 'great fun reading, but thank God poets are no longer allowed to waste their powers on such beastliness.' Shelley was a much greater revelation. *Alastor* and *The Witch of Atlas* made him feel 'bowed down and humbled'. It was poetry of an 'absolutely different and higher order' from anything else—leaving Arnold and Tennyson far behind. He read Tennyson, however, with great interest, and in his last spring term (1893) sent in a prize essay on 'Tennyson's poetry as literature', which was printed 'in its entirety'. It contained an attack on what he called 'Tennyson's anti-democratic principles' which conflicted with the growing radicalism of his own ideals.

It was at this time also that he began to be seriously interested in Carlyle. He read *Frederick the Great* and commented: 'I find reading F. the Great strengthens one's character and is a moral lesson; for it is the story of a man who loved pleasure much (chiefly fluting and the Muses) but who was called to give them up for duty, and at duty's call gave them up for ever, and turned himself sadly but resolutely into a hard-hearted iron warrior for the rest of his life.' In later years he was more critical of Carlyle's *Frederick* and thought the sage had allowed his passion for the 'hero' to lead him too far in admiration of the military dictator—a process which had begun in *Cromwell*.

Two books of a political character excited him greatly at this time—Wolfe Tone's *Memoirs* and A. M. Sullivan's *New Ireland*. For Ireland and Home Rule for Ireland dominated his thoughts unceasingly while Gladstone's second Home Rule Bill was making its way through the Commons. Of *New Ireland* he said: 'I never read a book with such devouring eagerness since I finished Renan's *Vie de Jésus*'—a modernist classic of which there was a copy at Welcombe. Chapters of *New Ireland* were read aloud to Wilbraham Baker—'without any comment, but I saw it set him thinking.' All this Irish enthusiasm was enhanced by the fact that Charles now had a post as one of the private secretaries to the Viceroy, Lord Crewe, and actually lived in the Viceregal Lodge in Phoenix Park. During the Easter holiday of 1893 George visited his brother in Dublin, going with Charles into the south-west, where the men of "forty-eight" had hidden, and this visit gave a vivid background to his reading of *New Ireland*. Henceforward he added the greeting 'God save Ireland' to almost all his letters to his brother, shortened often to 'G.S.I.'

B

Charles, whose impatient radicalism smarted under the restraints of life in the Viceregal Lodge, even under a Liberal Viceroy, complained that he was 'a dumb animal here' and that the Lodge was 'swarming with Tories'. 'Talk to and enjoy the company of your Nationalist friends,' was George's advice, 'and do not make yourself miserable because the upper classes are idiots, which everybody knows they have been for 250 years, ever since the generation of Presbyterian country gentlemen who beat Charles I . . . The raison d'être of the Liberal party is that the upper classes are not fit to govern, and therefore the democracy shall. Leave them to the pursuits of their own choosing and enjoy the friendship of a larger number of clever people than it is the lot of most enthusiasts of two and twenty to know.'

He was deeply concerned for the cultural growth of 'the Democracy'. 'I like T. P. O'Connor's paper [the *Weekly Sun*] better every week,' he wrote. 'He is trying to spread love of literature, of art, of the refined, the beautiful, the noble, among the People . . . We who love literature second only to the People, ought we not to rejoice over every attempt to unite these two things we love best?[6] If the poet and the painter were to yield altogether to the statesman in the Democracy of the future, it would drive me frantic, though not tory.' And then he added: 'We want another Tennyson, for after all he *was*, with all his Toryism, a poet whom the people read, partly understood, and greatly reverenced.'

Though loving 'the people', he was not satisfied by the attitude of many of the Liberal rank-and-file towards Home Rule for Ireland. There was, he said, a 'lurking suspicion in the minds of half-educated conscientious voters, that if Home Rule is passed the Catholics will bully the Protestants in some vague sort of way.' George believed this suspicion was 'spread among all the low church people', particularly the women, and that if women had votes 'the religious side of the question would ruin us'. English people had unfortunately been brought up to look on the Irish priesthood as 'bigoted, bullying tyrants of their flocks'. Charles's diary—letters of his travels in Ireland—had shown that this was not so, but that 'they [the priests] are playing the part of the village curés in France at the beginning of the French

[6] *The Sun* often printed poems by great English poets, thus introducing poetry to 'the working class'.

revolution and have, I suppose, been doing so for the last hundred years.'

Besides his excitement over Ireland, George tried also to look further afield into a distant and little-known world—that of the expanding overseas Empire. During his last autumn term (1892) the great explorer Stanley visited Harrow to give a lecture. He was now an old man, and had married a friend of the Trevelyans, Dolly Tennant, whose drawings of bare-foot children at play in the streets of London were greatly treasured by George in after years. A few years earlier she had won George's heart when one day she had entered the dining-room at the Chief Secretary's Lodge and found George 'crying over a long division sum'. This 'angel in human shape' soon had him comforted and showed him how to master the sum.[7] Now at Harrow he was asked to breakfast with the Head to meet them both. Stanley 'told very artificial stories in a theatrical manner—evidently having told them in exactly the same words scores of times . . . Dolly kept waking him up and putting him on, like a master putting on a boy.' But after breakfast he did talk to George about what he really cared about—the future of Africa. 'His idea was that inner Africa is a land of promise, healthy to Europeans, fertile, with vast sheep and cattle runs on high ground. If once people could get there, he says, they would be sure of success. But they all die on the way, for the road thither is low and unhealthy . . . But if you had a railway it would become a second Australia.' George was impressed, for at this time the future of Uganda was being discussed and argued over. He was not much concerned with what we should now consider the most important aspect of the matter—relations with the native inhabitants. 'I never cared a bit about Missionaries, savages or any such sentimentalism,' he said, 'but am really anxious not to throw away the *possibility* of a new and wealthy colony, if it was to be had for the taking.'[8]

His correspondence with Charles was a great relief. They wrote to each other every day. 'This, and the liberal papers,' said George, 'are, as it were, my religion, my daily prayer and bible-reading that keeps me brave and fresh for tasks less to my taste.'

[7] *Autobiography*, p. 7.
[8] The use of the word 'savages' for all the inhabitants of Central Africa by someone who held radical political views seems to our generation somewhat uncouth. But little was yet known of Africans or of the only Europeans who were as yet much concerned for their welfare—the missionaries.

Sometimes his letters contained poems such as this exhortation which he called a ' "creed" written for myself':

> To strike for right 'gainst wrong
> Or by the poet's song,
> Or by the subtle pen
> Stirring the hearts of men,
> Or by the statesman's tongue
> Moving the world along.
> And give these to some cause,
> Not seeking vain applause,
> But striving to do well
> As far as in thee dwell
> Unto thy fellow men;
> And God shall see it then
> And give thee wealth and fame
> And a remembered name . . .

Better than this however is a much more personal poem addressed to his brother in which the love of Ireland and of Charles are combined:

> Yon moon in the midnight heaven
> that sends its ray through my room,
> And lights the neighbouring housetop
> Till it shines again through the gloom,
>
> Yon moon in the midnight heaven
> With its turban of silvery cloud
> That floats away in the blackness,
> And leaves it alone and proud ...
>
> Yon moon shines high o'er Dublin
> Where the noble city lies,
> And it beats on Grattan's statue
> Where he preacheth to the skies.
>
> It beats on the silent Phoenix,
> On its every open glade;
> But the stags are hid from the moonlight
> Beneath the hawthorn shade.

It beats on the white Viceregal
Where beats a heart right true;
O moon, creep in at his window
And say I love Ireland too.

Before the end of the summer term of 1893 he had received
£24 in prize money, having won both the prize poem and prize
essay, the former with a poem about America called *Columbus*,
the latter with his Tennyson essay. With the money he bought
Ruskin's *Modern Painters* and *The Stones of Venice*, 'with all
the proper pictures', which helped to prepare him for Italy and
for mountain scenery, and the beautiful edition of Rogers's poems
with Turner's illustrations, 'which,' he said, 'I like better than
any other pictures of that class in the world.' These books remained a pleasure to him to the end of his life. For lighter reading
there were *Gulliver's Travels* and above all Pepys's diary. 'I read
a little of Pepys every evening just as a better Christian reads his
chapter of the Bible.'

Early in the summer of 1893, George being then seventeen,
his father wrote telling him he might choose between leaving at
the end of the term and going straight to Cambridge, or staying
on another full year at Harrow. There could be for George but
one answer. He felt he was making for himself 'an artificial atmosphere in an uncongenial clime'; that though he could willingly
have stayed another 'footer term' for the sake of the House,
another year 'in this blessed place' would be unendurable. 'I
want,' he said, 'to get into a world where the bat and the betting
book are not mightier than the pen and the poem. Here I am
"gagged" . . . If I "strive to speak", as Carlyle says, there is
none to listen but one dear friend [probably Philip Wilbraham
Baker] who only half understands . . . Another term would sicken
me; another year drive me into open revolt.' But once the question of his leaving was settled in the way most agreeable to him,
he could enjoy his last term with 'unmixed happiness'. He told
his brother on 1 June that there was 'no prospect of my having
anything to grumble about for the rest of my time here. The only
thing I can compare myself to is what Ireland will be like after
Home Rule.' But he would not allow himself to relax either his
work or his political and literary enthusiasms. 'I must return,' he
wrote, 'to the abstracting and delightful occupation of making an

29

abstract of dear old Stubbs.' He was anxious about the Home Rule Bill, anxious too not to compromise his own 'democratic' ideals, on which his conversations with Mr King were shedding a fierce light. King thought Cambridge was 'a place for the suppression of democratic enthusiasms.' George understood and in part agreed. 'If I can ever do anything for democracy,' he wrote to Charles, 'it must be through literature. Now the point is that literary people are not, most of them, democratic, and it is more than probable that unless I keep the fire ever kindled within me, I shall soon forget my "motif" and become a mere "littérateur"!'

A small event this summer strengthened his determination. The Duke of York (afterwards King George V) was about to marry Princess Mary, and the school was invited to contribute to a suitable wedding present. 'My money can be better spent,' wrote George. 'It is right that this aristocratic school should give her something, but I am the democratic exception in this high class establishment.' And he observed: 'It is curious that whereas everybody I speak to, Master or boy, says in so many words "What beastly rot the wedding present is", no one except myself has had the ordinary moral courage, or rather common sense, not to give anything. They have got a clock that everyone admits looks as if it cost £10, but which on account of its inside really costs £120 . . . Now why in the name of all that is useful, couldn't they have got a £10 clock, and given £110 in the name of the Duke of York to some charitable institution? O horrible abuse of utilitarianism! Everybody admits it would have been more sensible, but nobody does it!'

He was reading at this time Jessop's *Coming of the Friars*, which introduced him to the story of St Francis of Assisi. To his mind St Francis was 'a true *democrat* in the highest sense of the word—the first person since Christ was crucified who really understood that true Christianity was the gospel of the poor . . . It was Christ who said "It is *hard* for a rich man to enter into the Kingdom of God." It was Christ who made Lazarus go to heaven *simply because he was poor*, and the rich man go to hell, *simply because he was rich*, or rather because his riches led him unavoidably into sin.' If only Christianity could be freed from its trappings and preached as its founder preached it, 'it might yet do a great work among the People.' Such was his interpretation of the Christian religion—'the only thing I can believe in for certain—the progress of the human race. What people usually

30

call religion, the immortality of the soul and so on, I am in absolute darkness and doubt about these things. But in Democracy I have got hold of something definite.' '*It*,' he said, 'has disgusted me with Harrow.'

'I love the People,' wrote the young radical, 'and our party [i.e. the Liberal Party] more than many speech-days, more than many reading-prizes, almost more than my own poetry.' For George at this time was thinking of himself as a future poet. 'I am writing a song of the people,' he wrote on 6 July, 'or rather a tirade against the aristocracy, which I intend to be my biggest work as yet . . . I am putting my life-blood into it.' It was called 'The Prophet', and was indeed a tirade, more against the 'idle rich' than the 'aristocracy' proper.

> Listen all ye great and wealthy, thus saith God who gives
>   you all,
> Think ye that your wealth and riches are to spend at rout
>   and ball
> At the race-course and the theatre—those the riches that I
>   gave—
> Till soaked with wine and fat with pleasure, ye sink to an
>   unhonoured grave? . . . . .
> Look around you! See your duty! where the poor and
>   hungry crawl.
> Leaves that only blossomed sadly, withering to an early fall.
> Stunted children of the cities!—ne'er a glimpse beyond
>   their street—
> In their very dreams they see not rippling brooks and
>   meadows sweet—
> And the toilers of the country, packed in houses fit for
>   swine,
> —Thou hast built their hovels, landlord, and the curse of
>   them is thine!

In the last verse, the prophet, having failed to make any impression on the rich,

>   turned from them with a sigh.
> Suddenly his face was brightened, and his eyes no more
>   were dim,
> —Lo! a sea of eager faces, grimed with labour, watching
>   him!

He was also, he said 'writing ballads for the *Harrovian*', but nothing of a ballad nature appears in the *Harrovian* of this summer. His best poems, however, were not for the *Harrovian*. 'I wouldn't publish any of my spoony or literary poems there, for it is not the place for them,' and 'the *Harrovian* is non-political,' he wrote, meaning that poems of a radical tone would not be acceptable. By 'spoony' he probably means poems addressed to his brother in terms of strong affection, like 'Yon moon', for he was not yet interested in the other sex. He admired the poems of Ebenezer Elliott, 'the Corn-Law Rhymer', and hoped 'to write so some day, and put the poetry, the spirit, the soul of liberalism before the literary world.'

Some lines called 'Ancient History', which he wrote out of 'malice prepense' in the fly-leaf of a volume of De Quincey in the Vaughan Library, seem to give a foretaste of what 'history' was coming to mean to him.

> Like to some traveller mid the Alpine snows
> Who sees his comrade on the summit high
> Of some tall mountain; but the mists enclose
> The vale between in gloom and mystery;
> So we, who gaze across the ages black
> With mist of ignorance and crime, may still
> See the stern Roman triumph and the track
> Winding up the Sacred Hill,
> And Athens making holiday to see
> 'Ajax' just acted. From our higher place
> We smile to see how history was begun
> By simple men of old. Yet haply we
> Shall so be seen by some great future race
> From heights yet higher, nearer to the Sun.

'The book is safe not to be taken out again for another twenty years,' he commented, 'by which time I shall be either somebody or nobody. If I am nobody, they will tear it out and put it in the waste paper basket; if (as is highly improbable) I am a great poet, it will strike the librarian that it is in my early style, he will put it under a glass case in the Vaughan, and it will be a joy for ever.' A search through the volumes of De Quincey in the Vaughan in 1973, however, failed to reveal the poem, though no fly-leaf appeared to have been removed. The imagery of these lines fits well with an earlier letter to his mother in which he longs to be

32

'an eagle or some bird of passage, with a man's intellect, and to live for a year or so about 600 or 700 BC and what an interesting book you could write about it afterwards.'

As his last speech-day approached he was in good spirits, for he was to take an active part in it. He was given leave to read his prize essay on Tennyson, which contained some good 'democratic' criticism, and evidently leant a good deal on Matthew Arnold. 'I shouldn't think the frequenters of speech-day would hear anything of the nature of the *Forts of Folly*[9] read to them out of a Harrow essay, for some time to come,' he wrote afterwards to his father. 'I was determined to read it . . . I had made up my mind that if Welldon would not give me leave, I would *take* leave and read it all the same. Luckily he struck [i.e. gave way] at the last moment.' He also made another contribution. 'I am going to spout *Naseby*,' he announced; 'that's fun isn't it?' This was Macaulay's ballad about the final overthrow of the Royalists in the Civil War, as told by one of the fiercest of Cromwell's soldiers. But it contained at the end two somewhat controversial verses—the first attacking the Crown and bishops:—

Down, down, for ever down with the mitre and the crown—

and the next the Church of Rome:—

And She of the seven hills shall mourn her children's ills.

Authority suggested to George that he should omit the verse about the bishops, but George very sensibly said he would either read both verses, or omit both. 'They struck at once', and he omitted both.

In one matter this last speech-day was a disappointment. A scene from Sheridan's *The Rivals* was prepared, in which George was to play Sir Lucius O'Trigger, armed with a pair of pistols that had belonged to Byron. This, of course, delighted him, and great was his wrath when the Head announced that the programme would have to be cut down, so as to enable guests to get to London in time for the royal Garden Party at Marlborough House. The chief casualty was this scene. But what comforted and flattered him 'more than 50 Sir Lucius O'Triggers' was a notice of his prize essay on Tennyson in the *Daily News*. 'It

[9] See Matthew Arnold's poem 'The Last Word'

33

touched me in the tenderest part of my pride, and made speech-day a success to me.'

Before leaving Harrow for ever, he had 'long conversations' with three of the masters—Warner, Lascelles (the Science master) and Arthur Hort (son of the New Testament scholar)— 'on the faults of Harrow and how to remedy them . . . I made them promise to try to do something next term.' More boldly, he tackled the Head. 'I went to say goodbye to Welldon. He began a very pompous "farewell speech", which I bore with patience till he said, "I only hope, Trevelyan, that you will enjoy Cambridge as much, or nearly as much as you have done Harrow." At this I could put up with it no longer, and put a stop to his nonsense by telling him a bit of my mind, in as polite a way to Harrow as was decent. This at once brought him down from his pomposity and he talked very sensibly and sympathetically about it for a quarter of an hour.'

The three friends, Geikie, Baker and George Trevelyan, all distinguished themselves at this speech-day—Geikie carrying off the Greek Epigram prize, Baker the Greek Iambics, and George the Prize Poem and English Essay. Geikie and George went on to Cambridge, leaving Baker to be Head of the School, before proceeding to Oxford.

'I left Harrow in roaring spirits,' wrote George to his brother, 'on the best of terms with everybody, but I fear shocking some people by my brutal callousness at parting with "the Hill".' Wilbraham Baker was invited to visit Wallington in August. 'He shooteth but doth *not* swagger about it and hath only just got a double-barrel gun last year, yet withal he ought to have *one* mild day at the grouse, which are to him an unknown bird.'

He was 'eating up literature like a glutton', he said, but promised himself that it should not prevent him from doing his 'history work' at Cambridge. But he had deliberately sacrificed his classics to literature in his last term, 'with the magnificent result of reading *Past and Present*, *The Revolt of Islam* and coming out *28th* (!), all that last fortnight of the term. But this I did with my eyes open, because I knew that I should gain more by reading the aforesaid books and coming out 28th, than by *not* reading them and coming out 10th.'

The holidays began in London at the Trevelyans' home, which was now No. 8 Grosvenor Crescent. It was Gladstone's last ministry. 'The G.O.M. came to dinner on Friday,' wrote George.

34

'We were a small but select party—the Gladstones, the Edward Greys, the Playfairs, *Lord Acton,* and Papa and Mama and self. Gladstone I at once recognised as the greatest talker I have ever seen. Papa says he is the only worthy successor of Macaulay. I sat between Lady Grey and Lord Playfair who was roaring fun . . . After dinner the Old Man, who was in roaring spirits, insisted on the two "Lords" [Acton and Playfair, both of whom he had created] going out of the dining room first, as belonging to the "upper house". He talked at dinner as if he would enjoy the battle with the upper house[10] more than anyone. His joviality and bubbling wit, was what struck me most. Papa says he is far less "formidable" and far more jovial than he was.'

The underlining in this letter of 'Lord Acton' shows that George was already aware of Acton's importance as a historian and as a Catholic who was also a Liberal. Two years later they were to meet again in Cambridge when Gladstone's successor, the Tory Lord Salisbury, made Acton Regius Professor of Modern History.

A letter to Charles from Wallington that August shows him somewhat anxious about his own ideals and a little envious of Charles's more straightforward political career. 'For my part I must be one of those who sit and watch the battle fought out by such as you. My ideal, my enthusiasm, is the wedding of the modern democratic spirit, the spirit of "duty" in its highest form, to modern literature. The worst of it is that whereas you will live to see your ideal realised, realised by the efforts of the thousands fighting on your side, there are very few who care about my ideal, fewer still who have the talent required to accomplish it. I am afraid I have not any great literary talent, but what I have I intend to cultivate, in the hope that I have some part, however small, to perform in the scheme of creation, by means of that talent.' He then explained, with great shrewdness, his fears about the next stage in his life. 'The worst of it is that intellectual people are as much pleasure-seekers as the rest of the non-working aristocracy, except that their pleasure is intellectual instead of consisting of betting and drinking. Everyone who is intellectual is not serious, and everyone who is serious is not intellectual.

[10] Over his second Home Rule Bill, Parliament sat continuously throughout August and September, a most unusual proceeding. The Bill passed the Commons on 1 September and was rejected by the Lords on 8 September by the enormous majority of 398.

The reason Baker was my friend was that he was serious. He recognised that he had a duty to perform in this world, and intends to perform it. His duty was chiefly being a good landlord on a great estate. He had already begun to do good work among the people in his neighbourhood. He was fond of them . . . He hated the non-working pleasure-seeking aristocracy of Harrow only a little less than I did. In a word he was serious, but he was not intellectual. As far as I can make out the Cambridge people are intellectual but not serious.'

Not long after leaving Harrow George learnt that there was another kind of school in the world of a much more 'democratic' kind. 'This morning,' he wrote to Charles from Welcombe, 'I went into Stratford to see the grammar school . . . I was very much impressed. It seems to be a sort of demi-public-school, where a certain number of upper-class people's sons are educated with a certain number of middle and lower class boarders. £66 a year for boarders, who are the gentlemen's sons *mostly*. Result—a tone superior I consider to Eton, and certainly to H—! The rich man's son must work or the haberdasher's son licks him in form. *There is no jealousy between the two classes* . . . They secure on the average as many scholarships as Harrow. I was shown over the forms working in the dear old Elizabethan rooms; a very well-mannered *gentlemanly* set of boys all, especially the elder ones I was introduced to—boys of the primitive savage age at Harrow. In a small inner room I found the scholar of the year, and consequent hero of the school, working by himself—a tradesman's son called Garlick—as gentlemanly a fellow as you find in any drawing-room. They act a Greek play every year. There is an education for £66 *better than that of Harrow*. A good argument for the reduction of the leisured classes' incomes . . . Tell Mama I seriously think it would have been better if we had gone there than to Harrow. Certainly I should have had companions I should have liked better'.

George had visited but one of the hundreds of small grammar schools which had been the priceless legacy of the Tudor age to the nation. Harrow itself had begun as such but had sold itself to the monied class.

Yet Harrow, much as he disapproved of its ethos and was bored by its inhabitants, was still a concern to George at least for a term or two after he had left it. He went to an old boys' match at The Grove, and was distressed to find the house 'in a miser-

36

able condition,' and Bowen suffering accordingly. Bowen's unhappiness gave him some reproaches of conscience at having 'run away' so soon, when he was only seventeen. 'This is the one chord in my heart that Harrow strikes,' he wrote, 'this feeling for Bowen.' But he saw Baker 'happy and energetic' as Head of the School, and believed that by his warnings to him before leaving, he had done as much as anyone to make him so. His final conclusion was 'I *did* my duty at Harrow, and had earned my right to go.' He was besides much pleased to learn that, thanks largely to the representations he had made during his last term, various reforms were really being put in hand. His informant, Searle, the mathematics master, was 'spending his days trying to *heave up* Welldon, as George II *heaves up* the Dutch in Carlyle's *Frederick*. Once Old Honesty begins to march, the new constitution will march too.'

Several years later, in 1898, he walked from London to Harrow, 'reaching Bowen's door in exactly two and a half hours. I lunched with him in our "ancient hall". The boys were going on a paper chase. All seemed the same as ever, only Bowen was still more the same than ever before.'

III

Cambridge, 1893–1899

George settled into rooms in Whewell's Court, a somewhat gloomy region opposite the Great Gate, known as 'the Spitoon' because it had a drain in the middle. Later he moved into rooms on the south side of the Great Court, which had been occupied by his brother Robert. His life was in many ways a continuance in much more genial circumstances of his last happy term at Harrow. He was at first lonely, and had 'an intense wish to supply the void of friendship that Baker filled for me at Harrow.' 'I shall not feel safe till I have a friend here,' he wrote, although from the first he had 'an immense number of delightful acquaintances'. Somewhat suddenly he found that some of these had turned into friends. Chief among them were the gigantic Maurice Amos, later a judge in Egypt; Ralph Wedgwood of the great pottery family (though he himself went into the management of railways); Ralph Vaughan-Williams, the composer; George Moore, the philosopher. The friendships were lasting, particularly those with Amos and Wedgwood. They were 'all good radicals'— and George had been afraid there would not be any radicals at Cambridge—but '*not* great metaphysicians'. 'All dread MacTaggart (the philosopher), that is they are all guided by *heart* and conviction not by *head* and word-logic like him.' 'And,' added George, '*all* the right set of people bicycle.' He himself soon acquired a bicycle and, tireless and swift walker though he was, the innocent machine greatly widened the range of his enjoyments in the English or Scottish countryside, and later in Italy.

While still at Harrow he had been afraid of not finding at Cambridge enough people to share his radical ideals but, although there were 'a few good men who are drifting down the pleasant sunny streams of selfishness and good nature', he had

38

not found any of his ideals 'combatted, much less pooh-poohed, in spite of Bob's forewarnings that I should.'

There was only one set-back in his first term—he was 'ploughed in Paley'—the examination in religious knowledge which included a paper on Paley's *Evidences of Christianity*. 'It is a great scandal,' he said, 'for I wrote a scathing paper that would have made the sceptic tremble in his very boots.' The Paley paper it seemed was responsible for three quarters of the ploughings, 'the examiner being a very pestilent fellow'.

He and his friends soon discovered that the Lake District was the ideal place for a reading-party, and there, at Seatoller in Borrowdale, at the foot of the Honister Pass, they spent the Easter vacation of 1895. Maurice Amos drew a sketch of the five for their Log Book (it is reproduced in *Ralph Vaughan Williams, a Pictorial Biography*) in which one of the party, almost certainly George, is seen reading *Treasure Island* with his feet on the mantelpiece. On this vacation George read 'all sorts of jolly books, some connected with history and some not, but none tripos work. I never had a jollier time.' In fact he did his hardest work during term time; the time-table of the Christmas holiday at Wallington in 1893 shows him devoting only two mornings hours to 'work', and that was not to history but to 'the struggle with the Muse, invariably resulting in a couple of very satisfactory stanzas of my new poem.' The rest of the day was divided between reading poetry, 'to induce the Muse', walking alone or with his mother or Bobbie, and listening to 'Papa' reading aloud. Wallington was a quiet household; late hours and revelry were unknown, and everyone went to bed at 10.30 p.m.

During this Christmas vacation of 1893 he finished his poem, 'The Prophet', having spent 'a week of mornings over it'. 'I intend now,' he said, 'to throw myself into a literary debauch, that is, read delightful books all morning for a day or two—like the good boy who helped himself to plum cake after he had finished his sum.' The 'debauch' was to include *War and Peace* in French, 'as much of Macaulay's *History* as I can', and then he would 'study Wordsworth under John Morley's directions'. 'It is useless,' he said, 'to tackle any of Wordsworth (except his sonnets) unless you take the selections recommended by some great man who has fared all through him . . . You will understand what I mean if you look at a *complete* edition of Wordsworth. He spent *fifty years* writing a large quantity of Blank verse every year.'

This was not strictly accurate, but it was near enough. He used Matthew Arnold's selection in the Golden Treasury series, which enabled him to 'get at' Wordsworth through 'the mass of rubbish with which he surrounded his throne'. On this principle he came to know the poet who, as the years went on, gained the firmest hold over his heart. 'What grows on one,' he wrote to his brother Robert, 'is that everything he says is *true*. That is . . . it is at least the real thoughts of a man as they came naturally to him, not the imagination of a poet forcing his fancy into shapes. And considering this, the fertility of his thinkings in the best poems is really marvellous.' He tried to get Charles, then in the midst of an unsuccessful love-affair, to 'lean on the hills and the lakes and the stars as symbolic of all that is noble . . . Wordsworth leant on them fifty years. I believe he really leant comparatively little on God. He could not realize God in the abstract. He had to see him in the Hills.' Hills and books were George's refuge and strength because 'they cannot be removed by chance or time'. They continued to be so in memory, even when old age had taken away the strength to walk the hills and the sight to read the books.

The poem had been written while reading Swinburne and William Morris, who, however, taught him to see 'how far behind I must be in pure beauty'. In fact he now saw that he was not good enough 'to be a poet pure and simple', like Swinburne. During the year 1894 he came to the conclusion that his destiny was 'to write *heavy books*, history and the like', and so to be 'a writer of books first', though he still hoped to be 'a dabbler in poetry second' and to publish volumes of poetry as well as history. Thus Clio gradually won the victory over Calliope.

Perhaps it was his failure to win the Prize Poem in 1895 which turned him away from 'a poetry and article-writing life' such as he had proposed to himself. And the reading of history, particularly of his special period, (the reign of Louis XI of France), helped him to see both 'how histories are compiled', and what possibilities lay in it for himself. 'If one could make alive again for other people some cobwebbed skein of old dead intrigues, and breathe breath and character into dead names and stiff portraits. That is history to me! Even as it was to Carlyle.' And to that ideal he adhered till he could write no more.

He was fascinated at the thought of the unknown fields of history. 'Great or small, Macaulay or Dry-as-dust, one is welcomed to join the great army of miners who have yet only discovered that there is a city beneath their feet buried. . . . It is the problems and riddles and not the answers that have as yet been discovered.' His enthusiasm was enhanced by making the acquaintance in his first year of 'the third year history man', G. P. Gooch, 'that extraordinary Colossus of history knowledge', with whom in the spring term of 1894 he went for weekly walks. 'Under his direction,' he wrote, 'I am doing what I think to be a very complete preparation for the Mays.'[1] Gooch had 'a library of several hundred history books all of which he has read, and most of which he has analysed and learnt . . . yet withal there is something uncanny about him, something of the hermit—he is not a human beast.' But Gooch was human enough to revolutionise George's ideas of reading for Mays by bidding him 'read endless books and essays'. This George gladly did, and his letters are full of comments on Matthew Arnold (*Culture and Anarchy* in particular), Ruskin's *The Crown of Wild Olive,* and Meredith's poems, which grew ever more precious to him until he came to write his one book of literary criticism, *The Poetry and Philosophy of George Meredith* (1906). Ruskin, he said, was 'the real prophet of the age, not so great perhaps as the voice of Carlyle, but truer and more rational because more cultivated and more hopeful. He represents the uncompromising morality of Hebraism allied to the make-life-beautiful ideal of the Greeks, which latter Carlyle absolutely lacked,' while Matthew Arnold 'pitches into the dead-alive middle class with the heart of a social reformer and the tongue of a literary man of the first quality.' George told his brother Charles to read the chapters of *Culture and Anarchy* which George prescribed and he would then 'realize what I mean about the great part literary men have played in our social questions. You will also realize what were the *Forts of Folly* to the man who first spoke of them.'[2]

But Carlyle was after all the master influence in forming George's naturally deep moral outlook on politics and on his own environment, and in uniting that outlook with his passion for the past. The past, and the appeal of its reality and its mystery,

[1] The name for the examination at the end of the first year.
[2] See Arnold's poem, 'The Last Word':
    Charge once more then, and be dumb;
    Let the victors when they come,
    When the forts of folly fall,
    Find thy body by the wall.

stirred his compassion and imagination as well as his curiosity and scholarship. In the summer of 1897, when he was working for a Trinity Fellowship, he and a young friend visited south-west Scotland, the countryside and mountains of Carlyle's youth, and the heart of the 'Covenanting country'. 'In the inn in this village (Moniaive),' he wrote, 'the only one within 10 miles, we have just been shown a little back room where the covenanters were hid, while the dragoons ransacked the room in which I am now writing.' He then added: 'We counted 10 sorts of scones and cakes on the table at tea.' They stayed at Brigton near Newton Stewart, first spending the night at a shepherd's cottage 'stowed away under the Cairnsmore of Carsphairn'. Here they found the shepherd and his wife and old mother, to whom the raids of Claverhouse's dragoons were still a vivid tradition. 'The dragoons visited every house in the valley, penetrating to the very head of it, "where there was great sin done," the old woman said.' Two years later, again in Scotland, he walked along the cliffs on the east side of Loch Ryan, watching 'the great steamers flying out from Stranraer, under the woods of Corsewall House, Sir John Moore's home, and steaming off into the distance towards a low black line—the unhappy land. So they go today, and so have gone ever since James I's reign, ships bearing Scotchmen to Ireland . . . the first Pilgrim Fathers of British Ireland, to their work of good and evil, fateful and fated men. Or again one seemed to be a Cameronian, delivered from long persecution, but anxious for the fate of brethren in Ireland . . . where Londonderry is besieged and so much is at issue. What white sails are those coming round from the South? The English fleet, pork-bearing, barrel-bearing? Can it be? Let us pray so.'

This is Carlylese perhaps, but truly and deeply felt. In sober judgement, he wrote: 'I will offer a prize of heartfelt estimation and worship for any book more *sage* about the past than *Heroes*, more *sage* about the present (1830–50) than *Past and Present*. By "sage" I mean full of the most important truths, as yet unseen by the seers of the time, and now first added to the common stock of ideas and knowledge by the "sage".'

For him, Trinity held memories and traditions of peculiar poignancy. Not only had his father spent three intensely happy years there, commemorated by his light-verse dramas *Horace at the University of Athens* and *The Ladies in Parliament*, but Macaulay had felt towards Trinity 'as an ancient Greek or a mediaeval Italian felt toward his native city'. On the flagged path from his rooms to the north of the Great Gate under the wall of the Chapel, Macaulay as a young Bachelor of Arts would walk 'book in hand, morning after morning throughout the long vacation', and there, 'in his failing years, he specially loved to renew the feelings of the past, and some there are who can never revisit it without the fancy that there, if anywhere, his dear shade must linger'.[3] So wrote his nephew George Otto Trevelyan, and George of the next generation determined to follow the same practice though in a different part of the College. 'Tell Papa,' he wrote to Charles, 'I have been working several mornings walking up and down under the Library reading my note-books. I shall always do so when I can in future.'

The Master of Trinity during George's time there, and for long after, was Henry Montagu Butler who had been Head Master of Harrow before Welldon and in youth had accompanied George's father (five years his junior) on a walking tour in the Tirol. Once during his undergraduate days George was invited to the Master's Lodge for an Old Harrovian dinner. It was 'dull —dull, deadly dull,' he wrote afterwards. After dinner 'I got hold of the Master and had some pleasant old world talk . . . I wish he would ask me to some sensible party.' There is no record of such an invitation, but George had no lack of friends among the older people at Cambridge. He delighted in the friendship of the Henry Sidgwicks at Newnham where Mrs Sidgwick was Principal of the College. Dr Sidgwick was a beloved friend of George's father—they had been undergraduates together—and George was well able to relish the wit as well as the wisdom of the author of *The Methods of Ethics*. He also enjoyed looking from the Sidgwicks' windows onto the college lawn 'across which "sweet girl graduates" are walking in romantic couples, bonnetless, and arm in arm. The whole place *breathes* of *The Princess*.' But he showed no desire to descend among them.

In his early days at Cambridge he sometimes spoke at the Union, but without making it a regular practice as he did not intend to be a politician. In October 1893 there was a debate on Church Disestablishment, on which he felt strongly. He made what he called 'a violent and somewhat entertaining radical attack on the Church, in opposition to the worthy but prosaic argu-

[3] G. O. Trevelyan, *Life and Letters of Lord Macaulay*, Ch. 2.

ments of which the Union debates are now composed. The result was I delighted my radical friends and ruffled up the other side . . . I "caught it" from the *Cambridge Review*.' The *Review* reminded him that he was 'a young gentleman just up from school', and therefore 'still very young', and the *Granta* also attacked him severely. George, for a time, felt that he need not speak any more. 'I find,' he said, 'I waste a day or more in preparation and uneasiness about the coming speech, though I say it off all right when the time comes. I have much too much to do without the Union.' In the following term, however, he did speak again in a debate on whether legislation was the true means of social reform, and with such success that he retracted his vow of silence. 'The feeling of being at home on your legs with a listening and admiring audience,' he said, had greatly cheered and exhilarated him. But his success as a speaker on political subjects did not beget in him any ambition for a political career.

It would be impossible to give a true picture of George Trevelyan during these years without considering the depth of his intimacy with his brother Charles. Charles, after leaving the Viceregal Lodge, worked in London, beginning to build his political career by nursing the borough of North Lambeth in the Liberal cause; he unsuccessfully contested it at the election of 1895. He shared with George the love of mountain-walking, especially in the north of England; he shared also the love of literature, though George was a little afraid that his brother's absorption in politics might somewhat narrow his enjoyment of poetry and letters. 'I feel,' he warned him, 'that there is just the off chance of your being in the course of years narrowed by your acquaintance with only a certain class of brave men, most of them only half full of sweetness and light. The Resource of literature, besides being a resource, is an education which prevents its votaries from being narrow . . . You appreciate Carlyle and Burns one year, you therefore appreciate Browning and Shelley the next. I always delight to have you writing to tell me your literary opinions on what you are reading. They are always good. If you understand a man, you always understand him for the right thing. I write as an apostle of literature, and I speak sooth.'

The brothers were both subject to fits of depression or 'blue devils', but Charles suffered more than George and was less able to extricate himself from them. He had indeed less self-confidence than his younger brother. 'Half your life,' George told him, 'you are in good spirits and can make yourself delightful to anyone, especially to the family, while the other half you are in the Blue Devils . . . and so unless I, David, am there with my harp, Saul sulks away in a corner, and spins ridiculous theories about Democracy absorbing his domestic affection etc. Out on it! *Know* yourself, don't theorize about yourself.' The 'blue devils' was 'that and nothing more' and should not be treated as a sign that his affection for his family was waning. 'Send for David the son of Jesse whenever the evil spirit troubles you,' he repeated, 'especially whenever it whispers such ridiculosities in your ear.'

As for himself, he believed that it was his Harrow experiences, painful though they were, that had 'forced him to be self-sufficing' and to rely on his own 'resources' and on literature and common-sense. 'I feel that if I had not had three years' consummate misery, and one year of defiance, at Harrow, I might still be going blubbering about the world, selfish because not self-sufficing.' Charles's low spirits were indeed complicated by his having fallen deeply but unsuccessfully in love. George tried to show him that 'identity' with any other person, be it brother or mistress, was an impossibility. 'Had Romeo and Juliet married,' he said, 'I doubt the result.' His remedy for the pain of un-requited love was 'Read'. 'I wish,' he wrote, as late as 1902, 'you cared more for ideal literature—literature as religion, not a study or business or amusement . . . Not success, hardly even service is so much the true object of life as is the *spirit* in which we work. Now that can only be an unconscious, muddled sort of spirit . . . unless we sometimes, often, think and feel about the spiritual world of which this unsubstantial fabric of imperialisms, literatures, Wallingtons, friendships, is a mere image. It is not necessary to become a metaphysician, but it is necessary to *feel* the inner truth of our great heritage of English poets, and of Carlyle's *Sartor,* to roll them under the tongue of our mind, to have by heart the *tags* that appeal to you, to live in them, to be converted to them since they alone are religion—!' Reading was in fact a resource which had comforted all the first-rate men in this world who had the least appreciation of literature. It com-forted Macaulay in worse trouble.[4] But Charles must read the right books. Let him drop *The Egoist,* which would only show

[4] After his sister Margaret died during Macaulay's absence in India.

him glimpses of his own lower self, and read Browning's *Para-celsus,* 'and find glimpses there of your higher self'. He urged his brother not to think of himself as a 'pitiful creature', but to read and to work at the tasks he had undertaken. 'You and I are made to do work in this world and thereby to get some share of fame, not enormous fame or work, but enough to satisfy us and the world we serve. I have Napoleonic determination that this shall be so for myself and for you too, and you are not going to drop behind.' And Charles might always rely on George's friendship: critical though it was, it was always at hand. In one letter written just before a visit of Charles to Cambridge, is a poem, most touching in its concern, and in phraseology curiously like those evangelical hymns which, under the guidance of Booa, he had known from childhood.

Is the burden heavy, brother
Is it hard to bear?
See my shoulder ready, brother,
Come and leave it there!

I know all your griefs, brother,
I have felt them too,
But if once we meet, brother,
They'll be light to you.

I will grasp your hand, brother,
You shall grasp mine;
Then our eyes in meeting
Shall breed a Faith divine.

And, lest Charles should feel such an invitation too overwhelm-ing, he wrote in a more matter-of-fact style: 'I discovered with surprise, that probably very few people have friends, intimate in the way we are intimate, on whose arm to lean when the unname-able darkness falls. Possibly other people are not troubled by the unnameable darkness as we are. But be sure I need you as much as you need me.' Letters of this kind which have survived are only a few out of a great number, for, many years later, Charles wrote across one of them: 'I keep this one though I have destroyed all the others he wrote to me at this time on this sub-ject [that is, on the subject of Charles's love] . . . I keep this one for his sake, to show what a friend he was and to account for this immense pile of vigorous writing to me at the time. I see

46

now how much it was. Then it seemed little, for it was the only food I could digest. It saved my mind, if not my life.'

Their democratic ideals were sometimes called into play by affairs at Wallington. In those days the agent of the estate was a Mr Gow, who lived in the principal house in Cambo village. He was a somewhat dictatorial man who liked to show his authority over the villagers. George discovered that he had forbidden public access to the road which ran along the front row of village houses (including his own), thus treating it as a private drive. There was no precedent for this, except a tradition that old Sir John Trevelyan 'was proposing' to close the road, when he died fifty years before. 'Man proposeth,' commented George, 'but God disposeth. A *dispensation,* this death of Sir John's!' So, in the Christmas vacation of 1893, George, finding that his father had written to Gow to have the road reopened, but without any result, 'went round half the village, and exacted a willing promise (from the villagers) to use it and to make the children use it.' It was just at this time that Parish Councils were coming into existence, and among their powers would be authority over rights of way. A lecturer came to Cambo to explain to the people their new powers under the Act, and this, says George, 'brought forth such a storm of cheering from the sturdy Northumbrians that the lecturer was quite overwhelmed and wondered what had happened . . . God save the People!'

George was no artist, and never could quite share the admiration felt by his brother Bob and Bob's friend Roger Fry for such examples of the primitive genius of man as the cult-figures from Easter Island. But he loved deeply pictures and statues which seemed to express or support his own spiritual ideals. His brother Charles once gave him a little figure of a Greek goddess for his mantelpiece at Cambridge. 'It springs at once to the place of soother of blue-devilry,' wrote George, 'and reminder of the beauty of the world. My other soothers are Mama's copy of the Turner[5] and the portrait of William the Silent.' The figure had 'the additional and melancholy charm of reminding me of the Greeks and all Hellenism whenever I see it. I have been debating whether to call her the Muse of History (that is, *my* history-work), or the Muse of Poetry that is mine. Now I have finally

[5] That is, of the water-colour of Bolton Abbey. Caroline Trevelyan excelled in water-colour painting and among her best achievements were her copies from Turner's *Liber Studiorum.*

determined that she is Hellas, the incarnation of all Hellenism, and of all the good and great and beautiful things the Greeks did and bequeathed to the world. I have now on the mantelpiece, *Greece* most beautifully represented; *Mediaevalism*—viz. the Knights[6]; and *Modernity* in its typical advance on the past—the appreciation of scenery, represented by the Turner. A most allegorical and beautiful mantle-board.'

In 1895 a new star arose over the Cambridge horizon—Lord Acton was appointed Regius Professor of Modern History. Although a Catholic, Acton had been educated in German universities and his Catholicism was very different from the ultramontane, Hibernian variety which prevailed in England. George could submit himself to his teaching and guidance with perfect confidence. In 1896, the year of his tripos, he worked so hard and with such enthusiasm that nature at length rebelled and he was obliged to go for a voyage in the spring to Madeira and the Canary Islands, feeling completely played out. But after walking, first in Yorkshire and then round the Cornish coast with Vaughan-Williams on his return, and visiting by bicycle from Welcombe the battlefields of Worcester and Evesham, he recovered completely, and in the Tripos examination had the luck to be called on to give an account of the Blenheim campaign for his 'Queen Anne special'. He had visited the battlefield the previous year with Charles Roden Buxton, whereas Roderick Geikie, doing the same 'special', had visited only the Belgian battlefields of Ramillies and Oudenarde.

From the Tripos, in which he gained a first—'If I get a second,' he wrote, 'I shall be the most unmitigated humbug since Tolstoi's Napoleon'—he went straight on, in the autumn of 1896, to read for his Fellowship Dissertation. The subject he chose was the Peasants' Revolt of 1381 and the religious movement associated with John Wycliffe. When he published it as a book in 1899 he called it *England in the age of Wycliffe*; it was his only specialised excursion into mediaeval history; after that the Stuarts or the nineteenth century absorbed him wholly.

A year earlier he had recognised, through reading G. Lowes Dickinson's *Development of Parliament during the Nineteenth Century*, the importance of that great new element in historical

[6] Some lead figures of jousting knights.

studies—economic history, and in particular the study of the labouring class. 'The marked thing,' he wrote, 'about this century, politically, socially, educationally, historically and even artistically, is that the lower classes are being considered instead of simply the upper and middle classes. Why is it impossible to say whether the lower classes are better off materially, morally and intellectually than in any given period before 1800? Because no one ever concerned themselves to investigate or record their condition. Why is economic history so far behind other branches of history in certainty? Because it more than any other must deal with all classes alike and cannot take the upper and middle class as typical of a period, as the artistic, intellectual or political historians can do. There will never be any certainty as to the condition of the lower class in any country before 1800, because no one at the time left any record of them, either in monument, art or writing.'

But the silence was beginning to break a little with the study of manorial rolls and accounts, and the great 'incident' of the Peasants' Revolt, well known of course in political history, was in need of deeper study in its social, economic and religious implications. Although his radical sympathies and his dislike of orthodox and established Christianity made the story attractive to him, he was determined not to make it simply a dissertation on his own inclinations. 'I am beginning to study the state of the Church,' he wrote. 'It will be necessary to be very careful and not state anything on hearsay as it is and always will be a touchy subject.' It was fresh ground that he was ploughing and he had all the fighting scholar's delight in the game. 'It is hard inch to inch fighting with the subject,' he wrote, 'for I am the first that ever compared the authorities in detail, and the damned fools disagree as if they were on the school board. [His brother was on the London School Board.] If only some bloody ass of a monk had known what trouble he would give by sticking down the first thing he heard, he might have taken a little more trouble. But John Ball and Co. are worth it.' In February 1897 he read a 'slice' of his work to the Trinity Historical Society which he had helped to found for 'solid papers and criticism of a specialised nature and not for mere interchange of intellectual ideas on History.' Acton, F. W. Maitland, Archdeacon Cunningham (the 'father' of economic history) and 'all the Trinity History men' were there, and Acton was greatly impressed. He advised George to go on, on the same lines, until he had completed the period and made a publishable book. This he did, sending it in for the Fellowship competition in 1898. He won a Fellowship which continued for six years, and three years later he was appointed a College Assistant Lecturer in history, giving lectures on Modern European History.

Work was helped and illumined by bicycle-rides into the countryside which had once been the heart of the Peasants' Revolt. On 27 February 1897, he set out for Bury St. Edmunds 'through a country devoid of main roads, a curious net-work of bye-roads' and lanes 'where the bicycle never passed before from one old village to another'. The only sign of modernity were the chapels left by 'the indefatigable John Wesley'. The people spoke 'a deep guttural tongue "to me unknowe"'.' Yet these were the people who 500 years before had 'risen against tyrants— imagine it if you can—and slow-moving Suffolk had rolled down the roads into Bury articulating gutturally to itself of its wrongs, and forthwith finding the Chancellor of England (Sir John Cavendish) loose about the town had put up his bloody head above the pillory, where an elegant fountain and eighteenth-century well now stands in its place.' In these sentences we again hear the tones of Carlyle. He wandered in the grounds of the great Abbey, now a public park, and felt that its present state symbolised an innocent revenge for the violent deeds of the deceased peasantry of those days against the Church.

In spite of his sympathy with the English rebels of 1381 and 1642, George Trevelyan was never a 'party' historian. The Pilgrim Fathers, he said, had carried to America three qualities —'Civil Liberty, Religious Intolerance, and Prudery'. Religious intolerance had led Cromwell to 'complete indifference to human suffering in turning out the Irish wholesale from many parts of their native lands', and in selling white men to Barbados as slaves. 'Such things,' wrote George, 'seem to me to show the puritans not one whit better than their contemporaries in the essential of Christian philanthropy.' Christianity had nobly organised Europe 'politically and socially in the dark ages . . . yet failed in what it chiefly pretended to do, to make men love one another. It failed in this twice, first in the middle ages, in spite of the desultory effort of St. Francis and a few others; secondly it failed in the great puritan revival.' This failure, he believed, had brought about the failure of the Puritan movement itself. 'Philanthropy', as a philosophy and principle, had been ushered in not by churchmen, but by the great agnostics of the eighteenth and nineteenth centuries, such as Voltaire.

The progress of his soul, his ethical faith and development, play a very large part in his letters to his brother throughout his Cambridge years. His first visit to Europe on his own in the summer of 1895 was largely a 'thinking holiday'. On the Rhine steamer he devoured Morley's *Voltaire*. 'I had come out with the intention of thinking over in the mountain solitude [he was on his way to Switzerland] the question of my duty to the world, and whether my historical intentions were mere dilettantism and ambition and laziness.' He had 'wealth to do what I like, position and education.' He had besides, 'talent'. He did not want to be a politician, or 'work by personal contact with the masses'—but, was 'scientific work' at history enough? 'No, I answer after reading Voltaire, for if I put up scientific work at history as the sole ideal, I shall drift into the selfish but worthy egoism which we know as "academical". I will *not* be academical, as I may have been tending to be lately . . . Service to mankind, though it may be the same thing as service of truth, must be put first, in so far as the two are separate . . . I must act,' he concluded, 'as interpreter of history, in its truest sense, to all those who can understand it, to those in fact who read books. I believe I am more fitted for that than for going further afield as specialised digger.'

He further resolved to 'do good' in his relations with his Cambridge acquaintance; he would be more 'social', 'give up my precious lunch and breakfast hours which I have reserved for reading, to social life, for the sake of what I may do to others.' His 'set' at Cambridge he felt was self-centred. 'We do nothing except for ourselves, in the way of personal contact.' Many of them were simply 'wrapped in themselves, as a set, and always thinking.' Finally 'my superfluous cash must go to aid mankind, whether to the Liberal party or how.'

At about the same time, after he had taken his degree, a younger man, Milnes Gaskell, opened George's eyes to the existence of a type of undergraduate at Cambridge whom he had not yet recognised, different from his own 'set' but of equal worth and perhaps more solid value. 'Cambridge,' said this young man, 'is now given over to the vulgarity of medicals and footer men who talk loudly and coarsely in slang of their own and care about nothing but their athletic shop.' 'This,' said George, 'I most potently believe, but his remedy is not, like mine, the reading and intellectual men, but the sporting men. He says the Magdalene men he knows are the sons of the old sporting squires, that they are thorough gentlemen, they neither nickname God's creatures nor mar the Queen's English, *nor bet*, but only hunt and shoot. They will spend days in the fens after wild duck.' It was a pleasure to George to find that people like his own seventeenth- and eighteenth-century squires still existed, and had existed since medieval times.

In the autumn of 1895 he told his brother: 'I have definitely, and I believe finally, chosen the amelioration and enlightenment of others as the first object, instead of the pursuit of truth as truth.' As we look back over his life now, this statement seems both over-dogmatic and somewhat condescending—and he would certainly in his later years have said that it was. Yet it represented what was for him an important distinction—the distinction between mere learning or literary achievement, and such learning and achievement directed to the mental needs of the public. His resolution to 'do good' and put the service of mankind even before the study of history was indeed a lasting one. It led, in the years after he took his degree, to teaching history at the Working Men's College in London and, by his personal efforts, forging close ties between the College and Cambridge, particularly Trinity. And in his correspondence with his brother, in which mottos had always played a part, there appeared late in 1895 a new one, replacing the earlier 'G.S.I.' ('God Save Ireland') and even 'G.S.T.P.' ('God Save The People'). It was *'Ich Dien'*—'I serve'—the old motto of the Black Prince. 'I have found *Ich Dien* a success without any question at all,' he said, when Charles enquired why he was not using the signature more often—had he found it a failure? 'It has opened out a great field of new friendship based on common service or on my service done to the man; it has opened out a prospect of work and service in Cambridge and London which was quite beyond my thought when I started off abroad in June, sick of all save history for history's sake, and planning how with greatest decency to resign the liberal club secretaryship. I never consciously made any sacrifice before to serve anyone save you; when you were in death grips with the devil you cried for my hand, and I was forced to break my then natural selfishness and self-absorption to give it you. I never let you see that it was an effort to me.' He became more aware of

52

the needs and difficulties of other men. 'When one's friends begin getting started in life,' he wrote, 'or begin trying to do so, one sees how lucky one is by comparison. I hope I shall be able to be of use to one or two of them in the next year or two.'

Perhaps his personal reading during this year, which included Froude's *Erasmus*[7] and Plato's Symposium, besides Voltaire, had helped him out of the rut of 'history for history's sake'. The character of Socrates, as depicted by Plato, greatly awed him. 'You just feel this man was the greatest that ever lived.' His suppression of all passionate exclamation 'is one of the things that raises him above his compotators'[8]. But there was also need, he felt, for 'a new Symposium', 'about Shakespeare or some person who showed stronger emotion' which would 'idealize passion and brilliancy rightly directed'. For this, George knew, was 'the only thing you and I can strive for'—Socratic detachment being outside their sphere.

He believed besides that it was largely Charles's example that had made him reconsider his social relations. 'You carry your latest notion to the first person you meet, and do him good with it, shock him perhaps, and certainly enlarge him. I shall try and be more like you in this and less like my other friends.'

But these resolutions had to have thought, solitude and reading for their source, whether it was 'going a-byking by myself to think' among English lanes, or up on the 'high mountain platforms' of Switzerland, with Matthew Arnold to show him

> Where the white mists for ever
> Are spread and upfurled,
> In the stir of the forces
> Whence issued the world.

'I have sacrificed reading to social duty,' he said, 'but I cannot afford to sacrifice "le droit de penser".' 'A quiet time like this in the hills,' he wrote to his mother from Königsee in 1895, 'is the only time when I can fairly criticize myself, and put my finger on

---

[7] Erasmus aroused his sympathy. 'I am sorry poor Erasmus did not like Cambridge. One can conceive him staring across the river into the grey Cambridge fog, from out of his little turret window in Queen's, thinking of the golden sunlight of Rome, the statues, the paintings, and the intellectual cardinals, and then looking down into the Queen's quadrangle see some old dry-as-dust Scotist don walking across the grass—grr ye swine!'

[8] Literally, a fellow-drinker.

the faults in my method of life at Cambridge and Wallington. Especially the only time when I can regard my life at Cambridge and Wallington as part of a whole, and see where and how one should fill the gaps of the other.'

Probably few young men nowadays would undertake an ethical analysis of themselves in this way. But George Trevelyan had inherited not only Macaulay's genius for historical writing, but more than a little of the evangelical spirit of both his Trevelyan and Macaulay forebears. His grandfather, Sir Charles Edward Trevelyan, had been a strong evangelical churchman all his life. 'I am forced to confess,' wrote George, 'that we inherit the moral stamina produced in Grandpapa by religion and apply it straight to our infidel sense of duty.' And he added: 'I am now inclined to think that Oliver (Cromwell) and Grandpapa Trevelyan both would have had the same moral stamina even if they had not put it in the form of religion. But their minds were educated to put it in the form of religion.' Macaulay had tacitly rejected evangelical doctrine; George Otto Trevelyan likewise, while finding a moral as well as a political faith in Gladstonian liberalism. His sons, in their generation, were more outspoken in their rejection of Christian doctrine. Certainly there were some aspects of Cambridge life in those days which made atheism and anti-clericalism seem very respectable. Chapel was still nominally compulsory, and in 1897 the Chaplain of Trinity unwisely tried to impose this duty on young Michael Howard, a son of Lord and Lady Carlisle and nephew of the redoubtable atheist Lyulph Stanley. The result was a 'row' in which George took an active part. Many years afterwards my father said to me: 'If there had been more sensible clergymen in Cambridge in my time I could have been a churchman.' He lived indeed to attend Chapel on Sunday evenings regularly during his time as Master, and even once to preach.

Yet through all his rejections, the Bible remained indispensable to him. It was not simply that he loved the ancient stories, historical or legendary, and the beauty of its language. He used some parts of it in a way that can only be called devotional. When he was in Cornwall, in the spring of 1896, recovering 'self-respect and will and cheerfulness' after his nervous breakdown, he wrote to Charles: 'Yesterday evening I sat watching the sun set into the sea, and held a quiet thanksgiving with myself, reading David's psalms of repentance and trust. The old

54

shepherd king had different sort of troubles from mine, and sinned different sort of sins, yet what he says is what I want to say.' And to his brother Robert he wrote from Switzerland in the summer of 1895: 'Shelley, Homer and the Prophets keep me company,' while before going to bed he read 'four chapters of the book of Job'. Neither Robert nor his companion on this holiday, Charles Roden Buxton, who came of an evangelical household,[9] could quite share George's love of the Old Testament. George accounted for this by telling Robert: 'It is as impossible for a Hellenist poet like you to feel the O.T. as it is for a Christian like Buxton.'

From 1895 onwards George spent the earlier weeks of the Long Vacation exploring Switzerland and Northern Italy, either by himself, or with a chosen friend, or with Charles. In 1895 and 1896 his companion was Charles Roden Buxton; in 1897 another Trinity man, William Finlay (his former Wixenford friend) who actually brought a copy of Macaulay's *Essays* with him. George in 1896 brought Plato's *Republic*, which he said helped him to realise 'the importance of every man's life, not merely of the wisest men's lives'; he also brought Shelley and Shakespeare. 'Today,' he wrote, from Fionnay, 'I had a very Shelley-ish adventure. I went out with Shelley and Shaker in my pockets, found myself on one side of a torrent and saw a lovely cave overhung with bushes on the other side. I determined to cross, carrying my clothes on me, was nearly washed away but got across by help of my Alpenstock, soaking. Shelley enjoyed being plunged in the elemental torrent, and Shaker cracked a joke and took a cup of sack to warm him. I had to strip and spent three or four hours naked in my cave and outside it in the sun, reading Shelley.' Shakespeare comforted him in homesick moods; 'he is so very English and makes one feel less lonesome.' He also brought 'Homer in English and Greek, Mat Arnold and the Bible', and instructed his brother when he joined him to 'bring me out *two* amusing novels, *one* being either *Peveril of the Peak* or *St. Ronan's Well*.' He and Charles Buxton read the *Odyssey* aloud to each other in the evenings in Greek with

[9] George once stayed with Charles Buxton's parents, Sir Fowell and Lady Victoria Buxton at Waltham Abbey, and was enraged by their habit of praying aloud, at family prayers, for all personal and family problems, great or small. He declined to accompany them to church on Sunday, a proceeding which met with Lady Victoria's strong disapproval.

55

Butcher and Lang's translation. 'There is nothing,' said George, 'which gives me the feeling of the "Romance of history", like the *Odyssey*.' It was more enjoyable in this respect even than the Old Testament stories, which had too many religious associations, such as boring sermons, connected with them.[10]

The great event of the 1896 vacation was the ascent of the Breithorn with Charles Buxton, under the care of a delightful guide, Matthieu zum Taugwald, a cousin of the two Taugwalders, who, with Whymper, survived the Matterhorn disaster of 1865. He had been to America, where he joined the US army and fought Indians, until the poor morale of the troops—who were of mixed nationalities with no 'esprit de corps'—disgusted him and he came home. 'We discussed Swiss warfare and history at great length,' says George. 'He had read the classics. He gave a very interesting criticism of the classical references to Switzerland showing why he does not think Caesar ever crossed the St. Bernard, as is said.'

They spent the night before this climb at a tiny little climbers' inn at Gandegg, kept by three women. 'We had a regular Swiss evening, sitting with them in the little kitchen. There was real democracy—Matthieu, the milkman of the inn . . . ourselves and the three women. We sang them Harrow songs, and they sang us Swiss songs'; one song particularly, sung by Matthieu 'in a deep strong voice, with the sort of feeling in it which a trooper of Cromwell's would have sung a psalm or a spiritual song . . . No constraint, no social differences. Real democracy. Why? Because we all saw and felt that the others were well-meaning.' Their good fellowship was enhanced by the arrival of a 'damned German', also on his way to the Breithorn. This man drank too much and in the middle of the night after the others were in bed began to insult the women. Matthieu however came in in time, ' "and I did beat him with my fists," he said. "That may be the way in towns but we do not like it here." Matthieu's strongest expression of hatred is "I do not like it." '

At about 3.30 a.m. he roused the two Englishmen, ' "au nom de Jésus Christ, it is a beautiful day." ' On the summit of the Breithorn, in the presence of an unparalleled view of almost every peak and range in the Alps, 'we rose shouting, mad, our minds reeling with delight too great for articulate words. "O Switzer-

[10] This did not apply to his enjoyment of the Psalms, the Prophets and the Book of Job.

land, mine country!" cried out Matthieu looking round at the panorama once more as we ran along the ridge, shouting together.' They ran down, parted from Matthieu on the Theodule Pass, and proceeded down the Val Tournanches to Breuil and then by carriage to Châtillon and finally by train to Aosta. Aosta, the little military city founded by Augustus with its splendid gates and triumphal arch, thrilled him. 'It was under this arch,' he wrote, 'that the Legions tramped in from the east, coming up the Aosta valley.' They noticed also the house in which St Anselm was born. 'When he lived in Aosta,' wrote George, 'he must have expected to be Archbishop of Canterbury about as much as Charlie Buxton expects to be President of the United States. The Catholic Church was indeed Catholic then.'

They then climbed the long road up to the Great St Bernard pass, down which Napoleon and his army had made their entry into Italy a century before. It was all a feast for George's imagination. 'The whole road is very old-fashioned, no new hotels or villas on it; the old inns and churches and dirty villages must have been very much those that gave his first notion of Italy to many a recruit of the "army of reserve".' At length they came, in bitterly cold weather, to the famous Hospice where they saw 'the great hounds walking round it, baying musically', and felt, with their knapsacks and alpenstocks, like genuine pilgrims who might be asked 'whether Hildebrand had allowed the emperor to come in out of the snow yet.'[11] Here they spent the night, and were much amused by some French guests, one of whom played the piano while the rest of the party danced to keep warm! When at length a fire was lit they all gathered round it to talk. 'As usual,' wrote George, 'the Frenchmen instructed us on the merits of Byron, and the comparative demerits of Shelley. One of them expressed the sentiment that after all there was nothing in Shelley that was such true poetry as Don Juan. In the French language, spoken with perfect gaiety and seriousness combined, the idea sounded quite sensible.'

In spite of his protestantism, George had found that he could both respect and sympathise with Catholicism in these democratic regions. The next year (1897) at Saas Fée he and William

---

[11] In the year 1077 Hildebrand (Pope Gregory VII), hesitating whether to lift the ban of excommunication from the Emperor Henry IV, kept Henry for three days standing barefoot in the courtyard of the Castle of Canossa at the foot of the Mont Cenis pass, a suppliant for reconciliation.

Finlay watched from a distance a true Christian festival, when 'the Bishop for the first time for twelve years, had come up to visit and to confirm'. The procession of villagers with banners wound up the hill, while the church bells were sending out sounds that 'echoed through the vast mountains around and seemed to consecrate them and make them the Cathedral for the little community to worship in.' In the evening, however, they sat by their window at the inn and 'read Macaulay's essay on the Papacy [i.e. on Von Ranke's *History of the Popes*] aloud', to reawaken their critical faculties. Macaulay, thought George, had exaggerated both the decline of the Church in the eighteenth century, and its revival in the nineteenth.

The culminating event of this year (1897) was his first visit to Rome. He travelled out to Milan in December with Lord Acton who told him much about the 'ancien régime' in Italy when he had lived in Milan under the Austrian government after the failure of the 1848 rising. In Milan, George climbed to the roof of the Duomo early in the morning and looked down on the old town below, imagining himself one of the Tyrolese who held the roof against the Austrians in the 'five days' of 1848. This was just the kind of historical scenario that he loved, but what impressed him most of all in Milan was, surprisingly, the church of San Ambrogio. Not only was it a little-changed church of ninth-century Christianity, but in a glass case on the altar lay the skeleton of the saint himself, 'with the skull and the teeth he clenched' when he disputed with Theodosius at the door of the very same church. George stood gazing at this strange sight long after his turn in the queue of pilgrims had passed and the officials were beginning to get angry.

At Christmas he joined his parents in Rome, and there, standing on the Janiculum at the foot of Garibaldi's statue, with the Tiber and all Rome at his feet and in the far distance the Alban hills 'in all the glory of a crisp winter day of bright sun', he listened to his father telling the story—which he had never yet heard—of Garibaldi's defence of the Roman Republic in 1849. After visiting Tusculum and Veii and viewing thence the whole arena of the wars and policies of ancient Rome, he plunged across the Campagna—still unindustrialised, the haunt of shepherds and their flocks—into the Alban hills. From Frascati he climbed Monte Cavo, and thence fought his way through the trackless woods to the top of Monte Algido, discerning thence with pleasure

58

how well Macaulay, in *The Battle of Lake Regillus,* had described the landscape which sent troops to the fight.

'I am supremely happy,' he wrote to Charles from Frascati, 'and drinking in delight and new ideas every hour.' He returned to Cambridge to finish *England in the Age of Wycliffe,* and to sit in the following autumn for his Fellowship examination. Having gained the Fellowship, (the first ever awarded for history), he settled down to regular teaching at Trinity.

Wycliffe was published in February 1899 by Longman and a second edition followed in June. 'There is no sign of immaturity in the book,' wrote G. P. Gooch after George's death, 'and the narrative flows briskly along . . . The whole work revealed that his interest in the social life of the masses was no less than in the story of the court and the records of Parliament.' George in his Preface said that the period he had chosen 'represents, as far as England is concerned, the meeting point of the medieval and the modern.' It was addressed, he said, to the general reader, and not to students alone, but the notes and appendices were intended for the historical critic. For it was his hope that the book, though not of the dry-as-dust kind, 'may claim to be a serious contribution to history', and for this reason he had based it on deep research into original documents, many of them hitherto unknown. This was the principle on which all his future work was founded.

Italy became henceforward the field of his vacation wanderings more and more, and, long before he became or even intended to become the historian of Garibaldi, he had travelled on foot much of the country between Rome and the Adriatic which had been the scene of Garibaldi's retreat.

From Rome he went on to Naples, climbed Vesuvius with a guide who walked 'as fast as even our family wants'—and visited Cumae, 'the hill on which Greece first planted herself on Italian soil in the far golden days, wherefore the awe-struck Roman spoke of the "Cumaean Sybil", thinking that what was above him was divine.'

At Christmas 1899 George paid a visit to Paris, to improve his French and take a closer look at the passions roused by the Dreyfus affair which was tearing France to pieces.

The Boer War had begun and Paris was in the grip of its worst outbreak of hatred against England, a militarist imperialism which hoped for her overthrow by the Boers and for a *coup d'état* by a Catholic military junta which would destroy the liberal republican government of France. George saw great danger in this, and was angry at Joe Chamberlain's tactless speeches, which only encouraged the anti-English party. With dismay he watched the crocodiles of seminarist schools in the Bois de Boulogne, 'the lay schoolmaster walking apart from the scholars, some yards behind, the priest always in the middle of them, talking to them and poisoning their minds from childhood against the Civil State.' Even the landlady of his pension, a cultivated woman who knew England, talked eagerly of a *coup d'état* and looked forward to what George called 'the reign of the ghouls'.

But there was much in Paris to admire and even envy. 'The Sorbonne lectures, for instance, free to the public on all subjects, especially historical and literary, by the best men in France, of the School of Renan and Taine. There are scores of such lectures every day, and you have only to choose. Imagine Oxford and Cambridge made literary without losing the character of scholarship, planted in London and set lecturing for the general benefit of mankind.' The public buildings also and perhaps most of all the statues 'show a sense of history and of art almost totally lacking in England. They have, needless to say, a far better-placed statue of Shakespeare than we have in London. Ours stands among the Music Halls,[12] theirs on the Boulevards as one approaches the Théâtre. I passed him the other night, and greeting him in friendly compatriotic manner asked him what he thought of Paris in the year of Christ 1899. But he only winked and asked how it went in Warwickshire, to which I answered "very slowly." "It always did," he said, and I vanished into the night bearing this cheerful oracle in my heart.'

He explored Paris, 'Carlyle in my hand', and there, unexpectedly, discovered a new hand-hold in his search for the true way of living and thinking. He met an old Waldensian pastor from the valleys of the French Alps, 'a heroic kind of old man, who had seen so much of horror and trouble come and leave their black mark for ever and yet in a sort of way pass, that even the Dreyfus affair and the War (the Boer War)—which the French Protestants feel as if it was themselves who were killing each other —fail to diminish his cheerful faith and vigour.' George went to

[12] In Leicester Square.

the Christmas service at his church, where he felt the congregation resembled the early Christians in Rome in their goodness and sincerity. He had been disturbed, largely by the Dreyfus affair, to discover how much more badness and evil there was in the world than he had previously imagined. The Waldensians and their pastor helped him to feel that 'the little good there is in this world was better than the great sum of evil in it was bad.' Here, he felt, was a real basis for optimism, not that good would ultimately destroy evil, for good and evil were alike indestructible, 'but a little good matters more than a great deal of evil.' He realised that the discovery had its dangers and could lead to selfishness—nevertheless it was 'one of the greatest chapters in the gospel of love'.

From Paris, still thirsting for Italy, he paid a winter visit to Pisa and Perugia, returned home in February 1901 to help in Charles's election campaign at Elland, then went out again to Rome with the Buxtons at Easter. On Good Friday he sat on the Palatine, reading Carlyle while the Buxtons went to church.

Pushing southwards once more, he joined his brother Bob at Ravello, and together they crossed from Naples to Sicily. George little guessed how much the strange island would come into his work and travels in the course of the next ten years. This visit was to the eastern end of the island only, and it is important in George's life because it introduced him to a lady—a first cousin once removed of his father's—who afterwards became his benefactress. Mrs Florence Cacciola was the only child of Spencer Trevelyan of Netherwitton in Northumberland. Her mother, after her husband's death, had bought a small estate, Hallington, about half-way between Hexham and Wallington. Mrs Trevelyan died there in 1877 and Florence then left England, as it turned out for ever. She went to Sicily with her cousin Miss Perceval. In Taormina she met and married Dr Cacciola, a physician, and, apparently at Bob's suggestion, her two young cousins called upon her there. When, seven years later, she died, they found themselves the beneficiaries of her will, George of her estate in Northumberland, and Bob of her Sicilian property.[13] Her husband, who had a life-interest in it all, survived her for twenty years, so that Hallington, which my father was to love so dearly as his

[13] The Sicilian property was loaded with debts and Robert never took it.

holiday home in later years, came to him in 1927, the year in which he became Regius Professor at Cambridge, and was beginning to need something a little more commodious than a cottage in the Lake District in which to entertain his friends and build up a library of the books he specially loved.

Having gained his Fellowship, (the first ever awarded for History) he settled down to read for his next book, *England under the Stuarts,* and to regular lecturing and class teaching at Trinity, for which purpose he was appointed College Assistant Lecturer in history from October 1901.

In those days there was no University Faculty of History; all lectures were arranged by the Colleges, but there was a 'Special Board' for History and Archaeology, a body which in some ways anticipated the Faculty which was created in 1926 after the Report of the Royal Commission.[14] Under this Board he lectured regularly on Modern European History from 1900 to 1903 when he gave up teaching work at Cambridge to live and work in London.[15]

[14] See p. 195 below.
[15] See p. 80 below.

IV

Work, Play and Writing, 1898–1902

Political events in the great world fascinated, excited and worried
George increasingly during the years following his settling at
Trinity to teach history. He began speaking again at the Union
whenever a cause moved him deeply. The Dreyfus affair was still
convulsing France, and Emile Zola's open letter to the President
of France, known as '*J'accuse*', revealing the perfidy of the per-
secutors of Dreyfus, had just appeared. In the Union on 8 February, 1898 George spoke, with some eloquence, to the motion
that 'the service rendered by M. Zola to the cause of justice de-
serves the sympathy of this house.' The *Cambridge Review*
described his speech as 'the best that the House has listened to
from a resident member for some time.' 'I was delighted to find,'
he wrote afterwards, 'the House with me, enthusiastically with me
in this matter, for I make it almost a test of good feeling in the
English "jeunesse".' The motion was passed by a large majority.
Later that year he was still intensely concerned as the struggle in
France showed no signs of abatement. 'There is really no second
side to the question,' he wrote, 'and if France goes wrong on it
now, it will be necessary to consider her outside the pale of real
civilisation . . . Events come swiftly, loud thundering in the
papers, quick like blows, and leave ineffaceable marks where they
have struck. You cannot go back on them. They are there, they
are history and the world has changed while you gasp.' Carlyle
had seen the 'bad, bloody silly side of the French Revolution
spirit', and George now felt that that spirit, 'combining with pure
mediaeval obscurantism seems to have got the upper hand of the
noble and glorious elements in the Revolution spirit. With a sigh
one admits there was something, nay much, in that Tory terror
of French ideas entering England in 1790–1800.'

The vacations of 1898 took him in March into the far west, to the ancient home of the Trevelyans—Nettlecombe in Somerset—and to Sedgemoor and Tintagel; and in July into the north of Scotland. He took his bicycle and rode or walked through the Somersetshire lanes or along the forbidding coast of Cornwall. At Nettlecombe he seemed to have passed back into an older world and to be 'walking about among my ancestors'. The young squire, Sir Walter Trevelyan, could not at first be found, but was at length discovered hunting a badger. He was 'shy and absorbed in the pursuit, so that the scene was really very like the "me" in *Rob Roy* first meeting his cousins at the ancestral home.'

The battlefield of Sedgemoor thrilled him. He was able to view it from the top of the church tower of Weston Zoyland, where the old vicar, a Cambridge man, gave him a glass of ale and talked about Paley's excellence as a theologian. This immense expanse of the 'moor' seen from such a height, the houses all contained in the villages with no outlying farms, was almost a map of the battlefield. He pictured to himself the scene at daybreak after the night-battle—'small knots of men making for the hills in both directions for miles away across the plain and red-coated horsemen riding them down and cutting them off, or carrying back small bodies of prisoners to cram into the church.' Still in his imaginative reverie, 'I rode on between lines of gibbets to Bridgewater', which was 'gradually recovering from the Bloody Assize—has indeed lately spread into a new quarter with manufactories etc.'

At Tintagel, George explored the great ruin, whose origins were unknown, and scrambled about the sea-cliffs on which it was built. In his work on the Peasants' Revolt he had learnt that a Mayor of London who had supported the rebels had been sent there as a state prisoner. 'He must indeed have thought he had come to the world's end. I wonder what the draper from the green banks of the Thames and its wharfs thought of this iron-bound northern coast where not a fisher can moor a boat. Whether he thought it beautiful, whether it made him think or only pine. I expect they let him walk about loose on the island-rock, for he could not have got off it.'

In July he fared north to Inverness, which he was surprised to find 'has no great manufactories connected with the sea that comes up to its doors', and that there were no trading ships in the Firth. His object here was to explore the battlefield of Culloden. He noted the 'little old homesteads' on the moorland road, thatched instead of slated, 'the old sort of Scotch cottage now rapidly disappearing'. Some of these had witnessed the 'march past of the 6,000 romantic savages[1] going to their doom,' and also the return rout, 'when they dropped so thick on the moor to right and left of the road'. His political sympathies were entirely with the British army, whose victory 'in quite unromantic but none the less valiant fashion, brought blessings to Scotland quite incalculable or only now beginning to be calculated.' But his heart also went out to the fallen Highlanders, whose dying eyes saw the distant hills to the north 'which to them were Simonside and Wallington combined, the home . . . which they could not reach, no, not though they were in sight . . . so they rolled over on the heath to die bitterly, and tramp tramp comes by the Red Soldier from the Somerset or Warwickshire village, on his way to those same mountains to shoot more savages there, break up the clans and open out the Highlands for the picturesque tourist and usher in Walter Scott. How romantic is every age if it could only see itself so! The eighteenth century dull!!??' Below in the valley he could see labourers building a great stone viaduct to carry the Highland Railway across the Nairn, within a mile of some pre-historic stone circles. This seemed to him in some way symbolic of what happened on Culloden Moor on that grim April day in 1746.

He then walked for a week through the Highlands from Lairg to Cape Wrath with a Cambridge friend—a Manchester Scot who was going into the Ministry of the Kirk—and finally arrived at Wallington to work peacefully at rewriting *Wycliffe* and to enjoy the company of his parents. Charles was in New Zealand, making a tour round the world. He was in America during the war with Spain which resulted in independence for Cuba, so George's letters to him are full of rejoicing over the defeat of Spain, and news of home grouse-drives and walks in the Cheviots. At Wallington literature and publishing were in the ascendant. Sir George was on the point of bringing out the first volume of his *History of the American Revolution.* 'I never saw him so well as he has been the last two months,' wrote George. 'This

[1] That is, the Highland army of the Young Pretender.

morning he went off in great spirits to London for the *great interview* with Longman.' Bob also produced a book of poems, *Mallow and Asphodel*, which 'has been accepted by Papa and all of us in a way which will make family life much happier than it has been for some time past.' George himself had sent up his *Wycliffe* to be judged for a Fellowship, but with or without a Fellowship he was eager to publish it, and was happy in his father's approval of his work. 'I admire and love Papa more and more every day,' he wrote; 'this year he has been, for the first time for twenty years, perfectly in his element and in practically perfect health and I have been able to see him in all his true nobility of mind.' Sir George was indeed enjoying his well-earned retirement from politics; he was still young enough at sixty to look forward to many years of life doing what he really loved—reading Greek, Latin and English literature, writing history and living at Wallington. He took pleasure in welcoming his sons' friends there.

George's home recreations at Wallington were, as he told his brother, 'the old sports' which were as dear as ever—chief among them walking alone in the Cheviots. The procedure then was to get a train from Scots Gap to Rothbury, drive in a 'trap' to Alwinton at the foot of the Cheviots and then walk up on to the Cheviot ridge by way of the beautiful Usway burn and so over on to the Scottish side, '*Sartor Resartus* in my pocket'; stay a night at a farm where the people were strong Liberals and keenly interested in the American war with Spain, and walk back next day over the almost trackless wilderness of moors into Redesdale and so, after tea at Otterburn, to Wallington, just in time for dinner.

On these moorland walks he made friends with the old Presbyterian Minister at Otterburn, Mr Newlands. He was Scottish and a great antiquarian, so they had plenty of common interests, but the greatest pleasure he gave to George was something rarer than talk. He used to sing to his young guest the actual ballad of 'The Battle of Otterburn', as his mother had taught it him in his boyhood in Scotland ,'she having learnt it by word of mouth "at the milking" from the other milking maids'. He accompanied himself on his old 'crowdy' (fiddle) as he sang. So George was able, like Walter Scott, to listen to the true 'Minstrelsy of the Scottish Border', still even then a living tradition among the people of the moors.

66

He enjoyed shooting, especially going out alone with his father and the keeper, Thornton, or, as once, with Edward Bowen, but he was never as brilliant a shot as Charles. He did plenty of execution however among the grouse, and the immense rabbit population in the fields round Cambo. Besides sport, George took an interest in the Cambo Exhibition which took place every August—especially when Edward Keith, the young head gardener at Wallington,[2] gained prizes for his fine wood-carving—but George declined with amusement to judge a hand-writing competition. Legibility was the one virtue his own hand possessed, though, as he often said later, he did not, like Hamlet, 'hold it a baseness to write fair'.

At Cambo also there were village concerts in which George sometimes took part. He could not sing (as Charles could) but he could read aloud, and a young woman who was present at one of these gatherings remembered throughout a long life how George had read some poems of Browning, which the Northumbrians appreciated more than the Gilbert and Sullivan songs which also formed part of the programme. These they thought 'childish stuff, but George treated us well and read out what we couldn't understand.'

George's life at Trinity had by now been enriched by the presence there of one who became his most beloved friend— Geoffrey Winthrop Young. This poet, athlete, climber, friend and teacher of the young, was eight months younger than George and came up to Trinity in the autumn of 1895. He twice won the Chancellor's medal for English verse, and founded among other things the clandestine sport of roof-climbing by night over the roofs of Trinity. There was scarcely indeed any activity or recreation requiring imaginative effort and skill, from Alpine climbing to dancing, of which Geoffrey was not a master. The only pastime in which George did feel himself somewhat superior was that of reading, and in that Geoffrey was 'quite willing' to improve, under George's guidance. Long afterwards George thus described his first lunch in Geoffrey's room: 'we ate roast duck

---

[2] Keith lived to a great age, dying in 1957. He wrote a novel about Northumberland in Tudor times, *The Keeper of the Rede*, and some delightful *Memories of Wallington*, where he was head gardener for nearly fifty years. He was a socialist, which led to much friendly disagreement with his employer Sir George. He was famous in the county for his growing of sweet peas.

and green peas and talked about Shelley'.[3] Their friendship had a special aura because it was a friendship of the second generation. From their own Trinity days George Otto Trevelyan and Geoffrey's father, Sir George Young—a great Victorian public servant and also one of the pioneer Alpinists—had been devoted to one another. Geoffrey's mother brought 'beauty, wit and Irish grace of living'[4] which she transmitted in full measure to her sons, especially to Geoffrey. No one more than Geoffrey Young fulfilled for his friends so perfectly Hamlet's 'Man': 'How noble in reason! How infinite in faculty; in form and moving how express and admirable! In action how like an angel! In apprehension how like a god!' Years afterwards when they were both old men, George Trevelyan wrote to Geoffrey's wife: 'He is the first man among us all, and has *done* most worth doing.'

Their chief joint contribution to Cambridge life was the creation of 'The Hunt'—a unique game of 'Hare and Hounds' played by themselves and their friends for four days at mid-summer over the Central Fells of the Lake District. It was based generally at Seatoller in Borrowdale; sometimes at Stool End in Langdale. The 'hares' had an overnight start to make their way into the high fells before the 'hounds' set forth to sight and catch them. The range was almost boundary-less; weather was not a consideration; both hares and hounds slept away from base, in sleeping-sacks on the fells, in barns or in farmhouses. The climax of the game was always the chase and here George Trevelyan's mountain paces were a by-word. He climbed hills very fast, but his running downhill over scree or boulder-strewn turf was almost legendary. Fourteen years later, after running off Snowdon 'in my Hunt style about twice as fast as anyone else,' he wrote to his brother: 'As it is my *only* athletic performance, I am the more anxious to be able to go on running downhill as long as possible.' In the first Hunt in June 1898 he was a hare. These extracts from a letter to his parents describe the final chase after he and his fellow-hare had eluded the hounds for three days: 'It was Geoffrey Young who organized the hounds (twelve in all) and who was most after us. One day he started after us without breakfasting and was out till 7 in the evening without eating anything

<hr>

[3] G.M.T. used to tell us that when he had friends to lunch in his rooms he ordered 'chicken for four and bread sauce for sixteen'—in order to ensure a plentiful supply.
[4] See *Mountains with a Difference*, by Geoffrey Winthrop Young, 1953.

68

all day, several times coming across us. No one except a Young
could possibly go without food so; it is a most extraordinary
power.' Finally George was chased down the head-waters of the
Esk 'for the most exciting five minutes I ever had in my life. We
both went as hard as we could possibly go over a chaos of wet
rocks, not looking where our feet were planted, but simply bound-
ing by instinct. . . . we both of us rolled over and over several times
among the boulders.' By hiding in a cave by the stream he eluded
his hound and at length made his way over Mickledore into
Wasdale, 'with a sense of having *escaped* which was a most
curiously new and real feeling; it gave me a knowledge of the in-
wardness of adventure novels, and I shall always henceforth read
Kidnapped with a difference. I really know what it feels like to be
hunted—and to escape, two different but kindred sensations.'

In the second hunt, in June 1899, he was again a hare, with
Geoffrey as his companion. They camped in a cave on Glaramara
(the long ridge stretching eastwards from the Sca Fell range),
selected a few days before the Hunt began, and there, parodying
Charles Kingsley's 'Invitation to Tom Hughes', George rhymed
to Geoffrey in that great morning of their day:

> Up a thousand feet, Geoffrey,
> Over Wasdale Head,
> Find some stones to leeward
> And make up our bed.
> Laugh at hounds and huntsmen
> Safe in slumber curled,
> Then to chat till midnight
> O'er this babbling world,
> Of the friends at College,
> Of the fall of Spain,
> Of the tree of Knowledge,
> Of the chance of rain.
> If the Church goes Romeward,
> If Verrall's book is true!
> If Lord Charles comes homeward,
> If our cave will do.
> Anything and everything
> Up there in the sky,
> Ten o'clock is close time
> And no hounds are by . . .

The Hunt proved no short-lived pastime; it continues to this day eighty years later, the 'Master' being a member of the Trevelyan family. George, after saying in 1899 that he would not hunt any more, in fact took part in twenty hunts, his last being in 1926 when he was fifty years old.

Meanwhile at Trinity he was trying to put into practice some Carlylean ethics, which were in fact essentially Christian because they rested on the motto he had earlier adopted: '*Ich Dien*'. 'I am very happy this term,' he wrote in October 1900, 'I have a feeling I am being of some use which I had not last year. My history class contains all the good men of the third year and I am getting to know them, and so encourage them as well as teach them I think. I have Wednesday evening at-homes for history men, which I believe will be of use to some people.' Some of these evenings were given to poetry. The late Professor Dover Wilson told me that he first 'discovered Wordsworth, together with Browning and George Meredith', in George Trevelyan's rooms at Trinity. 'There are a lot of nice, very nice, eager undergraduates and B.A.'s, history and otherwise, about the place,' George went on, 'not highly intellectual, but clever enough to serve. These I now feel able to get at. I am interested in them now more than in my extremely intellectual friends. I seem to be able to get intimate with those sort of people and to be of use to them individually . . . At my lecture on Luther I saw a man at the back of the room, an artist person . . . crying, or at any rate under the influence of strong emotion which I thought rather a triumph for a 9 o'clock lecture. However, it was only the subject. There is no such subject as Luther again in lectures on Modern History.' But one wonders, was it just 'the subject'?

He was indeed now entering another kind of teaching world, which brought him into close touch with people who had not the prospect of entering a University at all, even as 'eager' but 'not highly intellectual' undergraduates. For in October 1899 George Trevelyan became a regular teacher and lecturer at the Working Men's College in London. The College had since 1857 been established in Great Ormond Street. It is not difficult to understand the attraction it had for him, with his ideals of service to 'the people', and his determination, formed at Cambridge, to unite the writing and teaching of history with 'democracy'—in other words to bring the knowledge and love of history to many who could not then enter the academic world. The College's founders, the Anglican scholars Frederick Denison Maurice and his friends, were in the main Cambridge men, and chiefly from Trinity. Among George's friends were Theodore[5] and Crompton Llewellyn Davies, whose father, a clergyman who had spent his life promoting education in London, was one of the founders of the College and was now passing his latter days as Vicar of Kirkby Lonsdale in Westmorland, where George had sometimes stayed. From him he learnt the importance of Maurice's work and ideals. The College was the finest creation of the Christian Socialist movement, and although by the time George Trevelyan joined the staff more than twenty-five years had passed since the death of 'Maurice the Prophet', his spirit and vision still fortunately prevailed there. It was not an institution like the 'mechanics' institutes' simply for giving lectures to working men, but was established, in Maurice's words, 'first for the benefit of us the teachers, secondly for the benefit of those whom we taught.' Fellowship between all who frequented it, in social and recreational as well as academic activities, was the basic principle. This was the 'College spirit' which gave to the Working Men's College something of the atmosphere of the colleges at Oxford and Cambridge, although it was not residential. In 1904 when he had been teaching there for some five years, George Trevelyan wrote an article in the volume of *Records* edited by Mr Llewellyn Davies on 'The College and the Older Universities'. The 'College Spirit', he said, with which Maurice had been imbued throughout his life although he was never a 'don', could be identified as 'common education and common intellectual endeavour, inspired by the friendship of some and the good-fellowship of all the members of an educational institution.' Maurice's heart had been fixed on friendship, not on wordly honours, and the College had received from him the air of friendship and common endeavour towards the things of the mind. 'We are not,' George wrote, 'an Extension Lecture or a Night School . . . there is no distinction of college or academic rank between teachers and taught. The teachers at one class are often students at another.' George himself attended his friend Francis Cornford's[6]

[5] Theodore, a most brilliant Treasury adviser with advanced liberal views, was accidentally killed while bathing near his Westmorland home in the summer of 1905. George named his first-born son after him.
[6] Afterwards Professor of Greek Philosophy at Cambridge.

class on Plato's Philosophy with a dozen fellow-students and testified that 'he made me understand it to an extraordinary degree'. And it is amusing to find George in his first term at the College presiding at a Smoking Concert in the Coffee Room as the new Vice-President of the Musical Society—his musical talent having never extended beyond shouting Harrow songs. One other remarkable illustration he gave of what the College had meant to him. 'I have been through the war,' he said, meaning the Boer War, 'at the College and can witness that it was one of the few places where it was then possible to be happy for a few minutes together. I think weekly visits to College during the War saved several from the madhouse.'

He made it his business, besides teaching history, to forge closer links between the College and Cambridge, especially Trinity. He enlisted many of his Cambridge friends as teachers and visitors to the College, among them G. P. Gooch and Hilton Young, the brother of Geoffrey Winthrop Young, as well as Francis Cornford. 'The lecture list,' George wrote in October 1901, 'is nearly half composed of them now.' He recommended that partially idle B.A.'s should go up to the College once a week from Cambridge; 'they will learn much and perhaps teach something.' He also advised men who had recently left Oxford or Cambridge to join in concerts and debates there 'before the doors of their profession close for ever between them and all chance of experience and change of idea.'

The week-end visit to Cambridge by members of the College, first organised by George Trevelyan and Francis Cornford in the summer term of 1900, became an annual event. The first visit is thus described in the College records: 'Mr Trevelyan was ubiquitous . . . He arranged that while you breakfasted with one of his friends, you lunched with another, tea'd with a third and dined with a fourth, while his own rooms were a hospitable headquarters where our scattered groups were re-united.' Several senior dons were also recruited into the service of hospitality. Dr Butler showed them over the College and they had tea with Archdeacon Cunningham.

All through this year he was working hard to raise money, both at Cambridge and elsewhere, for the College Building Fund. He saw this as 'a dead lift effort to raise money to put the W.M.C. in a position to compete with other educational institutions, many of which, though they teach the same things are not of the same

72

social value.' He arranged a meeting at Cambridge in February, but the Boer War was going badly, and the meeting was postponed. 'The only buildings,' wrote George, 'that could attract public attention for the moment are forts and ramparts.' In the autumn, however, it was possible to go ahead and we read that 'owing chiefly to the energy of Mr G. M. Trevelyan, the Appeal Fund has had some considerable accretions'. George enlisted the support of his own family, the Fund prospered and eventually the College was able to commission an entirely new building on a site in Crowndale Road, where it still remains.

On joining the regular staff he started with a lecture on 'Social England in the time of the French Revolution and Napoleon', and made this the foundation for his history class during that year. 'As long as he comes to lecture,' says the College Journal, 'we may reckon pretty confidently on a good history class in the College.' In the following October (1900), however, he changed his subject to 'England under Charles I and the Commonwealth.' So he introduced the young men at the College to the two periods of English history to which he remained faithful all his life—the early nineteenth century and the Stuarts. His style was emphatic and vivid like his writing. It was the social history of the people, rather than the politics of the State, that attracted him. Thus he told them in a lecture on England during the Commonwealth how Puritanism, never, like Methodism, confined to the lower classes, was an influence felt equally among the gentry in the country and the tradesmen and business people in the towns. 'Apprentices who worked in the backs of shops . . . heard sermons for three hours together with as much zeal as their descendants watch a football match for one.' Soon a 'Literary and Historical Society' was formed under his guidance in which he was able to speak to a rather wider audience than his own history class on the Civil War. He was then in fact deep in the preparation of his next book, *England under the Stuarts*, which appeared in 1904. But in the autumn of 1903 a new title for his lectures appeared— 'The Union and Freedom of Italy, 1796–1870'. This is the first indication of his turning towards the subject that for the next seven years was to hold his passionate and devoted interest—the Italian Risorgimento and its hero-figure, Giuseppe Garibaldi.

Besides his lectures, he also took a literary class, which was really a Carlyle class. 'It is very light work,' he wrote, 'not lecturing proper as it only consists of reading bits of *Hero-Worship*

73

with eight very intelligent men and talking to them about it and Carlyle.' His pupils in this class were so responsive that he began to suspect 'that people of literary perception in the highest sense run all through the middle and lower strata of society—though not I suppose the very lowest.' So his 'love for the people' which he had discovered in himself while still at Harrow, seemed to be finding its own justification.

We have seen how sometimes it seemed to George that in the midst of the anxiety and misery of the Boer War, it was only teaching at the Working Men's College that kept him sane. His views on the war, however, were not, as might have been expected, wholly pro-Boer (as his father's were); he hoped much at first from the 'Liberal Imperialists' led by Asquith, Campbell-Bannerman, Rosebery and Sir Edward Grey, and wished for complete military victory 'to prevent another war' and to be followed at once by self-government for the Boers. But as the war went on, he became as disgusted with the Liberal leaders as he was with the 'jingoes' on the Government benches. They ought, he felt, to denounce the jingoes and Boer-haters—especially those who demanded the execution of rebel prisoners. Charles—now Liberal member for the Elland division of Yorkshire—was urged to speak out to his constituents: '*Teach* people the folly of the bloody paragraphs they read day by day in the press.' Jingoism he said, had always been one of our vices, in the Napoleonic and Crimean wars, and again now. 'We have "forgotten",' he wrote in December 1899 when the war was going badly, 'spite of Kipling's song (he was the first to forget) and we are being reminded.'

Neither the Government nor the Opposition commanded his respect. 'I must sadly and deliberately confess,' he wrote, 'that to my mind every important person has done everything either wrongly or at the wrong moment from 1895 onwards.' 'The leaders of neither party recognise that we are in a dangerous national crisis, and that things are more serious than they have been since Napoleon's time. It is nonsense to talk of the Crimea: Europe was not armed and dangerous then, and half of it was friendly.' Balfour 'seemed to regard the situation as another phenomenon for metaphysical classification', while the Liberals had no more sense of the seriousness of the crisis than the Government.

74

He and Charles were in agreement in their views of the war, and George was distressed that his strongly pro-Boer parents were inclined to think Charles was 'truckling to the Tories'. 'The middle position,' he wrote to his mother, 'which says *every one* has been wrong may be the right one.'

He was in frequent correspondence at this time with George Meredith, who wrote to him in November 1901: 'A "Day of Humiliation" will come to Europe for the treatment of the Chinese without invocation from an Archbishop.[7] As to the Boers, our errors and blunders are doing it enough: but the Boers also pay the penalties for their misreckonings. Were I younger I would undertake to show the two sides of the case, sparing neither . . . Don't think I fail in esteem for great Englishmen.'

George saw that it was useless to try to frighten the Cape Dutch by methods of terror—'they have a religion which we have not.' Through misunderstanding of the Boer temperament England was preparing to become another 'Austria in Italy'—an oppressive imperialist power. He believed that when the war was over the burnt farms should be rebuilt at Britain's expense. 'Are we,' he asked, 'to bring 17,000 Boers back from Ceylon and St. Helena and put them back on their *burnt* farms and expect them to thrive and be good citizens?' Then there was the dreadful business of the concentration camps in which the Boer children collected up from the farms were rapidly dying of measles. 'Can we lightly destroy the rising generation of a whole people?' he asked. 'I think we are very guilty to this nation.' In October 1901 he wrote a letter to *The Times* about the camps, urging that they should be moved from the veldt to the healthier regions near the coast. Charles and Cambridge friends should do the same about the execution of prisoners. 'The memory of the shootings will never heal,' he said. At Cambridge he got up a Union debate on the question of the executions and won it by 78 votes to 68, 'by combining,' he said, 'a good deal of emotion with a non-pro-Boer attitude'—by which he meant a military victory to be followed by self-government. Charles must preach these doctrines, 'again and again . . . It is crisis, political, moral and intellectual. "Statesmanlike utterances" are not heard. Make Yorkshire ring.'

[7] The Archbishop of Canterbury (Temple) had tried to arrange a 'Day of Humiliation' in the previous year but it was not approved.

His 'non pro-Boer' attitude had one amusing consequence. In January 1900 he joined the Volunteers at Cambridge. 'The spirit,' he wrote, 'is very good and has no connection with jingoism.' He made it his business to get the scholars and intellectuals to join, in rivalry to the boating men. He enjoyed drilling. 'It is just what we all want in this place—discipline voluntarily undertaken and a little waking up into actualities.' He even went to Aldershot in March, hoping that 'at the end of that I ought to be roughly efficient.'

Staying in Devonshire in May 1900 with Lord Portsmouth at Eggesford, he was surprised to find strong enthusiasm there for the unsuccessful general Sir Redvers Buller, who was a local man, to the extent even of threatening to 'mob' Lord Roberts when he came to Crediton. 'Just think,' wrote George, 'what local feeling must have been like in the time of Monmouth or the Civil War, if it can so isolate itself even today, when the fast train from London gets down here in five hours.'

Meanwhile he was active in the world of liberal literary journalism. In a review-article in the *Nineteenth Century* for December 1901 he turned his attention to a new theme—the danger to England's cultural inheritance through the spread of an uncultured urban civilisation and the proliferation of newspapers and magazines that were without any cultural tradition, or knowledge of and respect for art or literature. 'What good is it,' he asked, 'that the door guarding the stores of knowledge is now left open to all, if the way to it is concealed by rubbish heaps that in one generation have grown sky-high?' Hell, Dante had said, was filled with

> Le genti dolorosi
> Ch' hanno perduto il ben dell' intelletto.

George saw in these developments 'the gravest danger that has ever threatened the human race.' He saw also that it was no use trying to go back to a simpler economy based on village industries; and that modern industry was creating more leisure for the workers, to be used well or badly. There must, he said, be 'organised and common effort to make the good as presentable, as obvious, as cheap, as the bad is today,' and he knew that State assistance alone could check the 'grand destruction', and check corruption at the core. But the fierce spirit of nationalism in every

76

country was turning national enterprise more and more into merely warlike channels, so that 'art, literature, religious leadership, political common sense, have in our island gone down before the tide in one generation'. Much of this impassioned critique was also contained in a remarkable book of essays in social and religious studies, called *The Heart of the Empire*, published in this same year 1901. The writers were a group of young men who were troubled at the apathy into which the political world had fallen after the final withdrawal of Gladstone. Among them were G. P. Gooch, C. F. G. Masterman, and George Trevelyan, who supplied the title of the book and wrote the last essay, a short one entitled 'Past and Future'. All the writers saw that the immense growth of the national wealth through trade and industry and the accompanying inevitable concentration of working people in the great towns—badly housed, insufficiently educated, and as much cut off from the life of nature, beauty and imagination as they were from intellectual and spiritual influences—were producing new and formidable social evils, which no political party was at present facing or attempting to remedy. George placed some lines from Matthew Arnold's 'The Future' at the beginning of his essay and some more at the end—Matthew Arnold, whom he called 'the regretful and unwilling herald of our latter-day era', who saw the history of man as a river moving between shores for ever changing as man's life changes.

> Gone is the calm of its earlier shores,
>   Bordered by cities and hoarse
> With a thousand cries is its stream.

In the primary schools, wrote George, Britain had taught people to read, but there was as yet no educational ladder 'to teach people *how* to read and so become educated.' Even the better newspapers and magazines were content to encourage 'omnivorous inquisitiveness into the trivial and the important alike'. Yet, as everyone was now more or less literate, there was an absolute need for 'good intellectual food for habitual consumption, to meet this terrible free trade in garbage.' And we had housed our working people in 'little prisons each with its tiny gaolyard.'

This essay was more outspoken in political criticism than the article in the *Nineteenth Century*, for in it he named what he believed was the force most potent in creating and preserving this bad situation—the Conservative Party, with its immense majority of 150 in the House of Commons and its contentment with things as they were, which was destroying the spirit of active social involvement and reform among young men of the upper and middle classes. Worst of all, it was the party of the great 'political brewers'—combines of immensely wealthy firms who monopolised the trade in drink, who cared nothing for and in fact disliked social reform, who were content with the doctrine that Society would improve automatically by unimpeded wealth-making and the rule of great material interests. This was a comfortable doctrine, but George pointed out that the great evils of the past had been fought and overcome only by the efforts of individuals, or of dedicated bodies of men like the Clapham Sect. The Conservative Party and most of the upper classes, he said, were indifferent to injustice or at least felt no deep indignation at it. There was besides a dearth of prophets—no Carlyle, no Ruskin, no F. D. Maurice was now calling men to thought and action, although the future held hitherto undreamt-of opportunities. So it must be that 'by the enthusiastic *effort of individuals* in the spheres of economy, social work, religion, education, literature, journalism and art—all parts of the variegated whole—the glorious world of the future will be built up.' It would never come by hoping or wishing, only by acting and doing.

George Trevelyan saw, only five years after writing this essay, the downfall of the Conservatives and the coming to power of the Liberal government of 1906, in which Lloyd George did indeed lead the nation into the paths of social reform. He saw also the growth of the free lending libraries under the wing of County and City Councils, while organisations such as the Workers' Educational Association and University Extension catered for the growing demand for more adult education. His friendship in middle life with Albert Mansbridge brought him into close sympathy with these movements. In 1908 he took part in 'a philanthropic attempt to instruct readers at public libraries what to read', through a pamphlet circulated in some north-country libraries.

His radical thoughts are perhaps best revealed in a letter to his father dated 4 December 1901, in which he defended and further explained his attack on modern society both in the review and in the essay. He knew, he said, that he would be criticised for being

78

too general and for ignoring particulars. But it was society itself that had to be changed. 'I believe,' he said, 'that in order to get a new spirit in the upper and middle class, or rather in a small proportion of those classes—the classes that possess wealth and power and hold the country in the hollow of their hand—in order to get them to do things, the entire belief in "progress" and the "benefits of civilization" must be destroyed, or at least combatted tooth and nail. Only when there is a *general* discontent, not merely this or that, will the spirit of saving society even begin. It is to individuals first, rather than the masses, that I hope to appeal.' Ninety-nine people out of a hundred might think him a fool, but if even one was moved 'to seriously question the value of modern life, I shall be quite satisfied.' He must of course, somehow follow it up, and this he would do, putting his best into it as well as into history. Then he gave voice to the new and disturbing conclusion to which he had now come, and which in fact was to influence his attitude to life increasingly as the years went on. 'You see,' he said to his father, 'with the world going, as I conceive, to ruin, for causes much more fundamental than the mere South African error, or even the mere strength of Toryism,—with a world going to ruin,—it is impossible to act and work as one would act and work in a classical period of literature and politics. Once one has faced facts they are tolerable, and even interesting.' As the landscape of history and politics darkened around him, leading the world into war and destruction on a scale undreamed of, he was indeed able to 'face facts' and find interest and even inspiration in what the facts demanded of him, personally, although he had given up all faith in 'progress' and virtually all hope for mankind. Meanwhile he wrote two articles in *The Northern Counties Magazine* (published in Newcastle) for February and March 1901, on 'The Last Rising of the North, 1715'. The subject was full of attraction for him because the "Fifteen' was a rising led in England almost entirely by the Jacobite and Catholic squires of Northumberland, many of them neighbours of the semi-Jacobite Sir William Blackett of Wallington—who himself, however, had thought best to take refuge with his Yorkshire relations when the decisive hour came.

Then, in the autumn of 1902, George took a leading part in the foundation of a new Liberal monthly—*The Independent Review*. Money and support were forthcoming among the younger

Liberals in and out of Parliament.[8] The *Review* was to be 'a twentieth century Edinburgh' with advanced political views, but 'above party and above all party personalities. It is for the problems and ideas.' Articles on climbing and outdoor activities generally, and on education were also welcomed. Some of these were supplied by Geoffrey Young, who was a student both of the mountains and of the languages of the Continent.

To launch the *Review* George sold some of his investments and cancelled a projected trip to the Pyrenees with Geoffrey Young in August 1903. He also made a more serious decision and gave up his Assistant Lectureship at Trinity, in order to have more time for the *Review* and for teaching at, and raising funds for, the Working Men's College. 'Two important schemes,' he wrote, 'have sprung up in connection with the W.M.C., in addition to the *Review*, and I greatly fear I shall mismanage them all, not get on with my book [*England under the Stuarts*] and do my teaching badly too unless I throw something overboard.'

Probably this decision was made easier for him because in the summer of 1902 his father had increased his allowance. From Bergamo he wrote to Sir George that such an increase would be both pleasant and useful, 'because so many projects come upon me nowadays, and yet I want to put by a good deal each year. You hint,' he added slyly, 'unless Mama subtly suggested the phrase, that I might dress myself a little better. Well, perhaps I might, as Hamlet said when he pulled up his stockings. I have a tendency to act Treasury official, to Booa's and Mama's cabinet requirements in that matter. I dress better than the Italians of the twentieth and worse than the Italians of the fifteenth century.'

By far the most important contribution from George Trevelyan to the *Independent Review* was an article in the December number (1903) which he called 'The Latest View of History'. Some years afterwards he re-published it, with some alterations, in the collection of his own essays and reviews, calling it 'Clio, a Muse'. In it he revealed that vision of history and the writing of history which had been coming to its maturity in his mind since Harrow days. The spark which kindled his fire was the Inaugural

[8] Among them were C. F. G. Masterman and Lowes Dickinson, while contributions were also made by older friends—A. W. Verrall the classical scholar, F. W. Maitland the historian, and Lord Bryce.

Lecture by Bury, the new Regius Professor of History at Cambridge who had succeeded Acton. History, Bury had said in this lecture, was 'a science, no more and no less'. It was not the first time that George had come up against the purveyors of 'scientific history'. In his first year at Cambridge he had been told by the dying Seeley that Carlyle and Macaulay were 'charlatans'. Though very angry, he managed, out of consideration for the sick man, not to reply. But Bury's lecture ten years later gave him the opportunity he needed, and in an essay that was at once eloquent and thoughtful he spoke out.

First, he said, history, to be read and respected, must be presented in an artistic, literary form. All the great 'scientific' historians, including Seeley himself (the author incidentally of an entirely 'unscientific' work, *Ecce Homo*) had been men of letters as well—Creighton, Gardiner, Freeman. History must indeed be 'scientific' in its fidelity to facts and in the scrupulous accuracy with which it collected and sifted them. But it could not discover the laws of cause and effect of any event or series of events, for historical knowledge could never be complete on any one subject. 'No one can ever give a complete or wholly true account of the causes of the French Revolution.' The powers of intellect, sympathy and imagination were all needed in interpreting the facts and tracing the causes of actions, and those were the very powers used by Carlyle to discover the true character of the French Revolution and the true greatness of Cromwell.

But in any case, 'cause and effect' were not all. Events were more interesting than their causes, which were 'but the vessel tossed on the weltering ocean of chance. The precious cargo is the deed itself'. And the true narrative of things done was a beneficent gift to the mind, giving it both rest and illumination 'by the contemplation of the many-coloured and living past'. Here lay what to George was the specal quality and glory of history—it could keep alive for us 'the spirit of rest and beauty so alien from the spirit of our age', and the spirit also of sympathy with the men and women of past times who had suffered and loved and struggled in the cities, churches, houses and countryside in which we ourselves still lived. He felt, none ever more deeply, the power and pathos of *association* between the present and the past, afforded by places that had been the centre of historical actions or the scenes of tragic and decisive events. One of his most moving pictures is of what may be felt and thought by a walk in the gardens of St John's College, Oxford—the headquarters of Charles I's Court during the first year of the Civil War.

'Given over to the sad use,' he wrote, 'of a Court whose days of royalty were numbered, its walks and quadrangles were filled, as the end came near, with men and women learning to accept sorrow as their lot through life; ambitious men abandoning hope of power; wealthy men hardening themselves to embrace poverty: those who had most joy in life preparing to accept death, and lovers to be parted for ever. Imagination sees them strolling through the garden, as the hopeless evening falls, listening while the distant siege-guns break the silence with ominous iteration. Behind those cannon on the low hills to the northward are ranked the inexorable men who came to lay their hands on all this beauty, hoping to change it to strength and sterner virtue. And the curse of the victors shall be, not to die, but to live, and almost to lose their awful faith in God, when they see the Restoration, not of the old gaiety that was too gay for them, nor of the old loyalty that was too loyal for them, but of corruption and selfishness that have neither country nor king. The very silence of the garden seems unalterable fate, brooding remorsefully over besiegers and besieged, so stern to destroy each other and permit only the vile to survive.'

His heart was much taken up with Roundheads and Cavaliers at this time because he was engaged in writing *England under the Stuarts*. His own political views and judgments were with the Parliamentarians, but his warmth of heart and imagination enabled him to enter thus into the tragic dilemma of the Royalists as well. 'So it is,' he added, 'with every ruined castle and ancient church throughout the wide mysterious lands of Europe.' Thoughts such as these, he believed, were valuable because they cultivated 'true feelings about human life, its relation to time and circumstance and to those higher things that are above circumstance and time.'

In the following years, 1904 and 1905, he wrote three important articles for the *Review*—two on 'The Poetry of George Meredith', which he had for some years past held to be the most profound and universal of any the nineteenth century had produced, not even excepting Wordsworth—and one in December 1904, 'On Religious Conformity'—a very penetrating criticism of the unthinking manner in which most educated English people regularly 'went to church' for almost any reason except that of intellectual consent or conviction. Such an attitude, he believed, led to an intolerable habit of mind towards those who did *not* 'conform', and also to complacency or indifference about spiritual truth. Several years later, in 1913, he re-wrote this essay as a lecture, and gave it at the Cambridge 'Heretics' Society, with the title of 'De Haeretico Comburendo'—the famous Statute of Henry V's reign which had made legal in England the practice of burning people alive for heresy. In the following year he published it as a pamphlet. It was an eloquent plea for a much more complete acceptance and toleration of each other by both Christians and agnostics, who, he said, 'may be regarded perpetually in a work of mutual rescue'. He illustrated the absurdity to which an unthinking 'Christianity' could lead by quoting a recent case at Morpeth Police Court, when the Chairman of the Bench, Major Mitford, in trying a man for poaching who refused to swear on the Testament, had declared that 'no man is capable of speaking the truth who is such a fool as not to believe in God.'

The Meredith essays were written partly to explain and justify what many people regarded as Meredith's obscurity of language, and partly to define his teaching about Nature which appealed strongly to George, and to illustrate the splendour of an intellect 'more constantly vigorous and acute and coruscating than any other poet of the nineteenth century'. In the spring of 1900 he had gone away alone for a week into the remote valley of Wigmore in Hertfordshire, 'walking in the ancient Derefold Forest where Lollards had hidden, and spending many hours of each day in the ruins of Wigmore Castle and the Abbey down below, in an intensive struggle with the meanings of the obscure magic of 'The Woods of Westermain.' He believed that Meredith was the guide of human thought 'into the dimmer shades of intricate psychology, into "haunted woods", the birthplace of new aspirations, prophecies, religions, which can find no expression in the dogmatic statement, but only in the ethereal world of beauty, suggesting the undefined and making the unseen felt.' Thirty years later the same kind of language might have been used by the interpreters of T. S. Eliot. For George, Meredith's 'spirit of Earth' fulfilled all the thirst for 'religion' without imposing any doctrines of a personal God, or of personal immortality. Here Meredith even went beyond Wordsworth, who in the *Ode* only

83

allowed Nature to be man's 'homely nurse', not his mother, and so turned away from the 'breast upon which he fed his soul'. Less than two years later, in the spring of 1906, he published a short book, *The Poetry and Philosophy of George Meredith*, which developed the ideas of the essay. He discussed the book in detail with his friend Robin Mayor, and submitted the manuscript to him for criticism and suggestions. As with his views that history should be written to be read and enjoyed, so he hoped to make Meredith's difficult poems 'more readable to the puzzled', and he begged his friend, in reading the manuscript, to 'consider the effect on the reader, *not* a Meredithian, but potentially able to admire if rightly approached. The book is for him. Judge it so.'

Two other articles—'Poetry and Rebellion' (1905) and 'Party Loyalty in Evil Days' (1906) anticipated the direction of his work in English history after the Garibaldi trilogy was completed. They were both review-articles; 'Poetry and Rebellion', reviewing Brandes's latest volume of *Main Currents in Nineteenth Century Literature*, was reprinted in 1913 in *Clio, a Muse*. The age of the French Revolution and the Napoleonic wars had always been dear to George as the age of his most beloved group of writers—Wordsworth, Coleridge and Scott, followed by Byron, Shelley and Keats. He wrote of their genius with eloquence and wit, set as it was against the background of political repression carried on by Pitt and his successors. 'Four things, rarely united, combine to enhance their story: great poetic genius; great personal eccentricity and power; great principles come to issue in politics; and the picturesque surroundings of the old world in its last generation of untarnished beauty. Except Tolstoi, with his smock and his weather-beaten face, standing among the Russian snows and revolutions, there has been no figure in our own time that exerted the same sway over the imagination of Europe . . . For centuries to come, the eyes of men . . . will be turned to the funeral pyre of Shelley on the shore of the blue Mediterranean . . . the heart of hearts unconsumed in the flame and the doomed figure [Byron] beside it looking out to sea . . . Such is the romance that England once gave to mankind to show what poetry she can create when her heart is turned for a moment from the cares of the world to the things of the imagination and the mind.'

'Party Loyalty in Evil Days' was a review of Lord Holland's

84

Memories of the Whig Party, 1807–1821—showing how Fox and his disciple Lord Grey did for Liberal politics what the poets had done for literature—keeping them close to human needs and aspirations in days when they might have been crushed out of existence. This subject he dealt with at length in his *Lord Grey of the Reform Bill*, published in 1919 after the long interruption of the First World War.

He had meanwhile, during the years 1902–3, been drawing nearer to the chief historical work of his early life, as well as to the personal happiness which made the secure background of that achievement. In June 1902 he went once more to North Italy ('you see, I drift always to Italy,' he wrote), down the Val Telline in a workman's cart to Sondrio whence he walked up the remote Val Madre, 'unapproachable save by stout mountain walkers', and slept at the priest's house—'the house of the poorest man at which I have ever been entertained, not excepting hinds in Scotland.' They ate rice together, talking broken Italian and Latin, and in the early morning George saw the old man come back from ringing the bell of the church that woke the glen at three o'clock 'He sent me off under the moon and stars with a long draught of milk, refusing my three lire as "troppo", until I told him it was for the "poveri". He and his valley are the same since AD 1,000 in spite of your Luthers, Voltaires, Garibaldis, and will be so when our big world over which we grieve and hope and agonize has (in the next 1,000 years) undergone innumerable changes now not to be calculated.' After hard walking for fifteen hours he reached Bergamo, where he looked down on the Lombard plain straight beneath his feet, 'unbroken as far as the eye can reach save by the Mountains Euganean, a little island in the sea of plain. I cannot see,' he added, 'in the distance a place Shelley haunted without deep emotion.' Meanwhile in the little city, 'Garibaldi keeps guard in the Piazza before the old Lombard Cathedral . . . and I sit before him, almost in his shadow *al fresco*, and write and have tea . . . The statues of Garibaldi are the best thing in Italy. All else, beautiful as it is, is mournful love of the dead past; the Statue is in every town the symbol of the hope of resurrection after centuries of death.' But he had not even begun to think of himself as the historian of Garibaldi.

From Bergamo he went rather surprisingly to Hungary, where he spent three weeks in Buda-Pesth 'among deputies,

85

journalists, literary men, University students and professors, bound together by ties of blood or close personal friendships, all liberals.' He had met a Hungarian liberal in England and had imbued him with the ideals of the Working Men's College, so that already when George arrived lectures in science and history were being started by the radical-socialist clubs. What, one cannot help wondering, became of those Hungarian liberals in the disasters of the next seventy years?

From Buda-Pesth he went up into the Carpathians to walk in Transylvania, among ranges less familiar than the Alps or the Lakes. He called this strange country 'great in civilization and in savagery side by side'. The inhabitants of 'Wallachia' were especially remarkable, not only for their dress ('white dirty pyjamas, brown leather belt, pieds nus, long hair, slouch hat') but because they spoke a form of Italian as their natural language. 'It is the Italian of the Roman legionaries they talk,' he wrote to his friend Robin Mayor, 'changed a little in 1,500 years under another sky far from Italy, but still Italian. I think they are descendants of the conquered Dacians, for they resemble in face the Dacians of Trajan's column most *strikingly*. They have borrowed and kept the sweet tongue of their conquerors.'

In this remote district of what is now Western Romania (he was at Hatseg, near Deva, in early July) he was welcomed and entertained by a family of Calvinist nobles, in a hunting château where, in the hills above, boars, wolves and 'the biggest chamois in Europe' abounded, while bears often raided the peasants' maize-fields. The peasants were, however, on good terms with their lords. 'As we walk through the village the picturesque Wallachian savages bow low and the children kiss their hands—quite like a scene of 300 years ago—but in fact it is only admiration, not fear, as the Wallachians all own freeholds and are their own masters since '49' To his own great amusement George was 'treated like a prince, partly because I am an Englishman studying the Romanian question, but chiefly because I am Macaulay's grand-nephew. Everyone educated worships him here. Equally in politics and literature he represents all the Hungarians cherish. They have no German scorn of him.'

In Buda-Pesth he was shown the new and as yet unused Parliament House, 'Here I said,' he wrote, 'that tho' I had often before seen houses and palaces where great things *had been* done, it was a new emotion to see the place where for the next

86

thousand years great things *would* be done.' The Hungarians were so delighted with this 'mot' of the young English Liberal that they gave him and it a paragraph in their leading newspaper.

V

Marriage and the Garibaldi books, 1904-1911

Until the year 1899 George's life had been quite untroubled by any strong emotions about the other sex. He was not uninterested in women but he did not fall easily in love. Victoria Buxton, sister of his friend Charlie, was a woman whom he greatly valued and admired, and he tried very hard to prevent her from being over-influenced by her strongly evangelical parents, Sir Fowell and Lady Victoria Buxton. In 1895 Sir Fowell become Governor of South Australia and they went out taking Victoria with them. Great was George's wrath, and fear for the consequences for Victoria of being cut off from her more intellectual and free-thinking friends for so long. 'Finding her firm to go,' he wrote, 'I insisted on the *absolute* necessity of her coming back for a year in the middle . . . to travel with Charlie and see people and get in touch with things.' She must 'keep up intellect by reading'—he would give her a list of books. And 'I promised to write once a month an intellectual letter, and of course,' he said to Charles, 'you must do the same. Under these circumstances her mind may be saved.' Victoria seems to have survived both her stay in Australia and the course of treatment by the Trevelyan brothers. In 1907 she married Charles de Bunsen and lived happily ever after.

George certainly looked forward to marrying some time, for he wrote when he was twenty-one: 'I am studying girls carefully, with a view to knowing what I am about say five or nine years hence.' This he found a 'pleasant occupation, but most girls are terribly unoriginal and uninitiative'. Then, in the spring of 1899, he fell deeply in love. In every respect except one, a marriage between these two promised happiness if she could have returned his love. But she refused him, though sorrowfully, and he was fortunately able to accept his failure with fine good

88

sense, though also with deep suffering. For she belonged to a great Anglican family—one of many such who in those days supplied the Church with bishops and the State with generals and distinguished politicians. She was herself a believer and could not share George's free-thinking. In 1902, three years after she had refused him, he was still telling Charles that he had not given up hope, and that he believed he should ask her once more 'before I allow myself definitely to fall in love with anyone else, because I don't believe I shall ever "adore" anyone else again and her I shall adore always.' But he was also by now feeling strongly that 'in my own case and for my own work a definitely agnostic atmosphere is essential for my free development of work and of life.'

Throughout this experience his confidants had been only his brother Charles, two Cambridge friends and his mother. To her he wrote a long letter from Paris in December 1899, explaining to her how, having parted finally from his lady, he now 'felt rightly about it,' and though carefree enjoyment was not possible, he could still feel interested in the 'things of this world', 'just because I have felt the reality of goodness more strongly than ever before'. 'Things and people being so bad, or at any rate mixed, what joy I have (and that is a good deal) and what courage I have (and that is never enough) is drawn from my having once seen a perfect life, a character and a mind realizing my ideal, after which I strive myself and in myself so largely fail. To have seen that ideal in reality just long enough and closely enough to have it impressed on my memory, is what I now live upon without repining . . . A new joy springs up in me every time I remember that she walks the earth, being such and living so . . . It is to me the most real thing in this strange world of shadows and apes. Here [i.e. in Paris] the apes carry it.'

He had another comforter also—Carlyle. In June 1900 he spent a week-end at the Bush Hotel at Ecclefechan, Carlyle's birthplace, with *Sartor* as his companion. Here he felt how privileged his life still was in spite of having a broken heart. He knew now what his life's work was to be—writing history—whereas 'by far the greater part of mankind are bound down apprentice to some wearying and at best but half congenial task at which it is their duty to spend themselves. How rarely fortunate, then, am I in all this.' Then he looked out on the village street. 'Incarnation indeed was there here—here the *flesh* is still, the white stone house piled by the old father mason while the French Revolution was still brewing, the dirty burn down the middle of the street with the pots and pans in it—that was the flesh in which the spirit lately was, the spirit now fled for ever, transfused through the land.' *Sartor*, to his mind, was the chief messenger of that spirit, a charter of freedom 'to all oppressed by untoward circumstances . . . the postman of Lockerbie for instance with whom I talked yesterday, whose grandfather knew "auld Tam" here as a lad; to this poor postman and many another of all ranks and fortunes *Sartor* is and will always be the word of life, whatever Mr Balfour and other patrons of the Chelsea House[1] may say in smooth foolish speech to the long-eared newspaper reader.' George now believed that *Sartor* was 'the greatest book in the world'. Certainly it spoke to his present condition, and he felt that in its strength he could now 'take *whatever* comes to me in this world'.

The letter of October 1902 in which he told Charles that he still 'adored' his first love, was written from 'Stocks, Tring'. Stocks was the country home of the Humphry Wards and their two daughters, Dorothy and Janet. Mrs Ward, who was a niece of Matthew Arnold and granddaughter of Dr Arnold of Rugby, was at the height of her fame as a novelist and also as a pioneer in the welfare of London children, still so neglected. It was during this autumn of 1902 and the early months of 1903 that George came to feel that the wound left by the failure of his first love could be healed by Mrs Ward's younger daughter Janet, now aged twenty-four, if she would accept him.

Whatever the preparatory steps may have been, at Christmas 1902 Janet spent a few days at Wallington. She went for long walks, 'nearly always with George and liked him better than ever—he's so splendidly keen about everything, and has such a tremendous feeling for the trees and the earth. Also he's writing a solid History of the seventeenth century in England, and his learning (at 26) is something quite appalling. I found that Biblical Criticism was absolutely the only subject on which I could stand up to him at all. (Oh no, I'm forgetting Birds—he doesn't know about birds.).' Afterwards he told her that when she came to Wallington he 'loved her from the very first morning'.

[1] Carlyle's house in Cheyne Row, Chelsea, had just been opened to the public as a Carlyle Museum.

She had been taught to know about birds when still a girl by Sir Edward Grey himself (afterwards Lord Grey of Fallodon), for Stocks had belonged to him though he never lived there. In particular, when staying at Stocks, he taught her their songs and call-notes. All her life birds were her greatest out-door joy. Long afterwards she said 'I'm just a bird's-nesting boy', and there was a good deal of truth in that.

Mrs Ward was in the habit of renting a villa in North Italy for an annual spring holiday, and in May 1903 she took the Villa Bonaventura on the shores of Lake Como. Thither, to join a family party which included Janet's most beloved friend Maisie Cropper[2] from her Westmorland home near Kendal, came George, and all was happily concluded between 'George and Jan' on 20 May during a very early morning walk on the flowery hill-side behind the villa.

Janet Penrose Ward was closely involved both in her mother's social work in London and in the free-thinking forms of Christianity promulgated by Mrs Ward and her friends. Janet, however, though she translated heavy German books about the New Testament at her mother's wish, had no particular theological belief of her own, and therefore could accept readily what George called his 'puritan atheism'. In politics she shared his liberalism—he told Charles to talk to her about politics. More important, George soon taught her to enjoy Meredith's poetry, but, as he wrote to Charles 'the crown of joys of which only silence can speak, is that she has a mountain foot. We have tried it above Como.' She had indeed, though she never went scrambling or rock-climbing and did not attempt to keep up with George in his more gigantic walks. Her loves were more for the intimate delights of woodland and valley.

After a few days of bliss at Como, George plunged once more into the heart of Italy, walking across the plain of Romagna to 'the virgin fortress of republican Liberty,' San Marino, on its range of precipices overlooking the Adriatic—then on to Urbino, Gubbio and Orvieto. At home he was now living bachelor-wise in Sussex Villas with one or two Cambridge friends, having given up most of his Cambridge teaching; the Working Men's College, his new book *England under the Stuarts*, and the running of the *Independent Review* filled his life.

[2] She soon became the wife of Walter Morley Fletcher, also a Fellow of Trinity, afterwards Secretary to the Medical Research Council.

There was time for many joyful visits to friends before the marriage need be seriously planned. They went in July to the Youngs in their wonderful Thames-side house, Formosa, near Cookham, and from there took a train to Dorking and called on George Meredith in his cottage at the foot of Box Hill. 'We found him,' wrote my mother afterwards, 'sitting in an armchair by the fire, dressed in a dark blue-green serge suit with a red tie. We sat down and he began to talk straight away—asking me . . . whether I liked walking in the rain and when George said I did he went off into a wonderful description of his own feelings when he used to walk in the rain or hear the first low gusts creep up before a thunderstorm . . . He talked better and better as he went along and really got off at last on his views of things in general but we, mindful of his daughter's instructions, got up to go and had the felicity of being told to stay another five minutes, and in that five minutes he turned to me and asked if I'd begun to write yet, and when George told him I'd translated a fat German work on the New Testament he sat back in his chair and gazed at me with an indescribable look on his face.'

When at last they got away, they walked all the way to Guildford—'fifteen miles and the hugest success'.

Charles, who was now thirty-three, was at last settling into a successful engagement with Molly Bell, the daughter of the North Yorkshire iron-master baronet, Sir Hugh Bell and his wife Florence, who was an intimate friend of Mrs Humphry Ward. They were married in the following January, two months before George and Janet, and built themselves a house in Great College Street, Westminster, so as to be near the House of Commons. Robert was already married to his Dutch lady, Elizabeth Van der Hoeven, and so the 'Trevvy brothers' were all at last supplied with wives. Janet told her sister she was not 'nearly so frightened of them all' as she had expected to be, and she was particularly happy at Charles's engagement, for Molly was an old friend.

The wedding of George and Janet took place in March 1904. It was, as might have been expected, run on unconventional lines by the bride's mother, who wrote the service herself, and engaged her favourite free-thinking clergyman, Dr Estlin Carpenter to perform it in the chapel of Manchester College, Ox-

92

ford. The honeymoon was long and varied. It began at Borough Farm in Surrey, the loved haunt of my mother's childhood. Then they went to Cornwall—George walking from Truro to the Lizard in a day[3]—then to Italy, where they rode on bicycles (called Peter and Paul) from city to city of Umbria and Tuscany, finally joining the Wards once more at Como in May. What the Italian country people thought of this bicycling lady is not recorded. Janet took with her one of those important new playthings, a 'Kodak' camera, with which she, in all the long years ahead, recorded the family joys and adventures.

From Como, George went off for 'a five days' walk among the mountains', tramping through the snows of Splügen—in order to come back 'feeling like a god'. 'I know,' wrote Janet, 'what infinite peace and stillness the snows must bring to him —stillness from which he can look out upon our life ahead.'

They had taken a house in Chelsea—2, Cheyne Gardens—of no interest as a house except for the remains of a very old mulberry tree in the back garden, which itself had been carved out of the large garden of Queen's House in Cheyne Walk. From the top front windows of the house, the waters of the Thames could just be seen galloping along when the tide was high. A then rather slummy little street—Manor Street—connected Cheyne Gardens with the King's Road, Chelsea; the Royal Hospital for old soldiers—one of Wren's loveliest buildings— stood a little further down the river, its grounds providing one of our playgrounds; Battersea Park across the river was the other. The household consisted of a cook—Annie Taverner who eventually married and went to Australia; a house-parlour-maid, and after my birth in February 1905, 'Nannie'—Alice Fox, whose father had been a coachman. She remained with us until her death in 1954, beloved of three generations of Trevelyans. Among their humbler neighbours, George had been delighted to find that the local decorator who worked in the house before they settled in was a reader of Carlyle.

The routine of the year was divided between London in the winter, and the country from Easter to the end of September. George's parents had a house in Grosvenor Crescent until 1914, but already most of their year was spent at Welcombe or

[3] The statement in Bertrand Russell's *Autobiography*, vol. 1, that the journey to Cornwall and George's immense walk took place on the same day as the wedding, is incorrect.

Wallington; the Wards lived in Grosvenor Place, from which they fled frequently to Stocks. At Stocks there was a cottage on the hillside half a mile away and there we spent many a week in early summer, among the delights of beech-woods, open chalk downs and gorse-covered commons. At one time of my childhood an old shepherd drove his sheep every morning through the wood immediately behind the cottage—we could see them among the trees and hear the tinkling of the sheep-bells. And every morning before breakfast we went for an adventure-walk there with George. He could work at Stocks Cottage in perfect quietude; at week-ends friends came to stay and be walked all over the countryside.

Among these visitors were Charles Tennyson, grandson of the poet, and his wife Ivy Pretious, an ardent worker for Women's Suffrage; E. D. Morel, whose heroic labours at length liberated the Congo from exploitation by the Belgian king; and Ramsay MacDonald, who was busily creating the Labour Party and of whom George wrote in 1912 that 'he had more sense than the rest of the Labour men and all the Government put together', and he wished he could be Prime Minister. Most loved of all, however, was my mother's cousin Will Arnold-Forster, the artist, who was like a fairy prince to us children with his stories and drawings and also his wonderful use of words quite unknown to us, such as 'joker', and 'ripping', and his snatches of music-hall songs (bringing a much-needed element of robust vulgarity into our repertory), besides his paints and easel.

But an even more wonderful retreat came into the family in the very first year of their marriage. Dorothy Ward took an unfurnished cottage in Langdale. It was called Robin Ghyll. She furnished it, and in June 1905 George, Janet and myself (aged four months) spent the first of many joyous holidays there. Like Stocks Cottage, it was a perfect place for George to work in; much of the 'Garibaldi' trilogy was written there, in the dark little dining room which he used as his study, while outside the greatest of all mountain views in the Lake District—the Crinkle Crags, Bow Fell and Langdale Pikes with the green flat valley at their feet—called to him from the little garden that looked out from the fell-side. To Dorothy he wrote that summer: 'I . . . have lived in the mountains by sitting on this glorious terrace for the last ten days. I never got through so much work [he

94

was already writing *Garibaldi's Defence of the Roman Republic*] and at the same time kept so fit and I believe it is largely due to the place, which is not in a hole as most Lake Dwellings are.' The weather was fine, 'but we lived through two days of flood, the workings of which were very fine to watch in the valley below, all spread out like a play before us. Then, too, the coaches and waggons of happy people,[4] and the lithe-legged climbers swinging up the road towards their happiness, and their bits of songs and talk as they pass a hundred yards below the house, made the terrace like a front place in the stalls at some happy play . . . And when they have passed nature and silence resume their reign.'

Every now and then of course he pushed off into the hills for one of his tremendous walks. I have a vision of him now at the end of one of those days, striding along the road through the middle of the valley, his white sweater making him visible nearly a mile away, and finally arriving on the little lawn with his hair standing straight up on his head, as the mountain winds and his scrambles on familiar crags had left it. The white sweater was his usual garb for long walks or climbs, but his everyday dress when on holiday was for many years a dark brown corduroy suit of breeches and Norfolk jacket, in which he looked very princely. In London he always wore a dark blue serge suit with stiff collar and black tie; this was not nearly so becoming. He bathed every morning in a pool in the 'ghyll' which ran down the fell-side close to the house and he also had a wooden seat made under the very ancient yew tree behind the house whence he could look out at will over the valley in the intervals of correcting proofs or reading for the next Garibaldi book.

In 1911 he bought Robin Ghyll for £200.[5] Dorothy was thenceforward his informal tenant and it remained our place of holiday freedom until in 1927 he inherited Hallington in Northumberland and so became in a small way a landowner in his

---

[4] This was before the days of cars, and tourists were taken round the Lakes in open 'char-à-bancs' drawn by horses, the passengers descending to walk up the steep hills. Sometimes the coach-drivers pointed out Robin Ghyll to their passengers, somewhat incorrectly, as 'the residence of Mrs Hoomphry Waard,' at that time well-known for her novels.

[5] For many years it had no 'mod cons' and was not so popular with the long-suffering domestic staff as it was with us. It was really an old cottage attached to the farm next door (Harry Place), with two rooms added not long before Miss Ward took it.

native county, and also the neighbour of his brother Charles at Wallington.

After his marriage he carried on with his teaching at the Working Men's College and became a member of 'Mrs Ward's Play-centre Committee' which was organising evening play-centres for children all over London. In 1907—the Liberal party now being in power—he asked Charles to 'wire-pull' some of the members of the Government to get a 'non-contentious' bill through Parliament authorising the setting up of play centres in London and other big cities. This was effected through the Education Act of 1907.

The chief controversy of the election of January 1910 centred round the question of Free Trade—the Liberals being by tradition for cheap food and therefore free-traders. The Free Trade Union was running a poster-campaign on the subject in the weeks before the election—'partly I think,' wrote George to Charles, 'on account of my stirring them up by my proposal. It costs £500 a week to "do" London. I have seen all their proposed posters in sample: The "three loaves" (English, German, American), is one of the most effective . . . I gave them my £200 and said you would send £100.' The brothers had made an arrangement by which they gave each other regular sums of money out of their savings to be spent on public causes.

Evening life in Chelsea and Westminster was often enlivened by parties. My mother describes the first one at Cheyne Gardens in the summer of 1904 at which '7 of the 10 men were fellows of Trinity', so that the room was 'thick with tobacco smoke and brains'. George, of course, had to have regular country walks, even when in London, and unless they went to Stocks or elsewhere for the week-end, these were provided by the institution known as 'the Sunday Tramps'. A group of friends (usually Cambridge people) took train to some country station such as Dorking or Haslemere, walked all day on a pre-arranged route, and returned home in the evening. This kind of walk was very different from those gigantic solitary stridings across mountains and moors or along the lonely Cornish coast. The 'tramps' were, as he explained in his essay 'Walking', (published in 1913 in *Clio, a Muse*), essentially social; one talked as well as walked, whereas in the other kind of walking solitude and silence were an essential part of the business. The 'Sunday

96

Tramp' was simply 'a Sabbath-day refection for the tired town worker'; companionship was good, because 'the laughter of good company, ringing round the interchange of genial and irresponsible verdicts on the topics of the day' could, more quickly than solitude, dispel the depression accumulated during the previous fortnight of London labour, 'bus journeys and walks only on "pavements grey".'[6]

Marriage had in no way lessened George's thirst for historical roaming in Europe, if possible in a mountainous landscape. In the late summer of 1905 he went off alone to Northern Spain. He joined an assortment of Youngs at San Sebastian in the Basque country through which Wellington had taken the British Army into France after the battle of Vittoria. 'From a blackberry overgrown fort on a high hill near San Sebastian we saw a great view of the way Wellington came and went.' They took part in the local 'battle of flowers' festival in the town, got up in honour of the young king of Spain (Alphonso XIII) who was present. 'I saw the successor of Philip II pelting his subjects with confetti with the energy of an English schoolboy, whom I think it is his role rather to imitate. His Most Catholic Majesty threw much confetti and compliments in bad English into our carriage.' George then crossed the ridges of the Pyrenees and the river Bidassoa into France and at St Etienne joined a lunch-party of French tourists from Brittany. 'How civilized they were and what far better talk we had than could have been got from a corresponding class in England. The bourgeoise was a perfect treasure, so humorous, so intelligent—clearly a very good mère de famille. It was a charm to talk with them about nothing, and most interesting to listen to them when they got onto their politics of which they took the sane, half humorous view so little represented in the journals of either side—the spirit of the 'Bon roi Henri' [Henri IV] which saves France always in spite of its upper class, its journalism and its professional politicians.' These people were so different from the angry, bitter Parisians whom he had lived among six years before. 'The politeness and kindness, the human fellow-feeling of these people, the motherliness of the women who serve the cafés and shops, astonishes and delights me. I feel as if I had never seen anything like it else-

[6] The 'Sunday Tramps' had originated with Leslie Stephen in the 1880s. But with him the word 'Tramps' seems to have been applied to the people, not to the exercise.

where: perhaps I know England too well to notice, and as I don't talk Italian I cannot judge Italy. [He would soon learn to do so.] Yet I do believe that the word "fraternité" in the French motto is not humbug but stands for a national quality inherent in them, though often piteously belied by their incontrollable passions and hates. I can conceive these people in the French Revolution, their mutual kindness and humaneness to every passer-by, after a day of faction and perhaps massacre.' He then went on to join Janet (and the bicycles) at Toulouse, and they explored Carcassonne, Rocamadour and other old French cities of the south.

There was no break after marriage in his close fellowship with Charles who—greatly to the wrath of his parents—had not been included in the Liberal Government which took power at Christmas 1905. George, and indeed Charles himself, took it more calmly. 'Mama has boiled over to me already,' wrote George to his brother. 'I calm her down and take the high-and-mighty proud line. She will, too, soon.' Then he added a comment which perhaps contains a note of warning. 'It is a rule that no Trevelyan ever sucks up either to the press, or the chiefs, or the "right people". The world has given us money enough to enable us to do what we think right: we thank it for that and ask no more of it, but to be allowed to serve it. If more comes, well.'

The brothers collaborated on many public questions. On the Education Bill of 1902, which provoked a threat by Non-Conformists to refuse to pay rates unless the Church of England's influence in the primary education was reduced, George had written impassioned letters to Charles urging him to stop his non-conformist constituents at Elland from taking part in such 'arrant folly', which might involve them in disfranchisement and so lead to the defeat of the Liberals at elections.

George's in-laws, the Wards, were at first a little nervous of his strong radicalism, for they were already Conservatives and imperialists, and in 1910 Janet's brother Arnold Ward, largely through his mother's energetic canvassing in the local press, became Conservative MP for West Herts. By that time I was five and my brother Theo rising four; in Parliament great things were in progress: 'Lloyd George's budget' had introduced the first Social Insurance, and Liberal threats against the House of Lords, if it should dare to throw it out, were vociferous. George was in Italy at the beginning of 1910, reading and exploring for the third and last of his 'Garibaldi books',[7] and from there he wrote to Charles to do something for him which, he said, 'I am *much* set on.' Would Charles, he asked, 'see Mary and Theo occasionally, and . . . tell them about what you are doing in the House, according to their respective powers of understanding? Because I want them to think of *you* as *the politician* rather than Arnold. I was a strong Liberal at four; you remember how angry I got when you called me 'Tory' in 1880. Mary is a strong Liberal, but Theodore knows nothing yet, and inclines to call himself "Uncle Monster's (Arnold's) man", as he was at Stocks too near the election time. No harm has been done yet but I want them to get to think of you *as the politician* and connect it all with Liberalism. If you can arrange to do this while I am away, you may be doing real good, for as the twig bends the oak often grows. It will be a fierce fight for them,' he added, remembering Wixenford and Harrow, 'to resist boys and masters at school. Childhood memories and associations must be made as strong as possible against that day.' Charles in his reply evidently twitted George with being 'jesuitical', and George admitted it—'relics of election fever', he called it. But in substance he did not retract his wish, and he soon had the satisfaction of seeing both of us passionate Liberals, singing the Liberal squib about 'Tariff Reform' (the Tory nostrum) with impudent and deliberate purpose to our Tory relatives:

> 'Tariff Reform means work for all,
>   Work for all, work for all;
> Tariff Reform means work for all (*pause!*)
>   Chopping up wood in the work-house!

In the exciting days of the two general elections of January and December 1910, George did a great deal of electioneering for his friends who were Liberal candidates in various constituencies. 'It is a very stiff job here,' he wrote from the Yorkshire dales, 'because though the meetings are good they put several sons of Tory farmers onto the register, by making them joint tenants.' This was before the days of adult suffrage, a reform which George and Janet supported 'with purse and person' through the People's Suffrage Federation, which also advocated women's suffrage and a voting age of twenty-one for everyone. 'I don't think young

[7] *Garibaldi and the Making of Italy,* published in 1911.

people of the lower classes are so unfit to vote as young people of our class,' George said, 'A man or woman of the working class has come so much into contact with real life and its hard facts by twenty-one that he or she is far more formed than you or I were at that age . . . And apart from that I think it would be disastrous to have all the old fogies (who will increase in numbers and proportion of the population as care for the aged increases) voting, and *not* the young fools as well.'

Much as he loved the Liberal party, George was not enamoured of its 'bondage to Non-Conformity' and so to a narrow view of educational reform, temperance and of morals and religion generally. His sister-in-law, Dorothy Ward, was at first somewhat alarmed at the intensity of his agnosticism. But he reassured her. 'Don't you suppose,' he told her in 1906, 'I don't know what English religion is worth at its best. I've seen it.' His first love and Booa were 'the two most perfect people I ever saw and religion was them.' But, because he was 'of a *romantic* rather than *classical* disposition', perfection was not what finally attracted him in the human personality, 'but the rugged struggle to some new thing, dimly seen ahead', and he felt that Janet fulfilled this need for him.

So much for his personal temperament. Politically, this same temperament made him rejoice 'at the appearance for the first time in English history of a political party with a *secular* religious background'. Nothing short of this, he said, was enough 'to counteract the enormously paralysing effect of religious humbug in England—of thoughtless, man-worshipping conformity and intellectual fear which paralyses intellectual growth in our Universities and very generally in all the educated classes.' This was very much the line he had taken in his article 'On Religious Conformity' in the *Independent Review* two years before.

Foreign policy also stirred the brothers into action, particularly the fear that the Government was truckling to the Czar of Russia, whose government was loathed by all Liberals. In June and September 1908 George wrote two letters to *The Times* proving past doubt that during the previous year over 70,000 people had been sent into exile in Siberia, untried and unconvicted. In Moscow, he said, could be seen 'long lines of educated men, dragged from their homes, setting out as unconvicted convicts on their hopeless exile.' The public feeling at such revelations helped to put a stop to any arrangements for a visit of the Czar to this country and aroused criticism of King Edward's visit to the Czar at Reval. Meanwhile my parents, whose generosity to good causes and compassion for the unfortunate were to the end of their lives unceasing, were busy raising money for Russian exiles in England. I can remember a drawing-room sale in our house of Russian toys and embroideries, at which, as a tiny girl dressed in a Russian frock, I eagerly offered a pair of furry slippers to an old lady who was in fact Princess Kropotkin come to open the bazaar!

Among their wedding presents had been some books from Sir Bernard Pares, which included Garibaldi's *Memoirs* and Belluzzi's history of Garibaldi's retreat from Rome in 1849. 'Merely because Pares had given me the books,' wrote George many years later in his *Autobiography*, 'I began one day to turn over the pages, and was suddenly enthralled by the story of the retreat from Rome to the Adriatic, over mountains which I had traversed in my solitary walks: the scene and spirit of that desperate venture, led by that unique man, flashed upon my mind's eye. Here was a subject made to my hand: if ever I could write "literary history", this was the golden chance.'

He did not waste any time. At first he thought only of a book of six or seven chapters describing the Retreat, but he soon realised that it must be something bigger than that. Eight years before he had stood with his father on the Janiculum, hearing from him for the first time the story of the Siege of Rome, when Mazzini governed it and Garibaldi defended it against the troops sent by Napoleon III to the aid of the fugitive Pope. In the early spring of 1906 he went to Italy and studied all the sites of the siege—the Janiculum, and especially the area round the Porta San Pancrazio, where the fiercest fighting took place, and then, accompanied by Hilton Young, Geoffrey Young's brother, he followed the line of Garibaldi's famous retreat, from Rome across to the Adriatic, 'the wildest and most romantic,' as he said afterwards, 'of all Garibaldi's marches, with the diminishing remnant of his volunteers to whom he had offered, sitting on his white horse beside the Egyptian obelisk in the middle of the great Piazza of St. Peter's, hunger, thirst, forced marches, battles and death.' Hilton Young had a camera, and when in the following spring, *Garibaldi's Defence of the Roman Republic* appeared with its bright red binding, its maps and plentiful illustrations, it contained ten photographs taken by him of places which the Garibaldians passed through in their retreat. Two other photographs of the ruined Vascello—the villa outside the walls which the Garibaldians defended all through June 1849—were specially taken by George's sister-in-law, Dorothy, who was in Rome in April 1906. In Rome, in Genoa, in Bologna and in Paris he worked his way avidly through letters, diaries, and records of every kind that gave information about the siege and the retreat. The bibliography at the end of his book shows what thorough research went into its creation. It was no romanticised adventure-story, but a true account of an episode in Europe's history that, tragic and blood-stained as it was, ultimately gave to Europe a new destiny, by revealing the quality of Italy's patriot fighting men, and their leader Garibaldi.

As soon as he returned from Italy at the end of April he began writing the book, 'with ardour and fury,' said Janet, before he had made any arrangements about publishing. He afterwards said in his *Autobiography*: 'I can't conceive how I managed to do so much in the time'—for he finished it by Christmas and it was out in March 1907. The two other 'Garibaldi books' took a couple of years each, but 'that first year,' he says, 'I worked like one possessed and driven by a fierce imaginative excitement.' He thought the book came 'nearer to inspiration than I ever reached again', though he admitted it bore the marks of haste as well. It certainly reads almost like a great heroic poem. By way of relaxation, he made a model of the siege on the floor of the 'Museum' at Wallington that summer, putting up the lead soldiers with as careful accuracy as possible.

George realised that his brother Robert was a literary critic of great perception whose advice on style could be invaluable. He had sought his help over *England under the Stuarts*, and after the publication of the first Garibaldi book he wrote to him, 'I am glad you see a nearer approach to chastity (i.e. restraint) in the style. I do not claim to have achieved chastity altogether, but the nearer approach is something and it is largely due to your very kind and painstaking efforts over the "Stuarts", for which I shall always be most grateful. You really taught me not a little.'

And two years later, when *Garibaldi and the Thousand* appeared, he was 'immensely gratified by Bob's approval'. Some people still found the style 'unchaste in places', but 'it would be much worse but for your "taking me in hand" over the Stuarts. There are so few *critics*, and none of them appear, in print at

102

least, over history books, which escape all *literary* criticism.'
George, with his passionate belief in the imaginative quality of
history, and therefore in its value as literature, deplored the
current habit of treating a history book as an historical mono-
graph and consigning it to 'historical students' only, 'unless it
violently proclaims that it regards itself also as literature and
appeals to the general public.'

In the summer of 1907 he found time to write an essay for a
prize offered by the *Westminster Gazette*, the subject being 'If
Napoleon had won the Battle of Waterloo'.[8] He won the prize.
'With this,' he said, 'and the Garibaldi sales (which bring me in
well over £200) I shall be able to buy books and travel in Sicily
and Italy as much as I like as soon as I like, and so I can get on
properly fast with the next volume.' And he added: 'It is the
first time I have really felt I had a serious man's task worth
doing.' 'The next volume' was the story of Garibaldi's conquest
of Sicily and Naples in 1860, and it was published as *Garibaldi
and the Thousand*. The subject was as dramatic and gallant as
the *Defence of Rome*, but as the 'Thousand' were assisted by the
benevolent neutrality of England and the active though secret
support of Piedmont, with Italy everywhere breaking into freedom behind and before them, it bears throughout a more hopeful,
less tragic character.

To Hilton Young he wrote in June that he was 'feeling in-
expressibly the unreality of all historical events except only those
performed in a red shirt', and that he was 'getting to know the
Mille (the Thousand) as if they were the friends of my youth.'

Another bicycling holiday with Janet in Italy in April 1907,
starting from Ancona on the Adriatic coast took them, with some
help from the railways, to Spoleto, and eventually to Venice and
Como. George's main objective on this journey was to see the
battlefield of Castelfidardo near Loreto, where the Bersaglieri
defeated the papal troops in 1860—and the castle at Spoleto,
which the 'Irish brigade' vainly defended against another Pied-
montese force which had invaded the Papal States. They exam-
ined the field of Castelfidardo carefully, on their way to Loreto,
'and I took notes thereof for future use'. From the hill of Loreto
—'that great shrine of superstition' (the 'Virgin's house', sup-
posedly carried by the angels from Nazareth in 1294 was there)

---

[8] He reprinted it afterwards with other essays in *Clio, A Muse,* (1913). It is
highly amusing and brilliantly convincing.

—they looked back over it, 'and there,' said George, 'in sight of their damned miracle-mongering, the powerless saints watched the Papal rule over Central Italy smashed inexorably to pieces.' Staying a night at Tolentino, they encountered a commercial traveller with patriotic feelings who said: ' "There is an English-man who has written a 'splendido libro' about Garibaldi," and began quoting about it from a Bolognese paper . . . He knew all about Garibaldi's Retreat, and had visited all the proper Gari-baldian shrines at San Marino, whither his prosaic business had carried him. Such is the Italian commercial traveller.' On this tour 'in all we did over thirty miles a day bicycling, and took all our luggage for a week on the bicycles.'

The visit to South Italy, in which he would trace Garibaldi's own campaigns of 1860, was postponed until the following year (1908). But at Robin Ghyll that summer of 1907 he began to plan the new volume. 'It is an enthralling story,' he wrote to Charles, 'and every detail, or new minor personality interests me immensely. The pleasure of constructing, pulling to pieces and re-constructing the story of a battle or march from a score of more or less contradictory accounts, as one reads them one after the other, is very great.'

That working holiday at Robin Ghyll was made memorable by a visit from one of Garibaldi's grandsons, Bruno Garibaldi. He was quite young, not in the least literary—'he cannot even read novels'—but a delightful out-of-door companion. 'He cares for nothing but Italy and out-of-door adventure.' He and his five brothers were in fact planning 'a redshirt invasion of Trentino' as soon as the old Emperor Francis Joseph died! In the event they were caught up in a greater struggle. When 1914 came all the six—it being very uncertain then that Italy would enter the war—joined the French army, and Bruno and his elder brother Costante were killed almost immediately.

The first Garibaldi book gave something more than pleasure to some readers. A schoolmaster in York read the concluding chapters of the great story aloud to his wife just before she began to be fatally ill. During part of her illness he had to be away from her. She, however, felt sure that 'at the last she would not be deserted', and he ascribed her freedom from anxiety to what they had read together about Garibaldi. When she was dying she said to her sister: 'I keep thinking I hear Garibaldi in the storm out-side.' George, much moved, wrote: 'Ah! how many noble

Italians, perishing in prison or in hospital or on the field or sickening in exile, have had that visionary thought and died happy with it! But it requires some power of imagination and high sympathy to conjure up that feeling and have it in England now'— when the 'intense emotions and nobilities' of that age have vanished. 'What shadows we are and what shadows we pursue. But sometimes what noble shadows. The "hero" is one, the thought of whom, living or dead, gives strength to others.'

His autumn activities in London included lecturing on Garibaldi to several hundred 'non-conformist working men' at Whitefield's Tabernacle, the best audience, he said, that he had ever addressed. Then, in December, he and Janet went off to Rome where his parents were also staying. There he worked hard once more in libraries and archives, 'getting to know the ropes' about the Sicilian expedition. Returning home for a short break, he started off again in March 1908, for Naples and Sicily. Again, his companion and photographer was Hilton Young; Charles joined them for a short time in Sicily during the Easter Recess, and Robin Mayor also. This expedition was limited to western Sicily and Palermo which the Garibaldians captured in May 1860; the new book would end there, leaving the rest of the story to the last volume of the trilogy, *Garibaldi and the Making of Italy.* Having walked from Marsala to Palermo, George had the moving experience of meeting there Mrs Tina Whitaker, whose father had been a poor Sicilian exile in the 1850s. She was born into that condition, and even now found it strange to be rich and to live in a large house. (She had married a wealthy English wine-merchant of Marsala, where Garibaldi had landed in 1860 under the silent protection of some British warships.) 'She said to me, in her simple believable manner,' wrote George, ' "my people never had a thought about themselves. They never kept a shilling or a piece of jewellery or shirt or a coat in the drawer if a brother or sister in the cause was near at hand, and that was always. *All* the exiles I knew were like that . . . When the cause was won they retired to obscurity leaving the jackals to fight for the spoils . . . When I was a girl I was never told to be unselfish or given to understand that what my parents did was virtuous. I never saw anyone acting or feeling otherwise and thought it was natural and that everyone was like that." ' As she thus described the unselfishness of the patriots, wrote Mrs Whitaker in her diary afterwards,

'All at once I heard a great sob: Trevelyan had been so deeply moved that he was weeping. It was a curious moment—absolute though emotional silence on my part. Then he recovered himself and went on asking questions.'[9]

While in Palermo the four friends visited the famous puppet theatre, and saw the thousand-year-old play *Orlando*. ' It begins,' he wrote to his parents, 'with the Pope in prison, getting himself released (faute de mieux) by the devil—who continually stands on his head to indicate joy. Next scene Orlando is found a captive to the Saracens . . . when the Pope by the Devil's aid turns up in sulphur and the Saracens fly . . . Christendom is then punished for the Pope's mésalliance by the famous "pazzia di Orlando" or madness of Orlando, when, finding that he has been betrayed by his ladylove, he goes mad and flings off one after the other all his pieces of armour, dashing about the stage in the most wonderful doll madness, far more dramatic and human than that of ninety-nine live actions out of a hundred. It was a marvellous piece of art, and no doubt the tradition of it, both the voice used and the way of pulling the strings, is as old as Charlemagne, like the play itself. The theatre was a dog-hole half as large as your drawing-room and I and my friends were the only people present who were not working men. We paid 2*d.* each for the best seats.'

At Robin Ghyll that summer of 1908 he began to write the book. 'The few days,' he said, 'before one gets one's mind back into one's subject, and gets off writing a new book are always agonizing, but I hope to be absorbed and in full swing in three or four days.' He wrote while there the account of Garibaldi's wanderings in America and at sea from 1849 to 1859; the rest of the story during the winter months in London. It was published as *Garibaldi and the Thousand*. He dedicated it to both the Young brothers, Hilton, 'because you have deserved it by reading it all, and to Geoffrey, because it is impossible for me to dissociate you from him and him from you.'

Before setting forth again for Italy for his final researches and explorations of Garibaldi's campaigns, he lectured at Oxford 'on Garibaldi' for the University Extension, and in November he even visited Harrow and gave a lecture to the School. It was a happy visit, for he met there 'a lot of very first-rate masters,

[9] *Princes under the Volcano* by Raleigh Trevelyan, p. 342. Quoted by permission.

especially Hort'—the son of the great New Testament scholar. Bowen had died in 1901, and the Head, a 'nice and liberal-minded but in some ways second-rate clergyman, Dr Wood', did not impress him.

Then in January 1910 he went once more to Italy; first to Milan, then to Genoa, Bologna and Rome. Political affairs in England were in an exciting state, for the Liberals were preparing the Parliament Act after winning the general election in January, and George had both the *Manchester Guardian* and the *Westminster Gazette* sent out to him regularly. 'It's odd out here,' he wrote, 'watching politics there:—rumours and annoyingly curtailed telegrams in the Italian papers each day, followed at two and a half days' interval by the English papers to explain what it really is.' In Milan he worked so hard in the Risorgimento papers in the Castello that he was too tired even to read a novel in bed— 'They all seemed too hard; but I picked up Meredith's poems and read "The Empty Purse" right through in an hour without flagging. Its cleverness revived all my energies of mind like a stimulant. It might be called "The Budget Poem" for it is on the bad effects of wealth and inherited luxury.' He promised to read it to Charles when he got home.

Besides ransacking libraries and archives as he had done on previous expeditions, George was able this time to meet and talk with several of the survivors of the 1860 campaigns' He made notes of each conversation on the spot, and wrote them out again carefully within the next twenty-four hours. Several of these survivors were members of the original Thousand: some were Englishmen who happened to be in Italy or Sicily at the time (one, Dolmage, was an officer of the British Army on leave) and attached themselves to Garibaldi's army out of sympathy. One, General Primerano, had been a captain in the Neapolitan Army.

Having reached Naples, 'which,' he said, 'I hate as much as I like Palermo,' he stayed a fortnight working there and then took ship for Palermo, where he stayed in the hotel Trinacria, on the sea front. 'In 1860,' he told Charles, 'the proprietor offered all of the Thousand who chose to stay here a month without paying, though they all insisted on paying. It was then the only hotel in the town.' There he planned his Sicilian tour. 'I am going on a tour through central and N.E. Sicily, round Etna, and to Milazzo battlefield during the next four or five days, bicycling if it is fine enough; if not, chiefly by train.' Having done this, he returned to England for a ten-day break; then went back to Italy for the final explorations. He took Janet with him, and three other friends: Laurence and Barbara Hammond (the historians of the Industrial Revolution) and Robin Mayor. Characteristically, they read *Henry IV*, Part I, aloud together in the evenings. In Naples they met Janet's first cousin, the young Julian Huxley, working in Naples at the Institute of Marine Biology. He accompanied them to the Volturno battlefield, where he and Janet took photographs, afterwards reproduced in the book, of the places were the most critical events had taken place on that hard-fought day. One day, the party made an expedition to the mountain castle of Montefusco, in whose deepest dungeons King 'Bomba' had imprisoned fifty leading Neapolitan liberals in 1851, under conditions of almost unbelievable horror.[10] 'The prison was a most extraordinary place,' wrote George, 'a regular black hole of Calcutta,—a kind of vaulted cellar under the level of the rest of the prison with an earth and cobble floor; the heavily barred windows look straight out onto the vineyards and olives of the steep hill beneath, where the nightingale sang which the gaoler shot because it gave the prisoners pleasure. The view—the only good thing in that place of misery—was closed to them by outside blinds let down to hide it.'

They returned to Rome, and there George planned the last part of his journey—bicycling through Calabria to the Straits of Messina, in the reverse direction from Garibaldi's march. 'I shall hear the budget's fate,' he wrote to Charles, 'bicycling in the wilds of Calabria. I shall only be able to write two or three times at length, as we shall be at it very hard all day going over high mountain ridges.' His companion this time was Dr Thomas Ashby, the head of the British School at Rome, who acted as photographer. Fourteen of his photographs were reproduced in the book. Sometimes the roads through the wild mountain country were impassable from mud and rain, and once they had to take a train, late at night, in order to reach Sapri, where the inn could only offer a single bed. So they tossed up for

[10] It was at the trial of these men that Mr Gladstone had been, almost accidentally, present; he afterwards visited some of them in the prison of Vicaria, and his exposure of both the trials and what went on in the prisons after he returned to England, in his 'Letters to Lord Aberdeen', contributed greatly to swing English opinion round to support for the cause of Italian liberty.

it and George got it—Dr Ashby having the sleeping sack. This story gave great delight to us children when Janet told us, Theodore exclaiming with impish pleasure 'But Daddy had the bed!'

Returning home at the beginning of May 1910, he finished the book by the following spring and it was published, as *Garibaldi and the Making of Italy* in September 1911. It sold 'faster than its predecessors, the first edition of 3,000 vanishing in the first two days and leaving it impossible to fulfil orders for some days.'

Although living in London, he kept in close touch with Cambridge and was not forgotten by Trinity. In 1909 he was again appointed by the College to give a course of lectures on English History from 1660 to 1714. This he did in the Michaelmas Terms from 1909 to 1912, coming down twice a week from London to lecture at Trinity in the Hall which, his father told me afterwards, he always filled.

In the spring of 1911 a sorrow of the most piercing kind fell on George and Janet Trevelyan. They had three children, myself and my two brothers, Theodore Macaulay, who was born in 1906, and Charles Humphry in 1909. In mid-April we all went with the Charles Trevelyans to Swanage in Dorset for a seaside Easter holiday. After only one day of most joyous fun, Theodore fell ill; it was appendicitis. All was done that could be done, but the operation was too late and he died. His parents, at Charles's and Molly's suggestion, took him for burial to Langdale where so many of his and their happiest days had been spent. 'As we drove up together with Theo in a closed waggonet from Windermere,' wrote George, 'it was raining and mists hung on the hills, but we saw the primroses and anemones and green spring in the woods, and felt, not happy, but blessed and comforted.' Geoffrey Young, 'the golden friend' as they sometimes called him, came and spent two days with them at Robin Ghyll. It was now that George decided to buy the cottage. 'I have long thought of it,' he wrote, 'and now my bravest hopes lie buried here in the fell-side graveyard, beneath the bracken and the rocks, and this is the place of my heart.'

He was not embittered or despairing and wrote out his thoughts to Charles. 'I have never despaired less about the universe, I have never felt more firmly that my faith as I had thought it out in hours of happiness holds good in personal sorrow; the hills and the buds and birds delight me more than ever they did (in spite of rain!) My interest in others is intensified rather than diminished.' Only he had ceased to be ambitious about himself—as he once had been. He felt it unlikely he would write 'another book which people will care for like Garibaldi', though he was 'zealous enough to serve out my time in a profession I love'. But what he cared most for was the family, and 'looking at Nature'. 'She gave Theo and she takes him away again, thoughtless of us because bent on life in general. I bow the head and bless her.'

During that summer of 1911, he united his Muses of History and Poetry, by choosing and editing a collection of English poems which he called *English Songs of Italian Freedom*. Here his love for Italy and his devotion to her services in the labours of the last seven years identified themselves with the love that so many English poets had borne her ever since Shelley and Byron having, as Byron said, 'no freedom to fight for at home', exiled themselves from a reactionary England to find and celebrate in Italy the first stirrings of the movement which became after their deaths the 'Risorgimento'. Shelley's *Euganean Hills* and his *Ode to Naples*, much of the fourth canto of Byron's *Childe Harold*, and the *Ode on Venice*; Clough's *Amours de Voyage*, written after the defence of Rome in 1849 which Clough had personally witnessed—these and other poems by these poets represent in the little volume the earlier decades of Italy's struggle, while the Brownings and Swinburne, Mrs Hamilton King and Walter Savage Landor dominate the later, with Meredith's late poem on the centenary of Garibaldi's birth completing it. The introduction, and the paragraphs before each poem setting them in their historical and personal context, give all needful apology and explanation. There is only one great name lacking: the book contains no poem by Wordsworth. Yet that late group of poems written after his tour in Italy with Crabb Robinson in 1837 contains four sonnets[11] on the hope of Italian freedom which are in

[11] The best of them, called 'At Rome', commemorates a meeting with Sismondi, the historian of the City Commonwealths of the Middle Ages:—

They—who have heard some learned Patriot treat
Of freedom, with mind grasping the whole theme
From ancient Rome, downwards through that bright dream
Of Commonwealths, each city a starlike seat
Of rival glory; they—fallen Italy—
Nor must, nor will, nor can despair of Thee!

no way unworthy to stand beside his *Poems dedicated to National Independence and Liberty,* written nearly forty years before. But my father's generation was so imbued with the notion that Wordsworth wrote no good poetry after about 1806, and that his politics had become irrevocably conservative, that it is probable George had never even read these poems, devoted Wordsworthian though he was.[12]

Even as he wrote the last paragraph of the Introduction, his heart sank at the news that 'the warship *Garibaldi* is bombarding Tripoli'. The kingdom of Italy could not resist an imperialist adventure in an imperialist age, and 'the red, white and green'—the flag of Mazzini and the Risorgimento—'has become one of the least honourable of the "commercial assets" waving over a militarist and financial Europe.' To his brother he wrote: 'I didn't think the Italians wanted the *appreciation* of Europe, so much as its *notice* and *attention* and that they have got. And it is all they *will* get out of the business in the end.'

His thoughts and plans were now centring on English nineteenth-century history, and he had already decided to write the life of John Bright. In fact the Bright family had asked him to do so two years before, when he was deep in Garibaldi, and he was glad when they agreed to wait until he had completed that task. 'I shall have had just exactly enough of Italy when I have done this volume,' he wrote to Charles in April 1910 from Ravello, 'and shall be very glad to take to Bright, and do it during several years of what will be an heroic age of our English politics, fought out by so many of the men I know and live among on behalf of Bright's own principles.' This 'heroic age', as he called it, of the Liberal party was able to pass the Parliament Act after another general election in December 1910 and January 1911. For this election George again worked hard, speaking for his Liberal friends in their constituencies, and consulting his brother about making contributions to various political funds. 'I have given £100 to the League of Young Liberals. I have another £100 at least: what do you advise? . . . Is the Gladstone League a good electioneering medium? . . . Or does any *candidate* require

---

[12] Wordsworth certainly became severely conservative about most questions of home politics, but his views on foreign affairs scarcely changed at all. He believed the nations of Europe should be free, and described the despotic monarchies of Austria and Spain as 'those vile tyrants'.

financial help?' But he did not believe in running 'bad candidates for hopeless places'.

Before returning to London in October he had one of his classic mountain holidays with Geoffrey Young, this time in Skye. 'It is impossible,' he wrote, 'to exaggerate the gloom, grandeur and barrenness of the black iron crags above, and of the great slabs that floor the bottoms of the corries. Geoffrey was in raptures. We had two days of very fine sea coast walking besides the climbing in the Coolins . . .' At Glenbrittle they met 'the shooting tenant, Mr Colin Philip, an artist of no mean merit, devoted to the Coolins which he paints with great skill in all weathers, cares not a damn for the shooting . . . He is very interesting on the Crofters' Acts which he has seen working beneficially since they were started, and he says . . . that the mere fuss about the Access to Mountains Bill has slightly improved matters, as the shooting tenants are some of them anxious to meet the public half-way.' Sir George Trevelyan, when Secretary for Scotland in Gladstone's second ministry, had introduced a Crofters' Bill to give protection from eviction to what remained of the Highland crofters, though he had resigned over Home Rule before the Bill became an Act. Meanwhile Charles and his friends in Parliament were trying, perseveringly but without success, to get an Access to Mountains Bill passed into law. It was constantly thrown out by the grouse-moor landlords and their friends in the House of Lords.

When the Parliament Act became law early in August 1911, George and his family were at Robin Ghyll. Charles telegraphed the news and George replied as follows: 'Your telegram was brought up to the door of the cottage at 8.35 this morning as we were all at breakfast on the loveliest of mornings, after an ambrosial night which Janet and I had spent sleeping out on the lawn. The old gentleman who brought it up from Elterwater went back smiling to spread the news among his fellow liberals in the valley. . . . Mary has claimed a holiday and is decorating the "cave" in the fell behind the cottage. I have celebrated it by reading Macaulay's account of the battle of the Boyne.' A few days before he had been over to Keswick to see Canon Rawnsley, chief founder of the National Trust. 'I found the cheerful little town full of Wesleyans,' he wrote, 'on their annual gathering there, the shop windows full of photos of leading non-con divines and the right sort of pious literature. I liked

112

to see them all happy, and doubtless rejoicing together that
<blockquote>
God hath humbled the great House
That wrought His church such woe'[13]
</blockquote>
For non-conformity then, in its political aspect, was mainly Liberal, and disapproved of the almost exclusively Tory and Anglican character of the House of Lords, which the Liberal government had now 'humbled'.

But there was one person in the Lake District who was a devout Anglican and also a keen Liberal, and that was Janet's great-aunt, Miss Frances Arnold of Fox How near Ambleside. She was the only remaining child of Dr Arnold of Rugby, had spent her entire life in the old family home, and was now nearing eighty. 'I must tell you,' wrote George to his brother, 'that dear old "Aunt Fan" at Fox How says she thinks Asquith's letter[14] so strong and dignified and courteous. She says that it fills her with hope for the future generation she is leaving behind, to see the quiet, steady undisturbed way the government and party have stuck to the one point and policy for these last two years and are now reaching the goal. She thinks it a triumph of character and sense . . . It is delightful that she should adhere at her age to the *spirit* of her father's liberalism instead of to the letter of his views.'

Meanwhile, 'Janet and I in this remote valley are following it all, day by day, with the most intense intellectual pleasure and excitement. We get the *Manchester Guardian* by the first post, and *The Times* at tea time, and I spend at least an hour over each, sucking them dry.' But he did not approve of Lloyd George's speech about the Agadir incident at the Mansion House on 21 July, in which he warned Germany in truculent language not to offend British interests, or forget how, in the past, Great Britain had 'redeemed continental nations from overwhelming disaster'. This sort of language, said George, 'was in the very worst Chamberlain manner, and played into the hands of makers of war and hatred both here and in Germany . . . it is *most* disappointing and has put back the clock of peace a long way

---

[13] From Macaulay's *Ivry: A Song of the Huguenots*. The 'House' in the poem is the House of Guise. In the quotation it is of course the House of Lords.
[14] To Lord Lansdowne, explaining the intention of the Government and the consent of the King to create peers if necessary, to get the Parliament Bill though the House of Lords.
[15] See his *Grey of Fallodon*, pp. 226–7.

since a few months ago. And I say all this as a Lloyd Georgite.'

Later, he modified this opinion. Sir Edward Grey, though he had not instigated the speech, was glad it had been made, for Lloyd George, though he was the leading Radical in English politics, had thereby shown Germany and indeed all Europe that England could not allow herself to be ignored. It was risky, but the risk succeeded, and for the present Germany was obliged to come to terms.

VI

John Bright: The Balkans: The Outbreak of War, 1911–1915

In July 1911 George was asked by two Cambridge friends to consider being nominated Reader in History at Cambridge. He declined, and the reasons for his refusal, given in a letter to one of those friends, show how central the writing of history had become to his purposes, and how he felt himself now to be at a turning point in his working life. The question was, would the Readership, as he would feel himself obliged to interpret it, be compatible with writing political history and biography as he felt it should be written? 'The Readership,' he said, 'is anything or nothing; it is just what one makes it oneself, which depends on the amount of energy and time and thought and devotion to the Cambridge life in all its aspects (not merely history) which one can give . . . If I were merely to live in Cambridge seeing my fifteen "best young men", I should not be exerting enough influence to make it worth while abandoning our London activities and friendships. And if I really threw myself into Cambridge life so as to exert some considerable influence, it would take it out of me a lot indirectly. The wear and tear of "intellectual Cambridge" and "semi-intellectual Cambridge" is known to me of old; I would go in for it and enjoy it but it would take it out of me, and would not leave me at peace. Now what I want peace for, what I want to reserve my nervous energies for, is the life of Bright.' He felt that he had come to the parting of the ways. 'The question now is whether I am going to be a person who wrote three amusing volumes about Garibaldi and then tailed off, or whether I am going to go on writing first-rate books. I have undertaken now to write the life of Bright with papers supplied me by the family. I already perceive that it entirely depends upon my own creative powers and dead lift efforts, whether it is to be a failure or a success. Bright is very easily made dull, prosaic, dead, dreary . . . And yet in reality he was (till he took office in 1870) a wonder and a world's desire—more like Garibaldi than the Prince Consort tho' you would not suppose so to look at his statue . . . The life will not write itself, the whole thing has got to be passed through my mind, and the story of English politics and society in the mid nineteenth century has got to be told *interestingly*. I have not yet tackled the art of telling politics; any fool can tell the story of Garibaldi interestingly. This is quite a new sort of job for me and far harder. I have got to invent a new art for myself. For this I want all my energies, all my nervous system, and as much peace of mind and calm around as can be got in this world by a sensitive and excitable busy-body like myself.'

Cambridge could not give him that 'vacuum of the intellect' which writing *John Bright* seemed to require. In fact, he said, 'I am bad at doing two big things at a time.' If ever he returned to Cambridge, he said, 'I must fling myself into it in a way I am not prepared to do during the next few years, because my status as a writer will just be coming to a crisis.'

When he finally returned to Cambridge in 1927 as Regius Professor, succeeding the 'scientific historian' Bury, his 'status as a writer' was more than assured, not only by Garibaldi and Bright, but by *Lord Grey of the Reform Bill* and most of all by his *History of England*.

Three years before, in 1908, he had been approached in the same sort of way, and replied in much the same spirit, when Sidney Webb unexpectedly asked him to be Director of the London School of Economics. He had neither the inclination nor the qualifications for such a post, but he replied to the invitation in a way that illuminates his knowledge of himself and his understanding of his own work. 'It requires,' he said, 'a complete devotion of all my faculties; I work up to breaking-point as it is; I have got in my head now masses of special knowledge and thought which I must get off my chest in the next three or four years, or I shall forget them. The whole thing is in me, and I must pour it out or it will cool. I have not Macaulay's memory or his power of work, or even a twentieth part of it. I am a "little person" and like other "little people" must husband my slender resources and must *specialize*. History to me is both a science and an art; science and art are severally the most exacting things in the world. Together, when one is really writing a history book, they demand every mental muscle—it is like mountain climbing when you are half-way up a chimney, when it would be distinctly unwise to begin doing ju-jitsu as well.'

His pleasure in writing the latter part of *John Bright* was greatly enhanced by being able to draw on his father's vivid memories of the debates on the Reform Bill of 1867. 'Papa is helping me immensely,' he wrote in January 1913, 'over the 1866–67 franchise crisis. By his help, and by that alone, I can make that really live. It is at present the dark period of our history, forgotten by everyone except Papa, and not yet flushed by the gradually revolving sun of history—as the 'forties and 'fifties are now being flushed.' It is easy to detect in the book descriptions of those debates, and reports of conversations which his father must have supplied.

The Corn Law agitation in Bright's earlier years and the repeal of the Corn Laws he described as 'one of the lucky bits of our history, and a really grand drama of great men and great events. So no doubt is our age, but it (i.e. the Corn Law period) is a continuous drama, over a whole generation.' For Bright's campaigns for Repeal he used some notebooks belonging to Charles, who had started but did not continue an article or essay on the Corn Law agitation. 'I shall use it freely,' wrote George, 'and plagiarize as I don't think you will ever finish it.' And in July 1912 he wrote: 'I am finishing the Corn Laws today. Your work was most useful to me.'

John Bright was published by Constable in the late autumn of 1913 and by the end of the year had sold 7,000 copies—'good for a 15/- book,' said George. At the same time he published with Longman another book of quite a different kind. While at Robin Ghyll that summer he wrote that he was 'trying to write essays or *obiter dicta* about history, literature and things in general.' By September he had decided to publish them and did so in a volume called *Clio, A Muse and Other Essays*. The first essay, which gave its name to the book, was a longer and improved version of his old article called 'The Latest View of History' in the *Independent Review* in 1903. 'I have doubled it,' he wrote, 'and immensely improved it (a great deal of it was not good enough) and left out all mention of Bury', whose remarks about 'scientific history' had triggered off the original article. 'But,' he added, 'it must be *very* good if I am to publish it now, and it must be in perfect taste, or it will read like blowing one's own trumpet. It is very difficult and wants a lot of thinking about. But I am rather keen on it if it can be well done.' It was eventually 'done' to his own satisfaction and to the delight of that and the following generations of history-lovers. After its publication he wrote of his pleasure at John Morley's approval. 'That essay,' he said, 'has done what I wanted including making some people at Cambridge—and doubtless at Oxford—very angry.'

Other essays in the volume are among the best and most 'poetic' prose he ever wrote. Above all, *Walking* celebrates in passionate terms his most beloved recreation and unfailing source of joy. 'I have two doctors,' it begins, 'my left leg and my right. When body and mind are out of gear (and those twin parts of me live at such close quarters that the one always catches melancholy from the other) I know that I have only to call in my doctors and I shall be well again.' This held good even in the depths of sorrow and when Earth seemed 'as Hell'. But Earth could share his grief because she was the mother who bore him. 'At the close of a well-trodden day grief can have strange visions and find mysterious comforts. Hastening at troop of dusk through some remote by-way never to be found again, a man has known a row of ancient trees nodding over a high stone wall above a bank of wet earth, bending down their sighing branches to him as he hastened past for ever, to whisper that the place knew it all centuries ago and had always been waiting for him to come by, even thus, for one minute in the night.'

He loved walking at night, especially in Italy. 'The stars out there rule the sky more than in England, big and lustrous with the honour of having shone upon the ancients and been named by them . . . The chorus-ending from Aristophanes' *Frogs*, raised every night from every ditch that drains into the Mediterranean, hoarse and primeval as the raven's croak, is one of the grandest tunes to walk by. Or on a night in May one can walk through the too rare Italian forests for an hour on end and never be out of hearing of the nightingale's song.' Although road-walking (in days when it was still possible to walk on roads) was good for 'pace-testing' when one was young, and had been the chief joy of many great walkers whom he had known, such as Edward Bowen, it would not really do for George's soul. 'Pan,' he says, 'would not have appeared to Pheidippides on a road.' And then he enumerated some of the high pleasures and wonders of solitary cross-country walking. 'The sudden glory of a woodland glade; the open back door of the old farmhouse sequestered deep in rural solitude; the cow routed up from meditation behind the stone wall as we scale it suddenly; the deep, slow South-country stream that we must jump, or wander along to find a bridge; the northern torrent of molten peat-bog that we must ford up to the waist, to scramble glowing warm-cold, up the farther foxglove-bank; the autumnal dew on the bracken and the blue straight smoke of the cottage in the still glen at dawn; the rush down the mountain-side, hair flying, stones and grouse rising at our feet; and at the bottom the plunge in the pool below the waterfall in a place so fair that kings should come from far to bathe therein—yet is it left, year in, year out, unvisited save by us and "troops of stars". These, and a thousand other blessed chances of the day, are the heart of *Walking*, and these are not of the road.'

The essay called 'The Middle Marches', written some years before for the *Independent Review*, celebrated his love of North-umberland—'the land of far horizons where the piled or drifted shapes of gathered vapour are forever moving along the farthest ridges of the hills, like the procession of long primeval ages that is written in tribal mounds and Roman Camps and Border towers on the breast of Northumberland.' He had trodden that land so often, in all seasons and weathers, that he knew it almost as well as Scott knew Liddesdale and Tweed. The people of Redesdale and Tynedale, quiet and law-abiding farmers now, were de-scended from lawless and cruel cattle-raiders whose wild history we yet treasure and value—why? Because, said George, although like the Homeric Guards they were cruel, coarse savages, 'yet they were also poets who could express in the grand style the in-exorable fate of the individual man or woman, and infinite pity for all the cruel things they none the less perpetually inflicted upon one another. It was not one ballad-maker alone, but the whole cut-throat population who felt the magnanimous sorrow, and the consoling charm of the highest poetry . . . The Border Ballads, for good and evil, express this society and its quality of mind as well and truly as the daily Press and the music-hall stage express that of the majority of the town-dwellers of today.' They were more tragic in tone, more violent in incident, than the folk-songs and ballads of the South. 'To be a lover in a South English ballad,' he wrote, 'is to run a fair chance of "living happily ever afterwards"; but to assume the part in a Border Ballad is a desperate undertaking.' The pele towers on the moors, the bonny banks of Rede and Ettrick and Yarrow, were blood-stained with the violent deaths of fathers and sons, lovers and jealous rivals, in a society where vengeance was the only law, and 'the supernatural world consisted of ghosts of the departed, and of the fairies—those friends with whom the poets go on mysterious rides like that of *Thomas the Rhymer*:

> O they rade on and farther on,
> And they waded through rivers aboon the knee,
> And they saw neither sun nor moon,
> But they heard the roaring of the sea.'

At the end of the essay he described that 'glorious Border foray of 1388' fought at Otterburn in Redesdale between Percy and Douglas, depicted centuries later on the upper walls of the hall at Wallington. 'It was chivalry and love of the game, and no military considerations, that made Douglas wait for Percy . . . It was chivalry that made Hotspur attack the camp at nightfall when his English bowmen could not show their skill . . . The result was the midnight battle of heroes, ending in an English rout.'

Besides the earlier reviews ('Poetry and Rebellion' of 1905 and 'If Napoleon had won Waterloo' of 1907), the volume contained two other new essays, 'John Woolman, the Quaker', whose diary had been loved by his friend Theodore Davies, and 'Poor Muggleton and the Classics'. This last is really an amusingly disguised description of his own feelings about the way the classics were taught to English upper class boys. He, himself, is 'poor Muggleton' who never could translate English into Greek verse, though he loved the Elgin Marbles and Homer, and all that Greece stood for in the ancient world. This last little essay brings us to his next adventure abroad—a visit to Serbia in the summer of 1913, to watch the Balkan war of liberation against Turkey, followed by a dash to Athens.

In 1912, the Turkish power in the Balkans was unexpectedly destroyed by the uprising of the Christian states—Serbia, Bulgaria, Montenegro and Greece, who together, to the astonishment of the Great Powers of Europe, defeated the Turks in battle after battle, and drove their armies back upon Constantinople. The Balkan allies, however, were not satisfied simply with liberating the Christian populations of Macedonia and Albania. They soon began fighting each other for territories beyond the boundaries

a George, aged about six

b Wallington, the West Front around 1900

Three generations: George Otto Trevelyan, George and Theo, 1910

a The brothers on the moors: Charles, Robert, George, about 1934

b Welcombe from the air, about 1925

The Master of Trinity, 1950

hopefully arranged for them by the Great Powers. In the brief interval of comparative peace before the Serbs and Bulgarians went to war with one another, in the summer of 1913, George Trevelyan and Hilton Young once more set forth together into regions as yet remote from the tourist, to explore the new battle-fields and make the acquaintance of Serbs and Albanians. They did not go as newspaper correspondents, but merely out of sym-pathetic curiosity and no doubt with a feeling that the defeat of the Turks was a real 'risorgimento' and made a fitting epilogue to the Italian wars of independence whose scenes they had so lately explored together.

The memory of the Turkish massacres in Bulgaria in 1876 was still vivid, and a Bulgarian professor, whom George had met in London in the autumn, told him how he remembered, as a boy, hearing the Turkish soldiers in his village discussing whether or not they should kill him. Disraeli's failure, as Prime Minister, adequately to protest about the massacres, and his hostility to the establishment of a large Bulgarian state under Russian in-fluence—always dreaded with exaggerated hostility by most English people—were not forgotten there. But Gladstone's mighty campaign against the Turkish atrocities, and his thunder-ing demand for the expulsion of the Turks from the rest of the Balkans, 'bag and baggage', had restored faith in England. 'But for Gladstone,' said the professor, 'we should hate England,' and he told how, at Gladstone's centenary in 1909, they had closed the schools in Bulgaria and held celebrations all over the country in his honour. George and Janet Trevelyan shared this en-thusiasm to the full, and at one of their evening parties in that autumn of 1912 George set up a photograph of Gladstone in the middle of the table. However, when he and Hilton Young reached Sofia in the summer of 1913 they were relieved to find that the Bulgarians were treating their wounded Turkish prisoners well, and that the 'Sofia ladies are both tender and efficient'.

George had not wished to go away from home for so long, but he felt he needed 'real change of thought' in some place where he would be forced to think about new things and new people. 'Since Theo died,' he wrote, 'I have never been able to take a long holiday away from home. Nothing but the newly liberated Balkans could draw me away.' He and Hilton Young planned to go first to Belgrade, then Sofia, then either through Thrace and the battlefields to Salonika, or to liberated Serbia by the Uskub battlefields, and then from Salonika to Greece. They found the Serbian peasants 'very democratic and independent', for there was no big landlord class.[1] Serbian Albania was almost entirely uncivilised, with no roads other than the beds of torrents. The village houses reminded George of Northumbrian pele-towers, 'with small arched loop-holes just under the roof'. They had belonged before the war to the Moslem warrior-class, now disarmed. George took with him a volume of Shakespeare's comedies in which he recorded: 'Got for taking abroad to Servia. There read *Much Ado*, *All's Well*, and *Tempest* coming home, June 1913.'

The Englishmen were hospitably entertained by the Serbian army—'we are in fact State guests in a camp which is in the country,' George wrote. The army had succeeded in establishing some order in Albania and in distributing seed-corn to the peasants. They were not anxious to fight the Bulgarians, though war did in fact break out the very next month (July), ending in the total defeat of the Bulgarians. George's letters home about this expedition have unfortunately not survived[2] but Janet's to him show some of the excitement of it all—the journey up the Diva in Albania on horseback; staying in a remote mountain monastery; and her relief when he finally wired that they had arrived at Salonika. I meanwhile, aged eight, was thinking all the time of the dangers he was running, much agitated by the conviction that he would be taken prisoner by the Turks!

Finally, we must return to 'Poor Muggleton' and his visit to Athens. He went there alone from Salonika by sea, whence he gazed at Olympus as Xerxes had, the mountain which, after 2,500 years, was 'to a traveller from an island beyond the limits of the world the one sight that he could not endure to see without tears, though he had passed through lands just liberated and villages desolated by war.' Next morning, very early, he climbed the Acropolis and was taken by one of the guards up a staircase

[1] After his second visit to Serbia during the war against Austria in 1915 George wrote an article in the *Atlantic Monthly* entitled 'Serbia and South Eastern Europe', in which he pointed out the democratic character of the Serbian army as opposed to the military tyranny of Austria which after annexing Bosnia drove thousands of Bosnian peasants into Montenegro to starve and die. The extinction of more small democracies like Serbia, he said, 'would mean the extinction of human freedom and of all that is noblest in the spirit of man.'

[2] He wrote an article called 'A holiday among the Serbians' in the *Contemporary Review* for August 1913.

on to the top of the Parthenon, where he was locked in and left to scramble about the unroofed marble walls in solitary delight. 'A few inches under my left foot is the riders' frieze—for Elgin left the west side of it. I crossed onto the top of the outer or pediment wall, and thence looked back and saw the frieze at close quarters, hailing the youth in the felt hat whom I have long loved in casts and photographs.' (Afterwards he told us he had kissed him.) 'There he still rides, as Phidias taught him, with head half bent; only the back rim of his hat is broken off into mere outline by Time. Then I crossed by a breach in the marble cliffs onto the pediment—the ledge where the Elgin Marbles used to sit— and made my way along it, like a mortal on Olympus while the gods are away. At the other end of the pediment are the two remaining statues, male and female, in an awful religious solitude . . . waiting for the end of the world. Now I have stood beside them; I have made my pilgrimage and touched the gods of my idolatry.' 'Poor Muggleton' (alias George Trevelyan) may not have been able to compose Greek verses, but no classical scholar ever gazed on the Parthenon with more reverence and joy.

Just before he left for the Balkans, George was asked by Earl Grey to write the life of his grandfather, Earl Grey of the Reform Bill. It was a tempting offer, as there were 'stacks of papers' at Howick to which he would have access. He longed to be able to write a 'thrilling narrative' about the Reform Bill, but he delayed his decision until after his return from Greece. Then he wrote to his father: 'I was born and bred to write about Grey and the Reform Bill, and I believe it is the best way now of doing Fox justice, to show that it was he who made the Reform Bill possible.' Old Sir George's pleasure in this decision may be imagined, for Fox was as much his hero as William III had been Macaulay's. So at the end of September George repaired to Howick in Northumberland, the grey stone mansion in its woods of beech and sycamore, almost within sound of the North Sea waves, to immerse himself in the papers and enjoy the company of the fourth Earl, who, he said, 'has behaved angelically to me.' 'I am getting on well with Grey,' he wrote to his mother in July 1914. 'The difficulty is not to seem too partisan in telling the purely domestic history of the 1790s. Pitt was *really* such a mean cad, and the world doesn't know it and thinks it a "Whig tradition." But it will have to get accustomed to the truth about him again. It is awfully exciting and so deeply connected with everything that has happened since and is happening.' He wrote three chapters of the book, and then the catastrophe of the First World War cut short all such activities and summoned him to far other tasks.

It was in these years just preceding the outbreak of the War that George began his life-long campaigning for the preservation of the English countryside. It started in 1912, when Borran's Field at the head of Windermere, the site of the Roman station on the road through the fells to Ravenglass on the west coast of Cumberland, was threatened with being built over. At the centre of the movement to preserve it were Gordon Wordsworth, grandson of the poet, and Canon Hardwick Rawnsley, the chief founder some fifteen years before of the National Trust. George assisted with a letter to the *Manchester Guardian* and contributions from himself and his family. By October the money was raised and the National Trust acquired its first property in the Lake District. 'Rawnsley,' George had written in the previous year, 'is really a very admirable man. He is always saving public rights and pathways in this district by his ceaseless and well-advised activities. He has just this year saved . . . a right of way up Fairfield which a "nouveau riche" recently settled as Grasmere was trying to monopolise. He is constantly dashing about doing things for the public that are everybody's and therefore nobody's business.' In the years to come George became in many respects Rawnsley's successor in 'dashing about' the Lake District, inducing the Forestry Commission not to plant conifers all over the inner fells; and with the wealth that came to him in middle life, buying farms in the valley bottoms and their sheep-runs on the high fells and vesting them in the National Trust. But he was never a fanatic, even about 'preservation'. Even in these early days, before the car had penetrated into every corner of the Lake District, the question of a road over the Sty Head Pass from Borrowdale to Wast Water was under discussion, and found favour in the eyes of Cumberland County Council. George strongly opposed it, and in fact it was never proceeded with though often threatened, but he maintained that the track over the Wrynose and Hard Knot passes could legimately be made into a driveable road, as has since been done. It was, after all, the Roman road

124

from Galava (Ambleside) to Glannaventa (Ravenglass) at the mouth of the Esk.

Until the last week of July 1914, George, in common with most Englishmen interested in political events, was more concerned about Ireland, the Home Rule Bill and Carson's threats of war for Ulster, than about the German build-up of arms and the dangerous situation in the Balkans. Even on 22 July after the Sarajevo murders, he was expecting a general election on the Irish question 'quite soon'. But the Austrian ultimatum to Serbia (on 23 July) and the subsequent bombing of Belgrade started mobilisation in Russia and France, and the awful possibility loomed up that our *entente* with France would lead Britain into any conflict that might ensue. 'The worst danger of all,' wrote George on 28 July, 'is the claim of *The Times, Morning Post* and probably most, though I trust not all, the Tory Party, that if France goes to war, we must. It may in a few weeks or less be the great issue of our time . . . Our whole British civilisation may be made or marred by its decision.' But it was a question of days, not weeks. This day, 28 July, was in fact the day on which Sir Edward Grey's proposal of a peace conference in London was rejected by Germany, and also that on which Austria declared war on Serbia. Two days later the Czar ordered general mobilisation, and on 1 August Germany declared war on Russia. 'In all Central and Eastern Europe,' wrote George Trevelyan many years later, 'the soldiers were in the saddle and rode mankind'.[3] The danger to all Western Europe was now great, for it was known that Germany's vast military forces would be turned against France (Russia's ally), probably through Belgium, whose neutrality had been guaranteed by all the Great Powers. Although Britain was not bound by any formal agreements to go to war on behalf of either France or Belgium, it was not possible for her to stand by and see without active intervention the overrunning of her nearest neighbours by a militarist empire such as Germany's. But many Liberals, in the Cabinet, in Parliament and in the country, were so appalled by the prospect of war on such a scale that even after Sir Edward Grey's speech in the Commons of 3 August, they hesitated. John Morley and John Burns resigned from the Cabinet. More important for George Trevelyan was

[3] *Grey of Fallodon*, p. 248.

the resignation of his brother Charles from his position—which he much valued—as Parliamentary Secretary to the Board of Education. George, as he later confessed, was still a 'neutralist', even after Sir Edward Grey's speech. He wrote to his father on 5 August of 'Sir Edward who betrayed us', because he had laid too much emphasis on France and the *entente*. 'What I feared has occurred,' wrote George to his parents on 'Black Bank Holiday', 3 August; 'the system of Alliances and Ententes has, so far from preserving European peace as Grey said it would, plunged us all into war, when otherwise Russia, Servia and Austria would alone be fighting out their Slav question, which I felt sure would have to be fought out some day when I was in Servia last year.' But although he absolutely supported his brother in his resignation, which he felt had 'raised the level of public life' by its loyalty to conscientious conviction, he was certain that, once war had started, it must be won by Britain. He had rushed up to London on 1 August from Langdale to consult with Charles and some others including E. D. Morel, Norman Angell, Ramsay MacDonald and Noel and Charles Buxton about last minute hopes of preventing war—'last hour neutrality work' he called it—and was in London on the night when war started—Tuesday, 4 August. 'There was very little "mafeking" last night,' he wrote next day, 'attempts to sing the "Marseillaise" by crowds not familiar with the French language made me wonder what Burke, Fox and Pitt would think of a situation to them so paradoxical.' He returned to Robin Ghyll immediately, looking 'white and drawn', said Julian Huxley who was staying with us there, after a night journey, 'buried his head on his hands on the breakfast table, and looked up weeping. ' "It will be war, and millions of human beings are going to be killed in this senseless business," ' he said.[4] Charles, though perfectly certain of the rightness of his decision to resign, had likewise burst into tears, saying 'It's the end of all we have been working and hoping for.' 'It is,' said George, 'much harder for him than for me, as his *work* is the public welfare and mine is history.'

It was the German invasion of Belgium that most shocked him, not only because it was a terrible breach of faith and an evil deed carried out with considerable brutality, but because

---

[4] Julian Huxley, *Memories*, 1970, p. 101. I also remember this incident, but to my memory the words were: 'If we are all going to start killing one another how awful it will be!'

Western Europe was being threatened by it with German domination, and that was something he could not endure. 'My feeling for the defence of Europe against Germany is very strong,' he wrote to Charles on 7 August. 'I wish to see no one crushed . . . but I should like to see the South Slavs liberated (from Austria) if they want to be, and Alsace-Lorraine free to choose for themselves. The German military party must be defeated but not Germany destroyed. I support the war not *merely* for our own survival but because I think a German victory will probably be the worst thing for Europe, at any rate her victory in the West . . . Until I know France and Belgium are safe I can think of nothing else. Till then I support the war without approving the policy that involved us in it.' Years later, when he came to write the life of Grey of Fallodon, his greater knowledge led him to exonerate Grey entirely from the accusation made by many of his friends of having followed a policy of secret arrangements with France which was bound to lead us into war. In a footnote to that work he wrote: 'I confess I was a neutralist till the war had begun. Many of us did not realise how completely and how quickly France and Belgium would be defeated without our aid. We were wrong and Grey was right.'[5]

Charles could not accept the war and from the beginning worked with the Union of Democratic Control and other pacifist societies. George felt he could not join him in these activities, deeply as it grieved him not to be able to go along with his brother. 'Frankly,' he wrote on 13 August, 'I am not going in for any pacific or antiwar movements till the war is won to such a degree that I think peace ought to be made . . . whatever we may think of Grey's policy, the present awful struggle is to save England, Belgium and France from the Junkers, and to save our island civilisation with its delicate economic fabric from collapse.' He begged his brother to postpone his pacific work until after the war, when the nation would be ready to listen to and share in it. 'In that new age a great pacifist democratic movement is *certain* to be an enormous factor . . . But you can't give it birth now.' The country was changing with 'miraculous rapidity —into what I do not know—but for one thing our country is becoming in many respects a *socialistic state,* not a jingo flag-wagging affair as in the Boer War.' Most of the 'peace people'

[5] *Grey of Fallodon,* p. 254,n.

and newspapers who had opposed the war at the beginning of the month would not now support a peace policy, nor would the Trade Unions. 'To start it now would I think predoom it; whereas after the war it might have great influence and importance.' But although he disagreed with his brother on that point, he was as yet very uncertain what his own immediate duty was. He was thirty-eight years old and his eyesight would not serve for 'joining up', except for home service. He thought, if he survived the war, he would probably set to writing history and not dabble in politics. 'I am a fish out of water, for in fact I have nothing in the world that I am any good at except writing history and till civilisation is partially resumed it is an art useless to anybody.' Besides, the situation was changing every day. His brother wanted him to write in the cause of peace, but he felt he could think of nothing but the threat to France and Belgium, or judge Grey's policy save by events. 'I cannot write with clearness and force and heart until I know what is going to happen.' 'Excitement combats misery in me, and together they create a sort of vivid calm.'

A little light relief was afforded by the attitude of the Lake District farmers and villagers. 'People round here,' he wrote on 20 August, 'believe firmly that Lord Lonsdale has been arrested for treasonable correspondence with the Kaiser.' The Earl had indeed a few years before been host to the Kaiser at Lowther in very ostentatious fashion. 'People in this valley,' said George, 'take it all with an amusing passivity. One can see here what rural England was like during the twenty years war with France.' Most horses except those on the farms were commandeered, and the holiday char-à-bancs ceased to run.

With his father and mother he enjoyed perfect confidence and sympathy throughout the war. To his mother he wrote on 24 August: 'It seems to me useless now to discuss whose fault it was . . . *But things being where they are* we have got to save France and Belgium or we shall exist precariously under the German sword of Damocles—which will be a very remorseless blade if they *succeed* in this accursed Belgium burglary.' And he added: 'That one should find oneself scanning the papers eagerly for news of Russian successes in eastern Germany is one of the horrors of the situation'—for hitherto it had been the Russian rather than the German Empire which liberals and intellectuals had feared and hated. To his mother-in-law, Mrs Ward, he wrote
128

on 11 August: 'I hope England will prove able to hit hard and so have more say in a peace that will not *crush* Germany, who is our ultimate bulwark against "the barbarian" with whom we are necessarily allied at this moment. But to France and Belgium Prussia is itself "the barbarian", and he is "at the gates" just now.'

He tried to go on with Earl Grey, though feeling that the bottom had dropped out of writing history, but at the end of August came a sudden call from Sir Edward Grey at the Foreign Office asking him to go out once more to Serbia, 'unofficially, but with letters and introductions'. His task would be 'to win the friendship of the Serbs for England and make them feel England is watching and admiring their deeds of valour and sympathising with their "risorgimento".' Behind this lay Grey's scheme for reuniting the Christian powers of the Balkans in antagonism to Turkey, which was pro-German. The quarrel in the previous year between Serbia and Bulgaria must be made up, so while George went to Serbia, Noel Buxton would go once more to Bulgaria where he was 'justly adored', and they would be able to travel together as far as Athens and then be sent on, helped by friendly Greece, to their respective spheres. He would write articles for the *Daily News* and other papers which would bring in some money, and probably would receive much Serbian hospitality as he had the previous year. 'What I spend I shall regard as my contribution to the public service during the war,' he said.

This project, however, was delayed for several months. Grey, whom he saw at the Foreign Office on the last day of August, believed the Serbs were too busy at present with their fighting to attend to such a mission. So the autumn was spent in London, filled with various activities. He joined a sort of Home Guard known as the 'Old Boys' Corps' and drilled in early mornings in Regent's Park 'with squads of other middle-aged gentlemen'. But he was also quickly involved in relief work for Belgian refugees who were pouring over the Channel. 'I spent Sunday at Folkestone,' he wrote to his father in October, 'helping with Belgian refugees. We worked on the platform at Folkestone harbour for twelve hours.' Janet and her Chelsea friends formed an energetic committee for housing the refugee families, with Crosby Hall as the central living and dining room. Meanwhile the war on the Western Front was becoming 'a butchery past words', and as he saw many of his friends 'led off to the shambles' he felt the misery of it all was too great to write about. Only, 'we must win'. He gave lectures on Serbia and also began writing a 'weekly letter' for America. It came out in *MacClure's Magazine* and was cabled also to Spanish, Greek and Chicago papers. These articles prepared the way for his as yet unthought-of visit to America in the next spring.

Then in December he at last went to Serbia. His companion was Robert Seton-Watson, the historian of Hungary and the Czechs, whom he claimed to have introduced to the Foreign Office—'an important point as he is the only Englishman who knows the subject and has the confidence of those populations.'[6] This mission was diplomatic and political, though this side of it was not to be talked about. Sir Edward Grey had given them a much stronger letter of introduction than he had offered in September; they were to go to Niš and try to induce the Serbs to make concessions to Bulgaria in Macedonia so that she would not be tempted to enter the war on the wrong side, and also to encourage the Serbs by making them feel England was really interested in their cause—which was the union of all the 'South Slavs' into one strong people and nation.[7] Ostensibly, however, they went as 'Secretary and Committee man of the Serbian Relief Fund to visit our hospital'—one of those founded by the indefatigable Lady Muriel Paget on the eastern fringes of Europe. George had been helping during the autumn to organise the Red Cross expedition, and when it went out early in October, ten thousand copies of an important speech by Lloyd George went with it, translated into Serbian, so that it was, as George said, 'quite a big affair'. The Serbian Relief Fund allocated £3,500 to the two Englishmen 'with discretion how it is to be spent'. They went out by way of Rotterdam, Rome, Brindisi, Athens and Salonika. Having reached Niš he wrote to his parents: 'I don't know what the new year will bring us all. It is only a question of how much evil! I see here what even victory means!' (The Serbs had driven the Austrians back across the Drina and the Sava, but typhus and lack of medical supplies were playing havoc with their armies.[8] 'We are quite well,' he went on, 'and very hard at work

---

[6] He was the author of two important books—*Racial Problems in Hungary* and *The Southern Slav Question*.

[7] The 'South Slavs' included the provinces of Bosnia, Herzegovina, Croatia-Slavonia, Dalmatia, Slovenia as well as Serbia.

[8] In the winter of 1914-15, after the Serbian victories, 150,000 of their people died of typhus.

amid a mass of human misery and heroism indescribable. I literally have not time to write descriptive letters other than those I am already paid to write to the *Daily News* . . . The Relief Fund work alone is very arduous.'

It was indeed. At the excellent hospital at Skoplje run by the Serbian Relief Fund the Staff was being made ill by bad drainage, and a stay at a mountain health resort was being arranged for some of them. Twenty-five doctors died of typhus in the base hospitals during February alone, some of them Americans; there were no doctors left free to attend to the needs of the civilian population. A vast influx of refugee peasants from the north-west of the country, where the Hungarian Magyar troops had massacred at least 2,000 civilians and destroyed all stores of food and agricultural implements, were faced with starvation and destitution, while 60,000 Austrian prisoners, mostly members of the other Slav races and provinces of Austria's 'ramshackle Empire', wandered about with 'an extraordinary degree of liberty' among their friendly captors, but had no change of underclothes and of course, very little to eat. The two Englishmen, when they returned home in February, wrote to the press urging the despatch of British doctors to the hospitals, besides medical supplies of all kinds and large quantities of 'unbleached calico (thick quality) used in the manufacture of the rough peasant dress of the country'. The Serbian State, which had been fighting first Turks and then Austrians almost continuously for three years past, was unable to supply more than a fraction of these needs; it must look to its richer allies who, though hard-pressed themselves, were able to send help to Serbia through the Red Cross in generous measure in the course of the following spring and summer.[9]

On 3 January 1915 Seton-Watson and George Trevelyan had an interview with Crown Prince Alexander and his cousin Prince Paul at Kragujevac, and on the 4th dined with them. After dinner they were alone with the two princes for 'about an hour and twenty minutes'. It was not an official conversation, and Grey's letter of introduction was not mentioned, though they thought

[9] Thirty British army doctors were sent out by the War Office, in March, while the Serbian Relief Fund appeals produced not only money, but doctors and nurses. There was no nursing service in Serbia at all. *R. W. Seton-Watson and the Serbians, Correspondence 1906–1941*, Vol. 1, p. 199. (1976).

the Crown Prince knew about it. Seton-Watson talked with the Crown Prince, who 'peppered him with political questions,' and pored with him over maps; George talked mainly with Prince Paul. Seton-Watson's Memorandum shows that the subjects discussed were mainly the creation of a large South Slav state and the means of securing Romania's entry into the war on the side of the Allies. The Crown Prince was also concerned to remain on friendly terms with Italy (which had not yet entered the war) over Italian claims to Dalmatia. The Englishmen assured him that England felt the importance of a strong and independent South Slav state, and in their telegram to the Foreign Office they emphasised the absolute importance of not allowing Serbia to be overrun in any new Austro-German offensive. 'If Serbia once overrun, 'they said, 'all our hopes of help from neighbouring Balkan powers finally vanish and East European situation almost irretrievably ruined. Firmly convinced Britain should run considerable risks to save our solidarity with Serbia as ally.' Troops ought to be sent 'from anywhere'; even the small contingent of blue-jackets now at Belgrade were effective as an encouragement to the Serbians.

Romania was a very important potential ally and on 16 January the Englishmen went on to Bucharest. But first they separated for a few days in order to cover more ground. From Valjevo George went alone up to Northern Serbia, the district that had been devastated by the Austrian advance in the previous summer. At Valjevo, he wrote, 'I was valetted by a nice little Croat prisoner who had been ten years in USA and came back only to be sent to the war. He allowed he could have got away but he waited behind to be taken prisoner by the Serbs.' Going north to Šabac he saw the ghastly devastation; peasant women weeping over the bodies of their children who were dead of starvation—their men-folk all dead or in the army. He helped one such family to get a cart to complete their sorrowful journey to what had been their home. Šabac, in the north-west corner of Serbia, was 'like Pompeii'—silent streets between rows of empty houses. 'We searched in vain for a single room unsacked.' But the Serbs, despite the atrocities committed against their people, did not take revenge on their prisoners-of-war, greatly to George's relief.[10]

[10] Article by G.M.T. in *Contemporary Review*, March 1915.

Then, returning by train to Niš on 11 January, he found time to write to me (aged nearly ten) 'in the train between Valjevo and Nish', a letter which gives a vivid enough description of the war-torn land: 'I have been riding along the road by which the Austrian army ran away when the brave Serbians defeated them. The mud was two feet deep in places and one foot nearly everywhere, and there were the cannons and their limbers left sticking in it on the road or close beside it, just as the Austrians had left them a month before . . . There were poor horses lying dead and unburied along the road, about one every two hundred yards. The houses were all plundered of their furniture and most of them had their roofs knocked off too. And we saw the poor peasants coming back to their homes and finding nothing. War is a much more terrible thing than you can imagine and let us hope it will not come into England.' Then he turned to his dear Shakespeare, ever his faithful companion in all travels: 'I have been reading *Henry IV* and *Henry V* again all the time I was going through these dreadful places. I thought about seeing the plays with you and what fun we had, particularly with old Falstaff; and then, when it came to "imitate the action of a tiger" I thought of you saying it. Poetry's the best thing in the world to read, even in time of war. It makes you feel like peace, even if it's about Agincourt.'

From Niš they both went to Bucharest.

After he returned home he wrote to his father on 3 March: 'On assurances to Romania Grey positively took my advice, as he told me himself, and actually telegraphed in the sense Watson and I wished.' He even thought it possible that his letters to the Foreign Office 'about the need for British naval or military action' in that part of the world, may have had some part in turning the Government to preparing the Dardanelles campaign. He thought it possible he might be asked to return to the east, officially or unofficially. 'The use they made of me last time,' he said, 'rather depended on my being unofficial as people of all sorts talked freely to us and said things which they do not seem to have said to our diplomats. This sort of roving unofficial mission has its uses in countries where there are so very few English people and where so very little news reaches the F.O.' It was also economical, as writing for newspapers paid his expenses twice over.

The early spring in London was again a time of uncertainty. 'People don't like it,' he wrote to his father, 'if "those literary men" spend the *whole* war period writing pro-war articles from their studies.' He spoke and lectured about Serbia and the Balkans, and went on writing for the *Daily News* and began to make plans for going to America to do the same there. His private anxiety continued to be his inability to agree with his brother Charles about the war. There was nothing he dreaded so much as a breach with Charles and Charles was equally anxious. After an argument George wrote on 15 March, 1915: 'Thank you very much for your nice letter. I am afraid we are a bad family at discussing things on which we disagree. When you put your views to me I can never debate them for fear of quarrelling, from a knowledge of my own temper. And then I feel I may have let you think I agree more than I do, and write letters in which perhaps I overstate the differences . . . Things will be all right again between us on public matters after the war provided we avoid heated discussion now. . . . This I feel, that we still both *want the same sort of world*. It is only a question of the means how to get *back* to (or *on* to) that sort of world out of the present smash, on which we differ. I daresay it takes all sorts to fight a war—and make a peace.'

I have a memory of an evening about this time when Charles came in, while my father was playing a 'floor-battle' with Humphry (aged nearly six). Soldiers were arranged on the floor on a sheet of lino, and each commander threw an india rubber at the troops of the other, turn and turn about. (It was a simplified version of the old game of my father's boyhood.) I was watching, and I can remember distinctly the ashen whiteness of my father's face, as he flung the india rubber automatically while trying to discuss the real war with Charles.

During March 1915, however, a great opportunity arose for putting his literary talents to real use. He went to America to lecture in American universities about Serbia and the Balkan war and the aspirations of the Balkan peoples. It was not an attempt to enlist American support for the European War with Germany, for America was still neutral and as she had a population of some 12 million Germans, it was necessary still to avoid anything like propaganda for our own cause. There were, however, large numbers of Slav immigrants from Austria-Hungary whose sentiments were strongly anti-Austrian and therefore 'pro-ally'. He sailed on

3 April 1915, in an American ship—greatly to Janet's relief for the Germans were hard at work attacking British shipping—and spent six weeks lecturing in universities and to 'select audiences, academical and city', all down the Eastern seaboard, and in Chicago, Wisconsin and Michigan. To his father, whose history of the American Revolution may almost be said to have prepared the way for him, as the last section of it had been published in the previous year, he wrote from Boston on 15 April: 'words cannot exaggerate the kindness and flattery I get here for your sake and still more for England's.' The English-descended Americans were 'passionately pro-English'. At Harvard he stayed with President Lowell and lectured on five consecutive days; in New York he stayed a week, lecturing at Columbia and Princeton, and having meals at the Century Club, the American Athenaeum, but 'how much more lively than its British prototype . . . they *blackball the millionaires!*' He was, for the first week or two of his stay in America, exhilarated and cheered by what he experienced of American life. He felt that he had drunk a 'magic draught', compounded partly of the physical air of America 'which transmogrified the Pilgrim Fathers into Yankees', and partly by the 'sense of millions of free, intelligent, well-fed kindly people living peaceful, industrious, happy lives with no one to make them afraid.' And, rather surprisingly, he found that he 'adored New York, its architecture, its street life, its whole outward being. So there! ! !' 'I love these academic Americans,' he wrote to Janet from Chicago, 'and the best of their business men. I smell a great, good future here on lines I understand and am related to though not quite our English lines. The best here . . . are like our best *North* English types, practical, democratic business men but living on books and the best ideas in their souls. At the City Club here I sat next a City Councillor who had walked half way from Rome to Ravenna with my book[11] in his pack.'

His father wrote to his old friend Lord Bryce on 1 May: 'George is having the time of his life which he takes in his grave and sad fashion . . . At last I have found someone to envy. Fancy seeing America under such auspices, on such an errand and at such a psychological moment!' He found plenty of sympathy for the Serbian cause; American doctors were in Serbia helping to fight the typhus epidemic; some of them had died there, but this

[11] Presumably the first Garibaldi book.

did not deter the flood of volunteers from the universities and medical schools. In Chicago and New York he saw the leaders of the Slav immigrants from Austria-Hungary and found them organising politically to counteract the German vote in municipal elections. But the Germans themselves were by no means all 'pro-German'. Many were descended from the liberal immigrants who had left Germany after the failure of the democratic movement of 1848 and had no love for the Kaiser. And while George was in America came the sinking of the *Lusitania*. The outburst of indignation was tremendous; 'the President might have made war if he had wished,' George wrote afterwards in a report to the Government at home. But Wilson kept himself very close. 'The news arrived on Friday; Wilson saw no one at all, not even a member of his Cabinet, until Monday. He spent Saturday playing golf . . . and Sunday "with his God", being a very religious man . . .He takes no *personal* advice, either from his colleagues, his relations or his friends. . . . He has made a rule to see no foreigners till the war is over, so I did not see him . . . But all agree he is pro-ally at heart.'

George saw several members of the Administration, however, some of whom did not conceal from him their pro-ally feelings. He also saw ex-President Theodore Roosevelt, the friend and correspondent of old Sir George, who told him that if he had been President when the *Lusitania* was sunk he would have 'seized the German ships in the ports and only given them up when Germany had yielded to his demands.' If there was a war, he said he intended to raise a Brigade and go to fight with it in Flanders.[12]

But in spite of the comfort and pleasure he derived from the American scene, George suffered terrible anguish every day as the war on the Western front grew grimmer and the Romanians began to give way in the East. To Janet he wrote on 4 May: 'The agony of this war, which at present seems to be going far from well, is to me suffering more awful than one could imagine in a nightmare. One *wakes* to it all day. I read these dreadful news in the papers, trying to squeeze hope out of them with very indifferent success. Why *will* the Russians always give at the critical moment? Does Italy mean business after all, contrary to my expectations? These agonies of questions follow one on the

[12] He did indeed try to do this, but President Wilson forbade him to go.

other all day. What of the Dardanelles, ah, what?' He admitted that he found 'relief and forgetfulness in the shifting American scene, ever new faces of kindest hosts and hostesses, audiences and eager new friends, all full of the books, poems, ideas on which we have been brought up, and all seeing a sort of incarnation of them in one's humble self from the little green island of letters and of freedom. And that island all the while in danger and in loss unthinkable.' He wrote this letter from the University of Wisconsin, 'one of the most outwardly attractive places I have ever seen.' There, among many sympathising American academics, he tried ' "to let my frail thoughts dally with the false surmise"[13] that I am not a citizen of Hell (Europe). My Heaven turned hell. And shall the Devil conquer it and stand crowned on its ruins?'

With such agony of anxious love he felt he must return home somewhat earlier than he had planned. 'I have struck off a few later engagements and am sailing on the 22nd (May) by the *St. Paul* (American line) being unable any longer to keep away from England and Europe in this crisis.' He was as yet quite uncertain what he would do when he returned, but he did not have to wait long. For Italy did 'mean business after all', and on 24 May 1915, while George Trevelyan was on the high seas, she entered the war on the side of the Allies. From that date onwards his purposes were bent to serve the cause of freedom by helping her.

[13] Milton: *Lycidas.*

VII

Working for Italy, 1915–1917

In London the entry of Italy into the war was very welcome at a time the Western Front was engaged in a terrible struggle and in the east the Russians were withdrawing. At once the friends of Italy began to plan to help her, especially with her wounded. The 'British Committee in Aid of the Italian Wounded', was formed with two old Garibaldians and the Quaker MP Joseph Allen Baker among its members, and an admirable man, E. H. Gilpin, as its Chairman. It quickly decided that a Red Cross Ambulance Unit should be formed and equipped to work on the Italian front, and to this end George Trevelyan was despatched to Rome in June to ascertain the reaction of the Italian War Ministry to such a plan.[1] His mother-in-law Mrs Ward wrote at this time to Henry James that his 'Italian ambulance business . . . is the only thing that protects him from the deadly anxiety of war.'

He found Rome in a state of patriotic fervour which was in-spired by memories of and appeals to the Risorgimento, and expressed in posters, films and *revues,* in which Austria was wittily caricatured and derided, and the pro-German politician Giolitti made fun of, but good-humouredly. That a Red Cross Unit from England would be heartily welcomed in Italy was soon made clear to George by General Elia, the Under-Secretary for War, and an agreement accepting the scheme officially was soon signed between the Italian Government and the chiefs of the British Red Cross. Our ambassador in Rome, Sir Rennell Rodd, gave his powerful support. Between him and George a personal friendship grew up, based on their love of Italy, of poetry and of the ancient world.

But it was not only Red Cross business which occupied George

[1] See *Scenes from Italy's War,* pp. 28–30, for George's own account of Rome at this time.

in Rome. Italy's declared war-objectives, known and approved by the public, were in the north the acquisition of the Italian city of Trento and its surrounding territory, then in the Austrian Tyrol, and in the east the great port of Trieste, with a mixed but mainly Italian population. But besides these claims, there were others, allowed at least in principle by Britain and France in a secret treaty signed with Italy on 27 April, in London, before Italy had broken with Germany and Austria at all. These claims would have pushed Italy's frontier right down to Spalato on the Dalmatian coast and made her ruler over a long strip of purely Slav territory.

When this became known to Serbia's English friends, Seton-Watson, Wickham Steed and others, they were anxious to prevent any such claims being pressed. By June, Seton-Watson had already begun to write letters to the English papers. George Trevelyan, who was in no way an imperialist for Italy, agreed with their views, but was desperately anxious that their enthusiasm for the future South Slav State should not create enmity between Italy and the Slavs at the very moment when Italy was entering the war against Austria, their common foe. On 22 June he wrote a long letter to Seton-Watson from Rome begging him not to agitate the matter now. '*The less said the better at present,*' he wrote. 'If we leave the Italians alone they will learn by experience in the war; already they are having great trouble with the Slovenes on the Isonzo[2]. . . . Let them learn what South Slav sentiment really is, and meanwhile don't go on ragging them. If you continue your campaign by pamphlets or otherwise two bad results will follow.' First the Italians would get angry and write argumentative replies, agitating for 'The Treaty, the whole treaty and nothing but the treaty', whereas at present few Italians were really anxious to annex a lot of Dalmatia. Such things must wait for the end of the war and be settled at the peace treaties. Secondly, English opinion must be kept quiet too. 'Anything said in England for or against you will do infinite mischief here (in Italy). . . . An acute controversy on this subject now may be utterly disastrous and I am quite sure will not achieve the end that you and I have in view.' He was desperately anxious that the South Slavs and Italians must be friends both during and after the war and that nothing must be done to ex-

---

[2] The Italian war-front ran up the west side of the Isonzo valley. Most of the inhabitants of that part of north-east Italy were Slovenes, whose language and culture inclined them towards Croatia rather than Italy.

acerbate the differences which certainly existed. Pasitch, the Prime Minister of Serbia, fortunately took the same view. The final post-script of George's second letter (on 20 June) to Seton-Watson sums up emphatically his view of the situation: 'The Italian *people* didn't go to war for Dalmatia, but because of Trento and Trieste and because they hated the Austrians and couldn't abide German insolence and intrigue. The Treaty will never be fulfilled to the letter because the Italians will *find out* if left alone'.[3]

No time, meanwhile, was lost in creating the Unit. Most fortunately, a nucleus of dedicated people was just at hand, with the experience in front-line work among wounded and all the personal qualities most needed for such work. The Friends' Ambulance Unit, consisting largely though not entirely of young Quakers who were conscientiously unable to take part in fighting, but eager to serve wherever the suffering caused by war was most acute, had been working on the Western Front ever since October 1914, in and around the shattered city of Ypres.[4] Their leader and founder was Philip Baker,[5] son of Joseph Baker, MP; Geoffrey Winthrop Young, who had been acting as a very independent amateur war-correspondent in Flanders for the *Daily News*, joined them when they crossed the Channel to Dunkirk. He remained with them all through the dreadful days of the bombardment of Ypres, organising help for civilians who were completely ignored by the military. When by May 1915 the authorities on the Western Front seemed no longer to be much interested in the volunteer independent Unit, the great new opportunity of work in Italy was just opening up. That George Trevelyan and Geoffrey Young should be associated in close fellowship for the rest of the war in work for Italy of such a nature, and on a mountain front too, seemed like a gift from Heaven. It may be looked upon as the crowning blessing of their twenty years of ever-deepening friendship.

George was appointed Commandant, not by any official authority but by the united choice of the London Committee, and of

---

[3] *R. W. Seton-Watson and the Serbians, Correspondence 1906–1941*, I, pp. 227–230.
[4] For the story of their work in Flanders, see *The Grace of Forgetting*, by Geoffrey Winthrop Young (1953). Geoffrey Young was responsible for the adoption of the name 'Friends' Ambulance Unit', a name continued in the Second World War. He was not himself a member of the Society of Friends.
[5] Now the Rt. Hon. Lord Noel-Baker.

Geoffrey Young and Philip Baker. He and all the Unit members wore khaki, like other Red Cross personnel, but their links with the Red Cross, though friendly, were not of a restrictive nature. The Unit remained throughout the war completely independent financially of both the Red Cross and the British Government; all funds were raised by Mr Gilpin and his London Committee, who also saw to the assembly and despatch, as George said later, of 'cars, spare parts, almost the whole plant of the hospital, the much-demanded tea, jam,[6] tobacco for our own use . . . year in and year out, with an amazing regularity.' It was only because of the support of such a Committee that the Unit was able 'to ride through such very rough weather as we often encountered in the course of the greatest storm in European history . . . In troubles of every kind the Committee in London was our rock of refuge.' The Committee also engaged well-chosen recruits as drivers, mechanics and doctors, and when the Unit's hospital opened in Italy, engaged the nursing staff. For a fortnight in August 1915 the Unit camped in a great field by the Thames near Cookham—close to Formosa, the home of Geoffrey's parents. It consisted by now of some forty members, and a fleet of twenty-six ambulances, lorries and touring cars. The ambulances were mainly Buicks presented by the Red Cross; but one Ford lorry was the gift of Professor A. C. Pigou of King's College, Cambridge, who himself joined the Unit for the first few weeks,[7] and several cars belonged to, or were given by, members of the Unit and their friends.

Besides its three leaders, George Trevelyan, Geoffrey Young and Philip Baker, the Unit contained others whose names were well known in the world. Dr Thomas Ashby the archaeologist, head of the British School at Rome, George Trevelyan's old companion on his last Garibaldian journey,[8] was of great assistance as interpreter before most of the Unit members knew much Italian. His own Italian was fluent, and was tinged with an Ox-

---

[6] The Commandant was particularly insistent about jam. In *Trento*, the light-hearted quarterly produced by the Unit, is found, in March 1916, the following note: 'On leaving England in 1915, the Commandant made only one stipulation—that there should be abundant and continual jam. The occasional interruptions in its flow, its one-time over-indulgence in the satiating and plethoric Plum, the correspondence anent it, its price and partition, form an epicure epic in themselves, and mark the periods of prosperity or decline in the Unit's Chronicles.'

[7] He used to return to it from time to time, taking part once more as a driver in its work.

[8] See p. 108.

ford accent. He was known as 'Barbarossa' from the colour of his beard. He bought his own two-seater Ford car, learnt to drive it without assistance round and round the fountain in front of the Villa, and became the terror of the roads. He was put in charge of the hospital stores. Henry Tonks, head of the Slade School of Art, who had earlier begun his career in medicine, now for a time reverted to it, and, in the rather chaotic September days before there was a real hospital staff, undertook to furnish the wards which had beds but little else. 'It certainly is most difficult,' he wrote in his diary, 'to remember all the things necessary for a ward . . . The plumbers came today, with the result that the hospital was flooded on two occasions.' He brought with him Dr Dakin, a distinguished surgeon, and the sculptor F. W. Sargant who afterwards led the Second British Ambulance Unit. Later, Sir Alexander Ogston, formerly Professor of Surgery at Aberdeen, came and spent two years at Villa Trento,[9] the Unit's hospital and headquarters.

Among the members generally there was much literary, musical and artistic talent—Victor Silvester, afterwards of dance-band fame; John Alford of the Poetry Bookshop; Elliott Seabrooke, painter of mountains and our neighbour at Robin Ghyll; Sebastian Meyer, another artist, who filled one of the Unit's song-books[10] with his brilliant caricatures.

Of the original nucleus of old FAU members perhaps the most remarkable was Herbert Dyne, the car-officer, always known as 'Daddy' Dyne. Quiet, gentle and immensely resolute, he was a man of superb organising power, who knew the whereabouts, condition and problems of every car and its driver with uncanny accuracy. 'To look,' wrote George Trevelyan, 'at his open countenance, you would never guess the depth of his subtlety. To wait with the requisite patience for the ripe result of his meditations, you had to remember how many sides of how many personal and vehicular problems were flashing through his brain. We could each of us see our own point of view, but Dyne saw them all at once. That requires first-rate qualities both of heart and head.'[11]

[9] His *Reminiscences of Three Campaigns* (1919) contains a most lively and appreciative account of the Italian campaign, the Unit and the hospital.
[10] *Bolts from the Blues*. Geoffrey Young wrote the lyrics for this work.
[11] *The Record of the First British Ambulance Unit for Italy*, (privately printed for E. H. Gilpin) p. 22. Hereafter referred to as *Record*.

Each driver was assigned his own car for which he was entirely responsible, and with whose abilities and problems he became completely familiar. This principle meant that when a driver had to have a rest or break, his car must have one at the same time; it could not simply be handed over to another driver.[12]

From the same service in Flanders came Gerald Marriage who was in charge of the garage at Villa Trento, the Unit's headquarters. To him and his mechanics the hard-worked and often battered ambulances came for repair and renewal—never in vain. He was, said Geoffrey Young, 'a mechanical genius . . . . he kept all our cars running all the war, except the few we lost by direct hits and fires . . . We were unique in the proportion of cars entrusted to us which we brought back home at the peace.' 'That he should be in charge of our garage was,' Geoffrey also said, 'the one condition that I considered indispensable at our original constitution.[13] George Trevelyan developed a particularly close and cordial relationship with him.

On 21 August the whole Unit broke camp and proceeded by road to Winchester and then to Southampton, where a friend in the Admiralty (Vincent Baddeley) had seen to it that a ship was at their service to take them across to Havre. George and Janet had said good-bye to each other in London, whence George took train direct to Southampton. A few days before, Janet had received a letter from Henry James, to whom she had written thanking him for his difficult decision to become a British citizen. 'I couldn't,' he said, 'without unendurable distress, hold off longer from translating my deep participation into the only terms that would really mean something.' Then he went on: 'I think incessantly of George and yearn over him and wonder about him and in fact figure him as the backbone, quite, of that long and in some ways perhaps rather limp peninsula!—which doesn't however at all express mistrust of the adored Italy, but only my sense of George's animating virtue. How wondrous his opportunity and how interesting will be his story! The greater the interest often, alas, the more of the terrible goes to it—but goodnight now . . .'[14]

From Havre the Unit drove in convoy across France, to the

[12] Record, p. 78.
[13] The Grace of Forgetting, p. 278. Record, p. 53.
[14] Henry James died in February 1916 at his London home in Chelsea.

frontier at Modane in a week of perfect weather. 'Night after night,' wrote George afterwards, 'we bivouacked under the stars in the pleasant land of France, under the walls of some remote château long forgotten of men, or in the hollow of some wooded hillside.' In the remoter districts their passing aroused great interest among the villagers who as yet knew little of the war— they came bringing flowers and fruit with which they loaded both cars and drivers. At Modane officers of the Italian Army met them with a special train of enormous length which took all the cars and proceeded to Turin where they were feasted in the Station buffet by the mayor and military chiefs, and then driven round the town in 20 pair-horse carriages, cheered all the way by dense crowds lining the streets. Finally, on the last day of August, they reached Udine, the capital of the province of Friuli in which their work would lie. Another public reception there caused some per- turbation to the Commandant who was nervous about the speech he knew he would have to make in Italian. It is recorded that, having mislaid his 'Sam Browne', he stamped up and down the train 'venomously repeating, like a chorus to the chugging of the train, "Where's my bloody little belt?" ' Fortunately it was found in time.

The Unit was to serve the 6th Army corps of the Second Army on that part of the front which ran northwards from Cormons, along the western and northern sides of the great limestone mass of Monte Sabotino.[15] Sabotino summit was very strongly held by the Austrians; its eastern face descends precipitously into the Isonzo, which there runs in a deep gorge at its feet, until it emerges at Gorizia into the plain and flows out into the Adriatic near Monfalcone. That side of the mountain was too steep for any fighting. The Italians had however succeeded early in the war in capturing a bridgehead at Plava, where a side-valley enters the gorge; they held on to it for two years under constant and heavy fire from the Austrian guns on the mountains that rise steeply from the eastern bank—Monte Kuk and Monte Santo. It was indeed a mountain war, fought on steep, bare limestone slopes where the Austrians had the advantage of defending en- trenched positions hollowed out or tunnelled in the rock, while the Italians, attacking, had to crouch behind walls of dry stone as best they could as they crept forward under heavy fire. The

---

[15] See Map, facing Preface, p. 1.

wounded in such fighting had to be carried down the mountainside on stretchers, step by step, to the nearest point where an ambulance could pick them up and transport them, over execrable roads and often in pitch darkness, to hospitals in Cormons or Cividale, or to the Unit's own hospital, Villa Trento.

From the moment of their arrival in Udine, the Unit found that it was expected and desired not only to transport wounded but to run a fully-equipped hospital staffed by English nurses. For this purpose the beautiful Villa Trento, about ten miles west of Gorizia, had already been put at their disposal. It had ample outbuildings and courtyards which could be used as garages and repair shops for the hard-worked ambulances, and a large 'granary' which in time was adapted to take two long wards called 'Garibaldi' and 'Aosta', the latter after the great Duchess of Aosta who was organising the craft (new in Italy) of training Italian women as nurses for the field hospitals. There was a beautiful wooded park in the grounds where in summer the wounded could lie out in the shade, and where Unit members often slept out disturbed only by the nightingales. All round were vine-clad hills (the Villa made and still makes, its own wine) and pleasant paths leading through them all over the peaceful landscape. The large hall inside which became the recreation room for the Unit members was hung, or rather plastered with 'unframed oil-paintings in a solid mass very much as scraps are stuck on a screen,' wrote Mr E. V. Lucas after visiting the Villa in 1917.[16] The creation of the hospital was mainly the work of Dr George Brock. He was the physician to the British Embassy in Rome and had attended George Trevelyan's mother, Caroline Trevelyan, when she was seriously ill in Rome in 1913. By October 1915, when the Unit had been a month at work, the hospital was ready to deal in some sort with the rush of wounded from the bitter and unsuccessful offensive made in that and the following month in the attempt to capture Gorizia. Dr Brock insisted that all nurses should learn to speak Italian, for he, like his Commandant, regarded the hospital as something more than an 'outpost of mercy': it was a centre and symbol of Anglo-Italian

---

[16] *Outposts of Mercy,* by E. V. Lucas, 1917. He was surprised by the 'vivid interest in affairs' taken by these 'earnest motorists', when not on duty, but at meals conversation 'had a way of reverting to carburettors and sparking plugs'.

friendship in a great crisis of European history. The medical staff who were Dr Brock's colleagues included, during the two years at Villa Trento, three Italians, one of whom, Lionel De Lisi, a man of wide culture and imaginative outlook, later became Professor of nervous diseases at Cagliani, and, from Great Britain, besides the young surgeons W. E. Thompson and Walter Propert, there was Sir Alexander Ogston, who afterwards wrote that 'the care bestowed on the wounded Italians here could not be surpassed in the best private nursing homes of Great Britain.[17] Then there was Colonel Santucci, the Medical Director of the Sixth Army Corps, of whom George wrote that he was 'from his heart outwards the friend of England', and he added: 'In the ever-recurring seasons of disappointed hopes and unexpected disasters, when Rumania fell, and whenever Russia failed, nothing did me more good than either to see Colonel Santucci draw himself up with his good eyes kindling, and wave his hand saying *"Ho grande fiducia"* ("I have great confidence") or else to see Sir Alexander Ogston smile as he smoked his pipe. They were two different ways of expressing the same idea.'[18] The Unit in fact enjoyed the best possible relations with the Italian Army and medical staffs and was from the first accepted and welcomed without hesitation—whereas the Friends' Ambulance Unit in Flanders had had to contend in 1914 with suspicion and even hostility from the RAMC because it contained some conscientious objectors.

The work of bringing in the wounded from the front was organised by establishing permanent out-stations with accommodation for ambulances and living quarters for drivers as near to the fighting-line as possible. There were also smaller outposts of one or two ambulances whose drivers messed with the local Italian officers. These posts were strung out along the line of the front, ready for any emergency. The first out-station, established in September 1915, was at Quisca on a spur of Monte Sabotino, a high mountain-village, whose little piazza with its terrace 'crowded with guns and with my cars,' wrote Geoffrey Young, who was in charge of the station, looked out 'down a steep fall of orchard in gold and orange and scarlet autumn leaf and heavy with ripe fruit, over falling valleys of silver olive trees and across a blue and distant haze away to the

[17] *Record,* p. 21.
[18] *Scenes,* p. 107.

146

far-off glittering sunlight upon the Adriatic gulf.' From behind the house, 'if I climbed to the crest of the steep orchard, I could look up and out over folds of woodland, and all along the bare rocky southern face of Monte Sabotino', where there was constant and bitter fighting. From Sabotino the Austrian guns trained on Quisca had destroyed all but the central piazza which was protected by a shoulder of the hill. Here with Geoffrey Young were four cars whose young drivers became famous for their hazardous night-driving without lights up and down precipitous roads often under heavy fire. The Red Cross sign had to be painted out on these cars—in daylight it was too clear a target for the Austrian gunners, who deliberately aimed at it.

There was another out-station at Vipulzano, a few miles to the south, and a third in the valley of the Judrio (parallel with Isonzo to the west) under the care of Rupert Thompson, who later also established a post at Caporetto, the little market-town on the upper Isonzo to which the wounded had to be brought down on hand-stretchers from the battle-line on the summits of the Julian Alps, and which in 1917 was the scene of the disastrous breakthrough by German troops.

The Commandant had his headquarters at Villa Trento, but he spent a great deal of time in 'perpetual and indefatigable touring' between the out-stations, keeping each part of the Unit in touch with other parts and with the Italian authorities. One of the drivers who loved him well wrote years afterwards to me: 'He sometimes came in my ambulance, and would sit mum for miles with just an occasional exclamation, and yet now and then his face would light up and he'd come out with a torrent of words. He could get almost anything he wanted out of the Italian Army people, and all that work we did right up at the front was because they trusted him absolutely. I think he loved the Italians above anything.'

As might be expected, the Unit soon began to run a magazine called *Trento*, in which poems and rhymes, jokes and songs recorded their doings in light-hearted style. One of the rhymes celebrates the Commandant's peregrinations thus:

G.M.T. G.M.T.
    He roared from Tolmezzo right down to the sea.
Three blue stripes on his sleeve

And one on his chest,[19]
If you'll only believe
Oh, he never took rest;
And it's whispered indeed 'twixt the Alps and the Ocean,
He discovered the means of perpetual motion.

That first winter of the Italian war was grim indeed. On 19 October just a month after the Unit had been settled at Villa Trento and Quisca, the Italian offensive against Monte Sabotino began. It was hoped to capture Gorizia, but the Austrian defences were still too powerful, and the weather was appalling; the roads were mere farm tracks, up which all troops and supplies (often carried by mules) had to come, and down which the loaded ambulances had to make their way from the front-line dressing stations to the hospitals at Cormons or back to Villa Trento. 'For hours every night,' wrote George afterwards, 'it was impossible to get a move on at all in the one narrow street of Quisca, where the up-coming and down-going columns of lorries and mules met each other punctual as the clock every night at ten, and held each other up for hours. Night after night I used to call in our good friends the Italian officers of the 4th Sezione Sanità to help untangle the coil in which our ambulances were bound.[20] The line thus held fast often stretched a good mile on either side of the village.' The road was fully exposed to Austrian fire from Sabotino but by good fortune the enemy never fired on it at night.

The Italians, advancing slowly up the exposed slopes of Sabotino under heavy fire, suffered terrible casualties. 'How often,' wrote George, 'in the chill October sunsets I watched from Quisca hill the Granatieri[21] moving forward from behind their stone walls across the glacis of Sabotino into the falling cloud of night and doom; then in a few hours the tide of stretchers began to arrive in the courtyard of the old eighteenth-century Schloss where the section worked, dressing the

[19] This was the ribbon of the Silver Medal 'For Valour' presented to him as representing the Unit in December 1915 by the King of Italy, after he and some of the drivers had evacuated the field-hospital at S. Floriano under heavy shelling. (See p. 150 below.) The 'blue stripes' indicated officer's rank.
[20] In December 1915 the Commandant took charge at Quisca while Geoffrey Young went to Florence on business.
[21] A corps selected for their height; later they helped retrieve the Italian line on the Piave after the retreat.

wounded as they came in and loading them into our cars for Cormons. By midnight the whole place was littered with hundreds of prostrate, mangled forms, among whom the devoted surgeons, sleepless for days and nights on end, worked themselves far beyond their strength in the struggle to keep level with the insistent flood.'[22]

And in November an even grimmer kind of slaughter began: cholera, already busy among the Austrians, struck the Italian fighting men with dreadful violence. 'The difficulty,' wrote George, 'of coping with plague in the shell-broken hamlets at the front was great; there were spacious cholera hospitals provided below in the plain but the difficulty was to get the patients down off the hills . . . . Up at the front it was impossible to provide for them. I remember entering the door of a church, and finding myself alone in company with twenty men lying on the bare ground in various attitudes of despair. On looking more carefully I saw that fifteen were dead, and the remainder just dying of cholera, too far gone even to roll an eye asking for aid. The symbols of religion looked down on this silent section of the floor of hell; it was like a scene of an allegory from Chaucer or the *Faerie Queene*.'

The ambulances meanwhile did their best against terrible odds. There was a ruined farm, 'in and around which,' wrote George, 'the cholera patients used to lie in scores; one of our cars alone carried 85 patients from the ill-omened spot to Quisca in one long winter's night, the driver searching about with his torch to find the cases, and helping them into the car when found.' Geoffrey Young describes how the walking cases, 'terrified of being left behind, jostled and fought to be let into the car . . . and either Rose (the driver) or I had to hold them off until the other of us had stumbled and felt from stretcher to stretcher and body lying on the icy mud, and had decided by feel which were still alive . . . And not once but once and again, as I lifted and the sick man made his effort, he fell back dead upon me—so sudden was the plague death-stroke. . . . And at the end the dead and the living would once again have to be sorted out in the ambulances.'[23] George himself helped to load the ambulances and travelled with them to the hospitals. It was the same whatever the dangers—'Trevvy' as he was known in the Unit, was

[22] *Scenes*, pp. 55-6.
[23] From *Mountains with a Difference*, by G. W. Young.

always there—indeed he seemed to know in advance where the danger was most acute.

At the end of November after a battle lasting fifty days, a merciful Scotch mist, called by the Italians *'nebbia inglese'* ('English fog') came down and put an end to the fighting for several weeks, and early in December Villa Trento was visited by the King of Italy 'a surprise visit,' wrote the Commandant to us. 'He was very kind and asked about the time when we carried the poor people away from the two hospitals under fire.[24] He is a little man like his grandfather the great Victor Emmanuel who freed Italy in Garibaldi's time. He has grizzled hair and is beginning to get old, but he has lots of pluck and his eyes look straight and keen at you very earnestly as he talks. After he had gone,' added George, 'I went and helped our merry men to heave coal at the station.' On Christmas Eve the King came again, this time to confer on the Commandant the Silver Medal 'For Valour', which George accepted on behalf of the whole Unit. At home in England old Sir George wrote to Janet's mother, Mrs Humphry Ward, of this event as 'what is perhaps the most perfectly satisfactory moment of my life', and he added: 'It is a very great enhancement of the pleasure to think what an opportunity for that kind King, and that charming and ideal people, to express their sense of what dear George has otherwise done for Italy.'

The British ambulances and the Villa Trento hospital were extremely popular with the Italian wounded. The ambulances drove closer to the fighting front than any others, not because the Italian drivers with their Fiats lacked courage, but because the Unit men, being independent, had established close personal relations with the Italians at every point in their sector and were able to push forward their cars 'well inside the zone usually left to the stretcher bearers', thus creating 'a motor-ambulance service that functioned at least a zone ahead of the regular military cars.' In this way many a life was saved.

The Italian soldiers were grateful and full of admiration, and the Unit drivers became something of a legend. 'They are all doctors in the Croce Rossa Inglese,' they said; 'they drive gently

[24] This incident was on 28 November at San Floriano, a village not far from Quisca, when the dressing-station there was blown to pieces while Unit men were clearing it. They continued to search the ruins, and were joined by the Commandant, who arrived in the midst of the operation.

and they even remember we are inside.' Such a tribute, made under the conditions of that awful winter of 1915, was heartening. Some months later, after the capture of Gorizia—which was always under fire from the Austrian guns still entrenched on the hills to the north—Geoffrey Young driving out of the town northwards towards the nearest fighting line met a wounded infantryman, who stopped him. Geoffrey was just explaining that he was going in the wrong direction for him, when the man, with his unwounded hand, plucked a rose from a roadside bush and offered it saying, 'It was only for this—a rose for your courage.'[25]

The patients at Villa Trento were almost all privates, though there was a small ward for officers. All the patients greatly appreciated the 'Ospedale Inglese' because of the care bestowed so skilfully and gently by these utterly unknown and almost angelic creatures, the female nurses, and because all operations were performed under anaesthetics—which were not considered necessary in all cases in the Army hospitals. 'It was a good thing,' wrote Sir Alexander Ogston, 'to see the collapsed men blossom into new life and spirits under the care they received on arrival at Villa Trento. . . . All was so tenderly done that in a very short time afterwards one could walk through the wards and find all the freshly wounded asleep with everything done for them and everything recorded in the most admirable manner.'[26] When a battle was in progress three or four convoys might arrive during the night, and a steady flow during the day. Although there were ultimately 180 proper hospital beds, in times of special stress as many as 400 were temporarily catered for.[27]

When the time came for evacuating groups of patients to base hospitals or to their homes, there were scenes of desolation, and many, says George Trevelyan, 'in the literal sense of the words "lifted up their voices and wept." ' Often after reaching home in some remote hamlet, perhaps lacking an arm or a leg, they would write, or cause to be written 'whole series of letters of gratitude and affection to the "Signorine Inglesi" who had tended them so devotedly.' Even behind the war zone 'the fame of Villa Trento was spread far and wide by those who had been patients there.'[28]

[25] G. W. Young, *The Grace of Forgetting*, p. 309.
[26] Ogston, *Reminiscences*.
[27] Report of Dr Thompson, *Record*, p. 22.
[28] *Record*, p. 18.

December 1915 was something of a holiday for George, for while Geoffrey Young was away he spent most of his time in charge of Quisca: there was not much fighting, though the shelling went on. 'It is my sort of holiday,' he wrote to me. 'I go beautiful walks in the valleys of the hills, which are so peaceful and beautiful and lovely that it seems odd when a shell goes screeching overhead on some far off journey of destruction. I saw a bank of primroses, open and blooming, in such a spot yesterday. I did not know there were ever primroses in December.' And again: 'I am having *such* fun up at Quisca with Geoff's merry men. . . . We sleep on straw mattresses which Geoffrey rigged up, which are *very* comfortable. There is a grand view right down to the Adriatic, and they fire over our heads half the day. When the enemy fire at our cars, our merry men laugh and say "The Bosches are strafing us again." '

'We went out and mended a road yesterday,' he wrote on 30 December, 'a dozen of us, digging mud out of the holes in the road first and then putting in the stones from a wall that stood hard by. It was great fun. . . Now our cars can run over the road better with fewer bumps.' Every afternoon he was driven down to Villa Trento to deal with matters there, and driven back again after dark.

Christmas 1915 was celebrated at Villa Trento with a home-made musical play, in which George was the Pirate Chief and Phil Baker his daughter. 'They say,' he wrote to us, 'I did the Pirate Chief so well here, but that was because *I know all about pirates.*' ('Peter Pan' was one of our favourite games, played either at home in London or out on the fell-side at Robin Ghyll, whither his heart turned perpetually.)

Such a spirit as his could enjoy all that was beautiful in the strange war-landscape of mountains and valleys, illuminated at night by starshells and searchlights as well as by moon and stars, while he mourned over the ceaseless waste and horror of the carnage.

He was homesick too, with a longing for home that his 'war-happiness' and constant activity never could dispel. 'I wish,' he wrote to me, 'people fought with bows and arrows and swords as in Robin (Hood)'s day—then I think we should beat the Germans quicker and I could come home and live with you again. Remember Daddy always.' And a little later: 'This silly war keeps Daddy away and away from you, when we should all be having such fun

152

in the woods and hills and reading books together and saying Horatius.'

To his mother-in-law, Mrs Ward, he wrote during the December pause in the fighting: 'This place and position were miraculously designed to suit me for the war, whate'er betide. The Unit in general and I in particular *now* feel a sense of confidence and success that makes life a real pleasure whenever we avoid thinking of the situation of England and of Europe. The mixed mental and physical work and the largely out of door life, and the excellent and varied company keep one *very well indeed.*'

One tragedy in another part of the vast area of the war pierced him deeply—the terrible defeat of the Serbians after their advance in the previous autumn, and the forced retreat of their army into the inhospitable mountains of Montenegro and Albania where thousands of them died. 'Hilton Young,' he wrote, in the same letter to Mrs Ward, 'has written an article on the Serbians in the *Nineteenth Century,* but I cannot bear to read it. I keep whole chambers of my brain sealed up for my health, and one is labelled "Serbia".' Mrs Ward had written earlier to Henry James: 'He [George] is sick about the Balkan States—thinks everything has been mismanaged by our Foreign Office and that with the right men to manage our affairs there we could have brought them all in.'

His letters to me and Humphry are a delightful record of his adventures and activities, with every now and then more thoughtful passages conveying to us his own great and simple philosophy about the war, his love of reading and strong desire that we too should love books and especially poetry.[29] He read a little every day, usually before going to sleep, and usually Scott or Shakespeare. He advised me in January 1916 *not* to read *Antony and Cleopatra,* because 'no one can like it till they are *over 30.* So poor Hamlet would never have been *quite* old enough to like it!' 'Shakespeare,' he said, 'is as good as the war is bad.'

After his fortieth birthday, celebrated with turkey for dinner, in February 1916, he took his first home leave, returning in March to find the hills carpeted with 'masses and masses of yellow primroses and purple crocuses.' One day he had to go 'miles and miles' round because 'on our best road I was stopped

[29] He unfortunately destroyed, at the end of his life, all his letters to my mother and hers to him, except some saved from the bonfire by his faithful woodman at Hallington, Will Scott.

by a HOLE that a big shell called a 305 (I don't know why) had made. It was almost as deep as my bus was high and spread just over the whole road.' It was also full of water. He illustrated this adventure with a lively 'matchstick' sketch. April came and swallows built in the car-shed at Villa Trento. 'We delight in their large blood-red collar under their throats, as well as their lovely blue backs and white tummies. Don't you think we are lucky to have to do even our machine-work on the cars in such lovely surroundings and the sun in the spring green of the trees close around?'

One day early in May 1916 he was lying under a chestnut tree near Quisca reading Shelley when a shell burst ten yards away from him. He went to look at the hole, but 'the naughty Austrians strafed me again, bursting another shell just over my head and I heard the pieces of shell falling on all sides of me. So then Shelley and I walked up the hill and they burst another one at us. I thought it was very rude to Shelley not to let people read him quietly under the trees . . . They must have watched me going there several times through their glasses and thought "We'll make that Englishman in khaki sit up". I think Shelley would have enjoyed it.'

Two events pleased him in that month of May 1916—the first was the unexpected news that the Crown Prince of Serbia (afterwards King Alexander) had given him an 'Order' in recognition of his work for the Serbian Red Cross in the winter of 1914. But, he said, 'I feel the English do not deserve anything from the poor Serbians, since we failed to save them. I am more sorry for them than I ever was for anybody before.'

The other was meeting, at a lunch with General Elia's staff, 'an old man of 70, still a lieutenant', whose last war service had been in 1866 against the Austrians. 'He had won the same medal as I had, and we were both wearing it, but he had won his *fifty years ago*! ! He was a *dear* old man. After lunch they gathered round him and made him tell stories of that war when this part of Italy was liberated.' George then told them how, in the following year 1867, his own father had gone out to join Garibaldi and had arrived too late to fight. 'I never saw men,' he wrote, 'so much moved and delighted at a story of old times.'

The weather had by now become very hot and he went about in a 'pith helmet' often accompanied by the car-officer, Herbert Dyne, in a 'cow-boy' hat. He jokingly said they represented 'the

154

two parts of the British Empire'—India and the Colonies. And in June he wrote to me: 'I wish you could see the fire-flies dance here every night, in and out of the long summer grass or corn between the vines. They are like merry little Tinkerbells . . . They are all round the Villa and Quisca every night.'

About this time Geoffrey Young wrote a reassuring letter to George's parents in which he said: 'George's nerve and extraordinary endurance stand us in good stead, and he has his usual fortune which is an essential leader quality. He has really mastered the difficult art of leading such a Unit. . . "Bravissimo" they call him up here.' (i.e. at Quisca.)

'Up at Quisca,' wrote George early in July, 'they have now taken to giving our men their work to do by night instead of by day. It makes a funny sort of life but rather a nice one at this hot time of year as the days are so hot and the nights are so lovely. Our men sleep about half the night and run their cars the other half. In the day they sleep a little, and read the newspapers; and have fun with Geoffrey playing badminton in the courtyard of a shell-ruined house behind ours; and of course clean their cars like good drivers.'

The Unit had in fact undertaken a new and dangerous task at the end of April—the servicing of what became known as 'the Plava run'. Plava was and still is a village with a railway station and road bridge at the narrowest point of the Isonzo gorge under Sabotino; it had been captured and held by the Italians early in the war together with a small bridgehead on the opposite bank where the Italian and Austrian trenches were only a few yards apart. Plava was an important supply-dump for artillery and stores of all kinds, but there was only one road to it in 1916, a steep and narrow lane with hairpin bends leading from the village of Verhovlje on the top of the Quisca ridge down the wooded cliff-side. Down and up that road, everything, including ambulances with wounded, had to go, by night and without lights, usually under heavy fire from the Austrians who had got the range of the road exactly. The Unit undertook, from the end of April onwards, to send a car every night to fetch wounded up from the half-ruined railway sheds where they lay after being carried on stretchers across the pontoon bridge from the cavern-hospital that had been blasted out of the side of the mountain on the other side. 'We cannot go by day,' wrote my father, 'or we should be shot for a certainty. Imagine a place with mountains

155

as steep as the fell behind Robin Ghyll, and our car creeping along without lights down that mountain by a winding road at night, with search lights and star shells lighting bits of the ground up at intervals, and then getting to the bottom of the gorge by the rushing river Isonzo, and taking up our wounded within half a mile of the Austrians under cover of night, and creeping up the road again.'

In June he 'crossed the pontoon bridge by moonlight while our car was getting its wounded on board. I was taken over the new hospital set up since the house they used to be in a month ago was destroyed by shells. This is the way of it: it is a great gallery cut out in the rock with the rock mountain overhead, so that no shell can possibly get inside. The beds for a hundred wounded are ranged along the side of this long cavern which is more like a smuggler's cave than a hospital.'

Then in July a terrible event happened. The Austrians launched a poison gas attack on the Carso—the great limestone plateau to the south of Gorizia in the hopes, nearly realised indeed, of disorganising the impending attack on Gorizia itself. The destruction of life was enormous, for the Italians had not been properly supplied with gas-masks. The Unit cars were summoned to assist in the collection of the wounded and the gassed although the Carso was quite outside their area of work. (It was in fact being served by the Third British Ambulance Unit under Mr Alexander.) 'We carried 400 wounded and gassed men away from that place, Sagrado, that night,' wrote my father; and to us he wrote: 'Two days ago when I spent a long summer night seeing the poor Italian soldiers come in by the hundred poisoned by the wicked Austrian's gas and falling down and dying all around, I thought how very *very* angry Garibaldi would have been with the poisoners of his brave Italians. But he would still have been kind to the Austrian prisoners and so I am glad to say were his Italians. For although they were *very* angry with the Austrians, they put the wounded Austrian prisoners into the stretchers on our cars, same as their own wounded, which I am glad of.'

In the early summer of 1916 two new out-stations were established in the high mountains above the Judrio valley (parallel with Isonzo to the West)—at Ciubic and Lovisce. 'I have four beautiful mountain out-stations now,' wrote the Commandant proudly, on 2 July, 'the new ones in even higher and wilder mountains than Quisca and Vipulzano. It is fun for me going about from one to the other. And one of them, Ciubic (a funny

156

Slavonic name, not Italian) is on a hill-side, steep and grassy with trees growing wild on it that reminds one a little of the Lakes so I love it.'

A fifth out-station was far up the Isonzo at Caporetto. To arrange for its establishment the Commandant and Herbert Dyne drove together along the wonderful new road which the 'genio' (engineers) had made for many miles along the summits of the hills north of Sabotino, eventually descending to the triangle of flat land by the Isonzo where the small market-town of Caporetto lay. Immediately above it towered the gigantic peak of Monte Nero, always under snow. At first Geoffrey Young was in charge there, while George took his place at Quisca. 'Every time I see great Monte Nero's snow on top of the Northern sky-line,' he wrote to us on 12 June, 'I say "There's Geoff and his merry men at foot of that great mountain far away." ' Soon however Geoffrey Young handed over Caporetto to Rupert Thompson, of whom he afterwards wrote that 'a refinement of taste and a pregnant devotion to good causes set him apart in our Unit and through all his life'.

All through the spring and early summer of 1916, preparations were going on for another attack on Gorizia and the mountains to the north of it, but action was delayed by a dangerous Austrian push on the northern Alpine front in the Trentino which necessitated the withdrawal of some artillery from the Isonzo. It did not return until July.

When at last the battle for Gorizia was imminent, 'the big guns,' George wrote on 28 July, 'and their ammunition are dragged up by great slow cranking machines that we call "caterpillars". We pass them every night (for we work at night from Quisca) in great quantities, crawling, snotting and snoring up the hill roads.' Then, in the summer Sunday dawn of 30 July, 'as I was walking down the road (at Quisca) the bombardment broke out with a terrific roar, and the great battle had begun. It will go on for many days so I am very busy. But never too busy to read your letters and love you.' Two hours afterwards, 'I passed the King, sitting wedged in between two officers in a motor-car carrying seven. He smiled at me and moved his lips as if he was speaking as he sped by. I hope Gorizia will be added to his Kingdom for he is a good man and it is full of Italians.' Then he added an ominous postscript: 'It'll be a case of "Dicky Pink" with a lot of people here now I'm afraid.' Happily the Unit came through this battle unscathed without even the loss of a car.

Within a week Monte Sabotino, which had resisted all the efforts of the Italians in their previous offensive, was taken and its immense 'trincione' quarried in the rock of the summit gave up a vast haul of prisoners—not unwilling to be captured.

Then the lower heights of Podgora and Oslavia, south of Sabotino, fell, and on 9 August the Italians begans to enter Gorizia— 'the only city of capital importance which had been taken from the enemy in the whole war,' wrote Sir Alexander Ogston afterwards. Some Unit cars had been brought down from Quisca and Vipulzano to the flat country opposite Gorizia, where there was already heavy work to do, and on the moonlight night of the 9th Geoffrey Young, by dint of walking with each car separately across the traffic-jammed, shell-holed, quivering iron bridge, manoeuvred three ambulances and his Ford tourer into the city —the first wheeled traffic of any kind to enter.

That night, piloting the now loaded ambulances back across the ruined, collapsing bridge, he reckoned he crossed the Isonzo twenty-two times and walked over twenty miles. Just after the last two ambulances had made it to the west bank, two very large shells fell in the centre of the bridge and demolished it, until the wonderful engineers once more made it passable next day. Afterwards Geoffrey Young was awarded the Silver Medal 'For Valour', for these bridge rescues.

Meanwhile the Commandant, with another convoy of cars from Quisca, had come down to the shores of the Isonzo north of Gorizia where there was a footbridge. Crossing it he met the Italian Command in Gorizia and arranged with them to stand by that night for the attack to be made on Monte San Gabriele, the mountain just north of the town, where the Austrians were established, heavily shelling the bridges as fast as the Italians repaired them. However, all the cars got across into the town, and drove on to collect wounded in Salcano, the village close under Monte San Gabriele. In Gorizia itself, the Unit was assigned a large Villa at the north end of the town—'Gorizia North' they called it—where the 'four night-drivers of Gorizia', chosen for their skill, endurance and capacity to 'see in the dark'[30], lived under

[30] They were George Metcalfe, afterwards a most beloved and distinguished doctor in Bedford; Lionel Sessions, who lost a leg later on S. Gabriele; Philip Rivers-Arundel, later killed flying in France, and Hamish Allan, who also sustained a wounded leg.

Geoffrey Young's superintendence. One November night they carried 150 patients from a hospital encampment in Gorizia across the Isonzo bridges 'in heavy rain and pitch darkness,' wrote George in his report, 'without being allowed the use of lights.' Next morning early a large shell burst among these hospital tents, which fortunately by then contained only a score or so of wounded. On the night of 1 December the part of the house in which the four drivers slept was demolished; three of them were out on duty, but one, Hamish Allan, was in bed. He was at length found by Geoffrey Young buried under heaps of debris.[31]

During this battle-time George told us that he carried about with him a handkerchief which had belonged to Garibaldi, 'for luck, (but I don't *use* it) and I show it to an Italian if he's a great friend of mine, and then he's so pleased,' He lived now chiefly in Gorizia, 'with the Austrians only two miles away from our house. I like being there,' he wrote, 'but I'd much rather be at Robin Ghyll! !' Wherever we were we peopled the woods or the fells with our favourite characters—Peter Pan, Robin Hood and their companions. The games we played with them were largely his creations and he used to enquire after them as though they were living people and send them his greetings.

But for all his home-sickness he was careful to tell us from time to time what he felt about the war and how important it was that we should 'win' it. He had been convinced from the invasion of Belgium onwards that Germany would go on making wars unless she was defeated: he also longed for the final overthrow of Austria so that the Balkans and the Slav peoples could be truly free. 'Byron died for freedom far away in Greece, to set the Greeks free from the Turks,' he wrote to us. 'He always longed to see the Italians free from the Austrians and it would delight him today to see them a free nation fighting in alliance with free England for freedom. And Shelley would be more pleased than even Byron, especially with fighting for freedom on the snowy summits of the Alps.' He quoted to us Byron's lines:

> Yet, Freedom, yet, thy banner, torn but flying
> Streams like the thunder-storm *against* the wind

and said: 'Byron wrote that in bad days for freedom. And if the Germans and Austrians won the war it would be bad days for

31 *Record*, p. 29.

freedom again. But whatever it costs us we are not going to let them win. And the wind will be with freedom's banner and not against it.' Then, appealing to another bit of history that was already fairly familiar to us, he added: 'All the Cavaliers and all the Roundheads who fought in the battle of Naseby would be fighting together against the Germans today. Old Noll and Rupert would charge side by side for freedom and old England.'

With our terrible hindsight fifty years later this faith may seem over-simplified. But it was not out of place then, and those who held it most strongly were not the people who extinguished the lights of Europe a second time in the twenty years following the end of the war.

During the winter of 1916–17 George wrote a lecture on Garibaldi which was translated into 'very choice Italian' by Major Lionello Delisi, the Italian doctor on the staff at Villa Trento who had great literary gifts and great poetic enthusiasm. It was called 'Garibaldi and the art of revolutionary war', and he gave it four times, to crowded audiences mainly military, at Udine, Milan, Treviso, and finally Venice. At Venice where he was the guest of the delightful historian and 'Podesta', Pietro Orsi, he was filled with admiration for the way in which the Venetians had met the misfortunes of the war—which had entirely deprived them of their tourist trade. They turned to 'war-work' and auxiliary war industries of every kind with an enthusiasm that was not always present in the large industrial cities of the mainland.[32]

After Christmas entertainments, once more lavishly provided by the musical and theatrical talent of the Unit, male and female, and joyfully attended by Italian villagers from round about, and members of the British Artillery which had now arrived on the Carso, everyone settled down to prepare for the great offensive which was expected in the early spring. The mountains north of Gorizia—Monte Kuk, Monte Santo and above all Monte San Gabriele, which overlooked the town—had not yet been taken, and Gorizia was constantly exposed to heavy enemy fire from batteries scarcely two miles away. In February 1917, in the middle of these bombardments, the Commandant might be found sitting out in the garden of 'Gorizia North' in the Ford touring car reading Chaucer while the drivers cleaned their cars. Sometimes he read aloud to Unit members at Villa Trento, poems of Words-

[32] *Scenes*, p. 120.

worth chosen from the little volume of Matthew Arnold's selections which he carried about with him, and of Keats, Meredith, Macaulay and Browning. On one of these occasions a nightingale sang so loud that he could not be heard, and they had to move further away.

In March the Russian Revolution began and the Czar was dethroned. George was tremendously excited. His secretary Leslie Sheppard writes of that day: 'He came into the dimly-lit office on returning from one of the out-stations and I showed him the little Venetian newspaper which had just been brought in, announcing the fall of the Tsarist government in Russia. I remember his prompt exclamation: "This is the greatest event since the French Revolution!" To us he wrote: "Russia is free! I can think of nothing else, feel nothing else. You will remember, however long you live, that you heard the news." Much of his time before the war had been spent in helping Russian exiles and political refugees; now they were free and could go back to their own country. His only anxiety was, would Russia proceed to 'ordered freedom,' or dissolve into chaos? The actual event, as it emerged in the course of the next year, was another and unexpected alternative, the dictatorship of Lenin and the Bolsheviks. Even as it was, the immediate results, from the point of view of the Allies, were pretty devastating. The Russian army was disintegrating and the Germans were lifting vast quantities of guns and ammunition to the west, particularly to the Italian front, where that very autumn they helped to bring disaster on the Italians.

Another event which rejoiced his heart was the entry of America into the war in April. He was particularly happy because of the pleasure it brought to his father. 'I wish,' he said, 'I had been there (at Welcombe) to hear him talk about it.'

On the Isonzo the great summer offensive began in May with the Italians using their old bridge-head across the Isonzo at Plava as their one and only base for the capture of Monte Kuk, 'with the infantry climbing straight up the steepest part of the long slope', after heavy preliminary bombardment had destroyed the Austrian trenches. He told us to imagine what it would be like to 'storm Bow Fell in the face of machine guns and rifle fire of a determined enemy', for the mountain heights and gradients of the Isonzo valley were much like those of our Langdale. After ten days' very fierce fighting Kuk and its neighbour Vodice had fallen, and in less than a month the 'genio' 'had constructed from

161

base to crest of the mountain a winding road of seven kilometres with perfect gradient and surface, at the cost of several hundred casualties among the roadmakers. Three thousand men were engaged on the work of whom two hundred were killed or wounded'. Up this road the heavy guns now climbed, 'while lorries with military stores, and our ambulances bringing down the wounded, were passing and repassing on the road to the crest.'[33]

Meanwhile down in Plava bottom the Unit had established a new and very useful, though vulnerable, out-station. A fine new road had by now been opened, just before the battle for Kuk began, which was known in the Unit as 'the thirty-two hairpins'. It came down from Monte Corada in the north into Plava bottom, where a small side-valley called the Val Grune enters the Isonzo and is crossed by the railway viaduct. This road made one-way traffic possible for ambulances, lorries and guns which now descended to the pontoon bridge by the new road and returned from the bottom by the old narrow road to Verhovlje. But Plava itself was still within the range of the enemy guns and was anything but a safe haven for men or stores. As the battle for Monte Kuk proceeded, the number of Unit ambulances serving Plava was increased to ten, and the Val Grune became their station. Philip Baker was in charge. The cars were parked near the railway arches; a tent and a wooden hut were provided by the Italians, but the drivers were obliged to retire to some caves in the hill above where they were safe from the eternal shrapnel, and also where they could escape the exhausting heat of that summer in the airless valley. 'When at Plava,' wrote George to us, 'I sleep now (since our tent was knocked down once by a big stone thrown by a shell) in a lovely *grotto* in the hill above dug out in peace time by shepherds in the rubbly soil. It has two entrances and holds six camp beds. There is a beautiful dim light at eve and dawn coming in through the two entrances. You would love it. It is just like Swiss Family Robinson life there.'

His activities during the May battle were ceaseless, dangerous and ubiquitous, though divided chiefly between Gorizia and Plava. 'Our Commandant was darting about amongst his out-stations like a lightning-flash,' wrote Sir Alexander Ogston. He somehow found time to write letters to his parents and to Janet and us,

[33] *Scenes*, p. 135.

every three or four days; and from them we learn what life was like in 'Plava bottom', while the great battle raged on the summits above and the wounded in their hundreds were carried down by the Italian stretcher-parties.

The Pleasures of the Plava View, 1917, by Sebastian B. Meyer. From *Bolts from the Blues*, (rhymes by Geoffrey Young)

Thus on 15 May he arrived at Plava about 2 a.m., relieving 'Phil Baker who had been down there all night receiving our boys as they arrived again and again. They shrapnelled us heavily as we laboured at turning the cars in the crowded road covered with wounded in stretchers. One wounded man was killed in his stretcher. The rest of us were lucky. But the chance of shells hitting is really small, and I got off with a stone cast by a 305 that just grazed off the skin of my elbow. After that I turned off the path and climbed up the wet grass of the bank thinking of climbing in a curious happy way. It was a "great adventure".'

Or again: 'Last night coming back (with a load of wounded) into Gorizia at 2 a.m. on a dark night a shell burst in front of us and next moment the car dived into an immense shell-hole. The car almost capsized but not quite. It was very painful getting

163

them all out, poor chaps, as we could not attempt to move the car while they were in it. While we were struggling with the task five successive shells hit the house we were standing under, covering with stones and rubble us and the car and the wounded in the stretchers where we put them on the road. But the car came straight out of the shell-hole when driven, so the situation was saved.'

On 17 May he spent 'afternoon, evening and half the night down at Plava, on a great day when our five cars came down five times each, Toulmin six times. . . . In the intervals of one of our cars being down I sometimes helped the Italian officers in their loading organization, sometimes went up into the green wooded hill above and read Browning's "Before" and "After" (wonderful things both). An Austrian cannon from far away was planting shells on a green bank below the wood a few hundred yards away while I lay lazily watching. The white spurt of smoke leaving the scar in the green hillside seemed almost like a process of nature, so common has it become in this worst of modern times. . . . The worst of war and the best of peace, the worst of man, the best of nature were strangely blended.'

On 22 May he wrote from the Plava dell that they had lost 'Buick No. 1' by 'a large shell which brought down the remains of a ruined house it stood by, on the top of it.' This was the first car the Unit had lost. The mechanics came out from Villa Trento and carried off the engine which was unharmed. And that same day as he crossed the bridge 'a bit of shrapnel whizzed between me and the sentry—and it was touching the way the dear fellow ran up to express his concern that I should have been in any danger, quite regardless of himself, whose business it was to stand on that worst spot in Plava all day long. God bless the common people of all countries!'

On 23 May, an attack was expected on Monte Santo from Plava and Gorizia simultaneously. Having seen all well at Gorizia —the cars just starting out for their front-line stations—he went off to Plava, arriving there at midnight, after the long drive round by Quisca, for as yet it was not possible to go to Plava direct from Gorizia along the Isonzo gorge, owing to an exposed piece of road that was under constant shell-fire. 'I take charge at Plava and run all night to and fro on our cars between the gorge station below Sabotino (Zagomila), keeping tired drivers at it till the first birds sing thro' the darkness for dawn and thence on into broad daylight. . . . At 6 a.m. Phil turns up and takes charge again, just as we have cleared the lot. Then I hastily breakfast, excellent fried eggs done by Ashton at the baracca (the wooden hut) in two or three minutes, and Berkeley drives me back via Quisca to Gorizia again to pick up the news of the night.'

To his parents he wrote on 26 May: 'I have been four nights running at Plava and beyond, fetching in the many hundreds of wounded that stream each night off Monte Santo into the Isonzo gorge. The confusion and ready-made character of the arrangements in that narrow gorge bottom at night, with the great crowd of men and mules going to and from the Kuk-Santo battle above, calls for Baker's or my constant presence and I have 'officer's throat' today with shouting for four nights in that interesting inferno. It's grand work and a joy to be doing it so successfully . . . But M. Santo and these precipitous mountains are terrible places to take.'

The Unit cars—which were the only ambulances actually stationed at Plava—carried in that awful fortnight (15-30 May) over 8,000 wounded, about twice what they had carried in any previous battle in the same time.

Now came a few days' calm and he could recuperate at Villa Trento from loss of sleep and the 'officer's throat'. He began to think about the future after the war, and what he should write when writing again became possible, perhaps a history of England from the earliest times until now, or possibly only from Tudor days. Such a book, he wrote to his father, would not be profoundly researched, but it would, now that Green's *Short History of the English People* was getting out of date, fill a popular demand, and 'in this age of democracy and patriotism, I feel strongly drawn to write the history of England as I feel it, for the people.' Here he echoed those earlier hopes of his youth, to serve 'the people' by writing history which they could enjoy.

'The war,' he went on, 'has cleared my mind of some party prejudices or points of view and I feel as if I have a conception of the development of English history, liberal but purely English and embracing the other elements. It might be a success as a literary work (otherwise I would not touch it). The doubt in my mind is whether it could have elbow room to be a literary success without being so long as to prevent the wide popularity which would alone justify the choice of it.' The other historical work he longed to write was of course the reign of Anne. In the end he wrote them both, first the history of England, then of Anne.

The strain of the May battle had made him temporarily 'bored' and 'wearied to death', but he soon recuperated—reading Prescott, Scott, and an Italian history of the nineteenth century. But he felt acutely now the exile's longing 'for the mere *places* he cannot get back to, as millions have felt it throughout all history with less hope than I, from and before the times of Odysseus and of Thomas Mowbray, Duke of Norfolk, in *Richard II.*' Against this sentence his father wrote: 'I feel it for Italy.'

To his father he quoted Swinburne's lines:

> The Wansbeck sings with a' her springs;
> The bents and braes give ear:
> But far and far they blithe burns are,
> And strange is a' thing near.

A week at Robin Ghyll was his dearest hope, but it would have to be late—perhaps as late as October. Would that interfere with Dorothy's annual holiday there, he wondered? To her he wrote in mid-August, asking whether if this was so, she could not come at the same time as themselves. 'As to *room*, we must *make* it as a war-measure. And I feel so much more closely drawn to you by all the happenings of these years that *I* feel your presence would *enhance*, not diminish, the sacramental happiness and beauty of the one week.'

He did in fact secure a holiday at the end of September, returning on 27 October when the great retreat had already begun and preparations were being made to evacuate Villa Trento. But before that, before his holiday began, much had happened in the Unit.

First, on 5 August at Villa Trento, there was another pleasant ceremony of medal-giving. 'They proposed,' wrote George, 'to send up my name for a second medal, but (for the second time) I stopped this. I should not like to have a second medal before both Geoffrey and Baker had one each.' Colonel Santucci, whom they all loved and who loved them, gave the Silver Medal 'pro Valore', to Geoffrey Young, and then the Bronze Medal to two of the 'four night-drivers of Gorizia', Lionel Sessions and George Metcalfe. Two Colonels commanding the British Artillery came to the ceremony, greatly to Colonel Santucci's delight.[34]

---

[34] Philip Baker received the Silver Medal in January 1918; the two drivers Yates and Glaisyer receiving the Bronze at the same time. These awards were for their work at Plava during the previous summer.

Heavy fighting began again soon after, on 18 August, with the unbelievably difficult ascent, direct from the Isonzo gorge north of Plava, of the steep sides of Monte Jelenik. Within a week the Italians had captured the whole range of mountains from Jelenik to the great Monte Santo, and their infantry had rushed onwards east across the country behind—the Bainsizza Plateau. 'On the afternoon of the 24th of August,' wrote George afterwards[35], 'standing on a line of trenches in which the Austrians had been that morning, Baker and I saw a little string of men, black against the white limestone, struggling up those heights beyond Ravne, three miles away as the crow flies. At first we thought they were retreating Austrians, but presently . . . we realised that they were the Italians who had a few hours before stormed the ground we stood on.' They soon established a line which proved to be the furthest Italy ever reached before the great Retreat deprived them of all the ground they had won at such cost.

The problem for the Unit was how to get the wounded, for the Italian advance had in fact outrun its own lines of communication, and Austrian batteries from Ternovo, east of Monte Santo, were making the construction of roads almost impossible. On 26 August George 'walked across the moor to Ravne (a village in the middle of the plateau) to prepare the way there for our cars. Arriving after nightfall I sought the authorities and found General Gonzaga's headquarters . . . I came only for information and orders but I got a dinner, a welcome such as would have befitted a brigadier and finally the other bed beside the General's. He was in particularly good spirits having just been knocked over and slightly wounded by a shell . . . He invited me warmly to bring along the ambulances if they could possibly come.' Next morning George walked back and met some of the ambulances struggling through a crush of artillery. Two managed to get through and reached Ravne—where a field-hospital centre was being established, though under immense difficulties. More cars followed after dark.

The capture of Monte San Gabriele, the southernmost of the high hills along the east side of the Isonzo, overlooking Gorizia, was now the Italian objective. It was a terrible struggle—'a smoking altar of sacrifice,' George called it, 'seen afar off by all

[35] *Scenes*, p. 144.

the spectator armies between Carso and Monte Nero's top.' San Gabriele was connected with Monte Santo by a range of hills over which a pass called the 'Sella (saddle) di Dol' carried a good road from Gorizia to the Bainsizza region. At the top of it was a ruined inn; at the bottom the ruined village of Salcano. Up that road which was always under fire, the ambulances from Gorizia plied to a dressing-station just below the summit, whence the wounded were brought down night after night by the 'dauntless three (Metcalfe, Sessions and Arundel), driving 'ceaselessly, soundlessly, with infinite care for the wounded men and for their cars',[36] to the subterranean dressing-station at Salcano, under the Villa Principe. On the last night of August, when the full moon lit all the hills with splendour, Geoffrey Young, driven by George Metcalfe, was mounting the road when their way was blocked by some mules. He got out of the car and walked forward to drive them away, when a high explosive shell burst near him, wounding him in the left thigh. Metcalfe got him into the ambulance, and as they were about to turn round, George Trevelyan arrived in another ambulance driven by Lionel Sessions. At that moment George was probably suffering more than Geoffrey, who was somewhat dazed with shell-shock. 'It was a dreadful thing,' he wrote to me three days later, 'to come up and find him wounded, just put into Metcalfe's ambulance, and not knowing whether he was badly wounded or not. And I had to go on with Sessions (to collect wounded) and leave him to be taken down by Metcalfe alone, which made it worse.' However, a shell-hole in the road soon obliged them to turn back and they found him in the hands of his friends the Italian surgeons in the Villa Principe at Salcano. From there he was moved to Villa Trento. No one at first thought the wound dangerous; George's letters of the next three or four days are entirely cheerful. Then, on 7 September, the blow fell. Gangrene had appeared and the leg had to be amputated after all. 'Since Theo died I have had no blow like it,' wrote George to Geoffrey's brother Hilton Young (who in the following spring lost his right arm at Zeebrugge). But Geoffrey himself was cheerful and forward-looking. 'They say,' wrote George, 'there is nothing the body suffers that the spirit may not profit by. Looking at Geoffrey I almost think so.' He had indeed

[36] *The Grace of Forgetting*, p. 315. It will be remembered that Hamish Allan, who had been the fourth 'dauntless' one, had been put out of action in the previous December by the collapse of the ceiling onto his bed.

forty more years of active and happy life ahead of him, climbing many Alpine peaks (including the Matterhorn) with the aid of a carefully-designed artificial leg.

The Unit's casualties on this deadly road were not over. In that first week of September Victor Silvester and Lionel Sessions were both wounded there—Sessions also losing a leg.[37] After that the Italian authorities forbade any more ambulances to go to the summit of the Sella. The awful struggle went on with appalling casualties on both sides, inflicted mainly by heavy artillery. Gabriele in that first half of September, had become 'a gruesome slaughter-house', with little shelter for the troops.

To his sister-in-law Dorothy Ward George wrote on 12 September: 'This *must* be the last war. And I believe it will be just *because of* its length and unutterable horror. This month I have seen its very worst shapes and sights absolutely at first hand and I don't know if the worst criticism of war is not one's appalling indifference to them until one's best friend is shot down and he, the dear one, lies before one; one of these statistically calculated wrecks. *Then* one ceases to be indifferent and gets a glimmering of what the statistics mean.'

Such valour and perseverance as that shown by the Italians in the battles for Kuk, Santo and Gabriele seemed to deserve to be crowned with victory. But it was not to be. During October the artillery from the collapsed Russian front pressed more and more heavily on the new Italian lines. Then on 24 October, two divisions of German troops broke through at Caporetto, where the morale of the Italians, long isolated there without any fighting to do, was low and at the mercy of defeatist propaganda from the rear. It was like the breaking of a dam. The Austrians poured through and retreat along the whole front became inevitable.[38]

When it began, the Commandant was just returned from his home leave. He arrived at Udine early on 27 October and found preparations already in hand for abandoning Villa Trento. All the wounded were evacuated that day, but in the evening thirty more cases were received for the night, and some men arriving exhausted and hungry, were fed and allowed to sleep on the floor in the hall. George made two expeditions to Gorizia that

[37] For this costly service Geoffrey Young and Sessions were awarded the Silver Medal (Geoffrey for the second time), and Silvester the Bronze, 'al valore militare', on 5 October.
[38] For the causes of the disaster, see *Scenes*, pp. 163-178.

day, where Philip Baker and his cars were moving the last wounded from the town. The Unit cars which had been the first wheeled vehicles to enter Gorizia fourteen months before were now the last to leave it. 'I was back,' wrote George to his father, 'just in time to get up and be the last Englishman in Gorizia.' He left feeling he would probably never see their old house there again; yet twelve months later he and Geoffrey had returned to it, on the heels of the Austrians, and on the tide of victory.

Before the Commandant's return the Unit ambulances had also accomplished a very dangerous task—the evacuation of wounded from the exposed village of Ravne on the Bainsizza plateau. This was effected safely on 26 October under the direction of the driver in charge, F. G. Penman, who was awarded the unusual honour of the Silver Medal of the Italian Red Cross for that enterprise and also, on the next day, for the clearance of all the wounded from the Unit's original out-station at Quisca, which had now become an advance clearing-post. So all the old out-stations were quickly and effectively abandoned and no wounded left to fall into Austrian hands.

The cars began to leave Villa Trento at 6 o'clock on the evening of 28 October. It had been hoped to re-open the hospital at Conegliano, some sixty miles west, but this was not to be. Meanwhile the retreat had become an enormous traffic-jam with which no one attempted to deal. 'A hundred London mounted policemen,' wrote Geoffrey Young afterwards, 'and some organised gangs to shove the blocking vehicles off the roads, could have saved for Italy millions worth of guns and of material and even troops.' The panicking peasants were everywhere swarming onto the roads with their possessions piled on ox-carts, the slowest of all methods of transport. One by one the Unit cars had to be abandoned in the crush, full as they were of stores, and the drivers, heart-broken, made their way on foot. The story of Geoffrey Young's adventures during the Retreat has been told by himself—it is surely one of the minor personal epics of the war.[39]

The Commandant and his convoy of six cars were more fortunate. They took to roads north of Udine, which were compara-

---

[39] See *The Grace of Forgetting*, pp. 322–324. He was accompanied and tended by the Matron (Sister Power), Herbert Dyne, and in the later stages by Philip Baker and other Unit drivers deprived of their cars. He was on crutches and travelled, when these failed, by stretcher, horse-buggy, and an abandoned railway repair trolley, pushed by hand.

tively clear, and crossed the mile-long bridge over the Tagliamento, which was roaring in spate from shore to shore, on the evening of the 28th. In Pordenone he spent 'a wet and anxious night' in the main square, watching for arrivals, but none came. At morning light he started to walk back to the bridge (about twenty miles), but before he reached it he had 'the relief of his life' He met Geoffrey Young and his party and half the nurses with news of the other half. Twelve of these had spent a night on the floor of a deserted house just over the Tagliamento and had then walked on, nearly starving, beyond Pordenone to the railway line where they found a train going to Padua. It had two carriages in front full of bread, which was being looted by Italian troops. An Italian officer, however, managed to stop this and get the bread properly distributed. Some was passed down to the nurses.[40]

Eventually all Unit personnel were accounted for at Pordenone and about half the cars. They drove on to Padua where new plans had to be made. There, in the Piazza Garibaldi, was the statue of the Liberator, and beneath him passed 'hour after hour, day after day, the files of the dejected and unarmed—his countrymen. It was impossible not to think him alive and watching. In all the wonderful changes and chances of the year that followed, that graven image, hand on sword hilt, seemed to watch and know.'[41]

As for George Trevelyan, he was torn between grief and joy. 'My political heart is broken,' he wrote, 'but my love of my countrymen and countrywomen is greater than ever before.' The Unit, though normally a cheerful and good-tempered crowd, had had its times of grumbling and discontent. But during the week of the Retreat, with all its uncertainties, dangers and discomforts, everyone gave their best. 'I believe,' he wrote, 'it was the only week in which nobody grumbled about anything. Such are the British in misfortune.'[42]

[40] This incident was told me by Miss Roma Bonar, then the youngest of the VADs, in 1977.
[41] *Scenes*, p. 188.
[42] *Record*, p. 41.

VIII

Victory and Beyond, 1918–1923

The Unit, recovering breath at Padua, soon realised that it would
no longer be possible to continue the hospital. All stores had
been lost in the Retreat when the ambulances were abandoned,
and it was still uncertain whether the Italians would continue to
hold the Piave line. The Second Army having now disintegrated,
the Unit was placed with the Third Army which, under the Duke
of Aosta, had fought fine rear-guard actions during its retreat
from the Carso and was now linking up with the Alpine Fourth
Army on a line that ran up the Piave to Feltre and then west
along the Asiago Plateau to the high Dolomites above Arsiero.
The Unit was ordered, for the first time since it arrived in Italy,
to go 'in riposo', repair its remaining cars and prepare for further
service. The nurses went home, all except the Matron (Sister
Power), the housekeeper Miss Kemball, and two VAD's, Miss
Bosanquet and Miss Bonar, who remained to look after the
domestic needs of the car section.

Their first quarters during November were at a farm not far
from Mantua, where there was a huge threshing-floor on which
the first dozen cars could be serviced for the road again. While
they were there, large numbers of British troops began to arrive
at Mantua, where they detrained and started to march to the
Piave. The joy which the sight of them—'the first British Army
that ever entered the Lombard plain'—brought to George Trevelyan's heart may be imagined. 'Looking on such men, it seemed
impossible to think we could be beaten,' he wrote afterwards.
'What perfection of equipment, of drill, of discipline, and yet
what lively suppleness of individual will in every man. The
kitchen fires burning as they marched, the glossy-coated horses
and shining harness, even the hard-won brilliance of the objur-
gated buttons were not wasted in that march through Italy.' The

172

Italians were enormously pleased and excited. They loaded the British with flowers and little Italian flags which the good-natured Tommies stuck in their rifles. Moreover the arrival of these kindly allies had encouraged the Italians in their great campaign of self-rehabilitation after the retreat. 'The Italians,' wrote my father in January 1918, 'are drilling hard and march about in step, to make themselves as smart as the Tommies. It's a great movement nowadays. You see them all over the fields here drilling.'

Meanwhile the Unit had moved to its permanent headquarters —an eighteenth-century villa at the southern end of the Euganean Hills, called, hopefully, Villa Trieste. George's pleasure was great at finding himself within a mile or two of Byron's house where Shelley had stayed and written the 'Euganean Hills' lines. The population, both the peasants and the town-dwellers of this region, were intensely patriotic and anti-Austrian, for it was not so long since Radetzky, the commander of the Austrian army in Garibaldian days, had shot and hanged all those who ventured to oppose the rule of Austria. In fact, three such, Cesare Battisti and two companions, had actually been shot as late as 1916 at Trento, the Italian Alpine city still in Austrian hands. It was indeed a thoroughly Italian countryside, fertile and highly-cultivated, and with the additional attraction of warm springs in many places. One of these was close to Villa Trieste and provided the Unit men with a natural warm bath in which they could bathe at any time of year.

There was no furniture in the Villa at first; the four remaining ladies had to make do with a stretcher and three wire mattresses saved from Villa Trento balanced on two trestles each. However these deficiencies were soon remedied; the lounge was decorated with new pictures done by John Yates on sandpaper with chalks and pastels, and at Christmas a splendid dinner was served which included lobster salad, roast turkey, plum-puddings with hot sauce, cake, fruit, chocolates and coffee. Little Capitano Varaldi, the Italian member of the medical staff, was alarmed at the amount of food disposed of and kept on telling Miss Bosanquet who sat next to him: *'Ma mangiano troppo, Signorina! Ohmé! ne viene ancora!'* ('But they are eating too much, Signorina! Ohmé! there is still more coming!')[1]

[1] I am indebted to Miss Roma Bonar for allowing me to read her letters home to her parents at this time.

The first dozen ambulances were ready for service again by the end of November 1917. The Committee at home immediately sent out 'lots of nice little Fords' to replace the cars lost in the retreat, and by April some fine large Talbots also, very serviceable in climbing the steep Dolomite roads on the northern front. In November two out-stations were established just behind the Piave line and two more in January. On the northern, Alpine front, hill-stations were set up in February on the Asiago plateau, between the Brenta and the Astico, where, after a snowless autumn and Christmas, deep snow and a driving Arctic wind welcomed the Unit men up there in February.

'It is extraordinary,' George had written to Humphry on 1 December, 'how this winter of all winters it *will* not snow, but goes on fine day after fine day, with those glorious mountains still brown instead of white on our northern skyline—and all the little men fighting in their crevices though they look so quiet and grand far away. If only it would begin to snow in the Alps near here, the Bosches wouldn't be able to go on attacking there and trying to get into Italy that way.'

Unlike Villa Trento which was only some ten miles from Gorizia and Quisca, Villa Trieste was not less than forty or fifty miles from any of the fighting lines on which the ambulances were serving. The roads however were good, not like the mud tracks of that first Sabotino winter, though there were plenty of hair-pin bends in the Dolomite regions.

For a few days after the snow came, the Unit men on the Alpine out-station lived in tents and caves until their wooden 'baraccas' were set up. 'I slept in a tent there one night,' wrote George to Humphry, 'and the frozen wind was blowing the chairs over and flapping the tent about, and it *was* cold. The men were sleeping in a cave which was at least warmer.' They built their 'baracca' of inter-locking wooden pieces, 'in an angle of a great rock that keeps off the shells . . . I had fun tacking down strips of canvas paper over the cracks of the floor where the pieces joined, to keep out the draught.' With wood and paraffin stoves they kept themselves quite warm, while their Italian soldier-servants 'though not professional cooks, would always produce a hot and succulent meal of *pasta* (spaghetti) under apparently impossible conditions.'

The Unit had replaced its cars; but would it be able to retain its men? The needs of the British Army for men, after the

174

appalling losses on the Western Front in 1917 and the absolute necessity of stopping the German advance in the spring of 1918, threatened the Unit with what would have been a fatal loss of personnel. Some 'Colonials' and a few Americans replaced some of the crack drivers, like Metcalfe and Silvester, who had had to go, and at Christmas 1917 George rushed home to put the whole situation before the authorities. Certain key-men, such as Dyne and Marriage, were so essential that if they were taken the Unit would have to break up. This, it was explained, it was perfectly ready to do, 'cheerfully and without grievance', if these particular men were required for the army, but in the course of the summer, especially after the great battle on the Piave in June, the Chairman of the Red Cross, Lord Stanley, became convinced that the Unit's work ought to continue in Italy, and his opinion was endorsed by Lord Milner himself, the Secretary at War.[2]

This result was achieved in August when the Commandant came home on a leave of mingled business and pleasure. The War Office had refused to let the British Red Cross have any more cars from England or America for the rest of the war—'a monstrous ukase,' said George. After 'a great confab' with Lord Stanley, he and Sir Courtauld Thompson and E. H. Gilpin (the Chairman of the Unit committee) began lobbying the government offices. They enlisted the support of Lord Northcliffe of *The Times,* as well as the Foreign Office and all the Information Departments. 'We are positively famous,' wrote George, and on 20 August they saw Lord Milner, who, said George, 'went as near promising me all I wanted (except pensions) as he could properly go before seeing Stanley.'

As for cars, Sir Courtauld Thompson was told to order fifteen new Fiats in Italy, to be divided among the three British Red Cross Units working there. These the Red Cross would pay for, and at the same time it voted a grant of £100,000 for the work of the Units in Italy. 'Dear old Geoff,' wrote George to Geoffrey

[2] *Record,* p. 42. In May 1918 plans were being made by the officers of the Unit (Geoffrey Young and Phil Baker in particular) for transferring the remainder of the personnel and cars to some other front, in the event of its work in Italy coming to an end. It was expected that by July this would happen, unless a really big battle occurred which would change the whole situation. In fact such a battle did break out in June and, as will be seen, the Unit played such a part in it that its withdrawal was no longer contemplated.

Young on 1 September, 'this is a great triumph for our show. It is what one dreamed of rather than expected in the past. And both you and your leg have certainly helped greatly to bring it about.'

Meanwhile in the fighting zone, the arrival of British and French troops at the front often made the Unit's movements sudden and unexpected. 'Whenever,' wrote George, 'the energy of Baker had settled the drivers snugly into some new and well-shelled home two kilometres from the Piave line in January, or some icey hole in the snow-bound rocks of Puffele on the Asiago plateau in February, then the French or British at once took over that part of the line from the Italians and we had to flit. But we always negotiated new scenes, new work, and new Italian friends. Mobility and 'communications' became our strong point this year with a base always forty miles away . . . Our two most permanent homes at the front that year were Arsiero [which he nick-named 'Stool End' after the farm at the head of Langdale] and Vallarsa [west of the Asiago plateau], where we saw for the first time the real high-Alpine war . . . Our work lay at the foot of the *tele-feriche*, or aerial railways which fed the war on those astonishing rock citadels: the sick and wounded came down the wires in cages, hundreds of feet in air.' At Arsiero the town had been deserted by its inhabitants; two houses only were still in use— by the Sanità officers and, in March 1918, by the Unit men. But the whole party soon had to move into huts close under the cliff, and there, as on Monte Santo, a cavern capable of holding several hundred wounded was hewn out of the rock.

Vallarsa, their other mountain out-station, was actually in Austrian territory, 'the only British Mess on enemy territory in Europe,' wrote Geoffrey Young. On the north side of the watershed, it looked down towards Trento. There they lived in huts in 'a huge colossal Dungeon Ghyll, 2,000 feet from top to bottom,' said George, called Val di Prigione (Prison Valley), whence they looked up to a great range of Dolomite pinnacles every one of which had been made into an impregnable fortress by one side or the other, and among which, 'Italian and Austrian mined and countermined in the heart of the rock, swinging themselves about on ropes to give and take sudden death in night assaults at places usually left to the Alpine clubs of the different nations.'

The Italian front was quiet all through the winter and spring of 1918. Not so the Western, where the Germans made their terrible attack in March, breaking the British Fifth Army and pushing forward as far as Amiens. And our ill-fated expedition to North Russia entirely failed to stop the Bolsheviks. 'These are terrible days of anxiety,' wrote George to us on 26 March. 'They ought to stop us all from ever being selfish again, when we think of all those thousands and tens of thousands of brave men willingly dying to try and save England and the world's freedom.'

One or two personal experiences during this quiet time show how his heart and mind were being nourished. At the end of February he gave some lectures 'to a "school" of several hundred British officers in the Euganean hills here on Garibaldi and all that fun.' A little later he told us how his car broke down in Vallarsa and he and his driver John Yates had to be towed back over the pass to Schio by an Italian lorry, a somewhat hazardous run as the Italian driver *would* drive at fullest speed down a very twisting road with the ambulance and its two inmates bumping along behind. At Schio he found it would be a day before he could get another car from the Villa, 'and I had to spend a morning doing nothing in the Inn there and I should have been *very* much bored and very miserable if I hadn't had *As You Like It*. I read the lovely second act through very slowly lying on my bed and had a very happy morning far from wars and motor cars with Rosalind and Touchstone and the melancholy Jacques, and the dappled deer under the sunlit leaves.' (During the retreat he had lost his copies of Shakespeare, Milton and *Lorna Doone*, which he was reading because my mother was reading it aloud to us at home, but Shakespeare and *Lorna Doone* were soon replaced.) At home I had been to see *As You Like It* at the Old Vic and he commented: 'It is generally so beautiful on the stage that I can hardly bear not to have lived in Shakespeare's time instead of our own. But I don't suppose it was much of it as nice as the people in *As You Like It*.' He could only manage a quarter of an hour a day for reading, so busy was he 'planting' the Alpine out-stations.

In March 1918 the first stage of a very beneficial family up-heaval began at home. Partly owing to air-raids, which made our Ward grandparents nervous, and also for educational reasons, we left London and took a furnished house in Berkhamsted, thirty miles from London and quite near the Wards' house at Stocks.

Humphry and I began attending the two good schools there, the old Grammar School and the more recent Berkhamsted School for Girls. In the following year we got our own house where we lived very happily for the next eight years. What pleased George particularly about the move at that time was that four of his best Unit men who had been called up were now stationed at Berkhamsted training to be officers—'Rupert Thompson, Heathcote, Metcalfe himself and Silvester whom we used to call the "ardito",[3] who was wounded on Sept. 4, the same day as Sessions.' We did indeed see much of these wonderful people and even went to tea with 'Metters' in his digs, when he gave us butter from his home in Ulster, a treat in those rather meagre war days.

The great event for us all of that spring—so dangerous and terrible in all its public aspects—was the engagement of Geoffrey Young to Elinor Slingsby, and their wedding in April at St George's, Hanover Square. George had naturally been anxious about Geoffrey's future ever since the disaster on the Sella di Dol. A happy marriage would be the best and most reassuring of all possible blessings for him. Elinor, though nearly twenty years younger had, as George said, 'a soul worthy of yours and able to meet [this deadful time] simply, on your own heights.' She was a child of the Yorkshire dales; her father, Cecil Slingsby, owner of a cotton-mill near Skipton, was a pioneer climber in the Norwegian mountains. She and Geoffrey had long been comrades among the fells and rocks. We were enjoined to send very full accounts of the wedding, which we did (it was the first time we had ever attended one), but, though we children did not know it, a terrible anxiety hung over the principals, for news had just come that Geoffrey's brother Hilton Young had been severely wounded in a naval battle. The battle proved to be Zeebrugge, and Hilton on the *Vindictive* had lost his right arm—'Nelson's own wound,' said George. And to us he wrote: 'It's as good as knowing one of the "men of Bideford in Devon" back from the *Revenge* battle—it is really.'

May in Italy was hot, and the lake close to Villa Trieste was a most welcome refreshment to all the Unit members who could swim. It was nowhere less than eight feet deep even close to the shore, and, as scarcely any Italians could swim—'If we went in

[3] The Arditi were the boldest shock-troops in the Italian army.

178

we should die,' they said—they used to gather on the banks to watch the Commandant and his friends. Geoffrey Young came out again to join his old comrades, and to everyone's astonishment '*began* by diving into our deep lake from the *top* of a ladder platform seven feet above the water!'

Meanwhile the battle swayed backwards and forwards on the Western Front. On 6 April George wrote to Geoffrey Young: 'These are great days: never was such a battle between God and the Devil since they jointly made the round world and all that therein is. . . . I have great faith in Englishmen and Frenchmen when they've absolutely got their back to the wall as now, especially with sound of the distant hallo of America rushing to the rescue, in their ears. Was there ever such a situation?'

A week later he wrote from Rome, where he had been to 'stir up further the excellent American Red Cross's colossal push in this country for refugees, soldiers' families and soldiers' comforts at the front, which is being so big and so well done that it may do much to consolidate things here.' The soldiers' families, whose allowances were most inadequate, 'received in every village of the Peninsula the aid of the American Red Cross,' which, 'backed by unlimited funds, helped Orlando (the Prime Minister) greatly in the work of removing the discontent of the country and spreading a sense that time and victory were on the side of the Allies because America was coming along.'[4] The Unit worked on the best of terms with American ambulance units at the front. Only in one respect was there difficulty. The Americans in the Northern Alpine war-zone wanted to share the Unit's very advanced work among the Dolomite peaks. 'When I agreed to this,' wrote Geoffrey Young later, 'they manoeuvred further to push us out and to occupy the whole zone ahead of us.' But the Italians would have none of this; they would not even allow them to share the front-line work but relegated them to the zone behind.[5] The Unit with its long experience had the perfect confidence of the Italian command and of the Sanità officers, who were not to forgo this old comradeship for a new and untried alliance. Besides, the Unit men, because they remained in their stations while the army was constantly shifting its divisional commands, often knew the terrain better than the Military themselves, who consulted them on the details of front-line

[4] *Scenes,* p. 200.
[5] *The Grace of Forgetting,* p. 339.

positions, roads and bridges. There remained the question however of whether the Unit should stay indefinitely in view of the advent of 'enormous numbers of ever fresh Units of American cars'. But, as already stated, the authorities decided in favour of its remaining where it was, and in fact some of its finest work was done during the great Battle of the Piave in June.

On 15 June the Austrians launched their attack, along the whole front from Asiago in the north down the Piave to the coast. Initially it was successful, driving the Italians back from the Piave a mile or two, but it was not sustained. In the north, the British, furious at having been forced to give any ground to Austrian troops, counter-attacked so fiercely that by the end of the second day there was no need for further fighting in the mountain area. The Austrians there simply refused battle. But on the Piave front, where the Unit cars were now being concentrated both north and south of the main road from Treviso to Ponte di Piave, along which the Austrians had intended to make a thrust which would break up the whole Italian front, fighting of great intensity and peculiar difficulty lasted for eight days. It was in a sense an 'invisible' war. Vineyards and orchards closely covered the terrain which was completely flat, so that very often the opposing troops could not see each other at all until they were almost touching, so thick were the overhanging leaves and trellises of vines. Through this leafy labyrinth lanes and farm tracks ran, along which the small Ford ambulances could drive to the most advanced aid-posts, sometimes within two hundred yards of the firing line. The larger Talbot cars which could not penetrate the narrow lanes were fully employed along the main road, as were also the Unit officers in their touring cars, meeting the Fords as they returned from unloading their wounded and directing them to the points where they were most needed. The Unit carried, during that week, 4,578 wounded, of whom nearly 2,000 were stretcher-cases.

The battle ended with the Austrians retiring east of the Piave only eight days after they had crossed it. The river, which was more than a mile wide, a strange waste of white limestone shingle, had risen with the summer rain—the road-bridges were all destroyed, and the foot-bridges could not cope with the necessary supplies and reinforcements. Everyone now knew that Italy was saved, for Austria was already collapsing, politically and economically, and had not the means of launching another offensive.

'At the turning point of the battle in our sector,' George wrote to me, 'after a dangerous Austrian advance, the Italians rallied and drove them back. And the first sign of real victory was an Italian captain, wounded and brought back on a stretcher, being brought to the car by which I was standing, waving his hand and crying out with joy and excitement "We've driven them back! We've surrounded and taken 300 of them! *Voglio andare colla Croce Rossa Britannica!*"[6] And then he shook my hand heartily and we put him into the ambulance. All that afternoon we kept carrying Austrian wounded, some of them nice gentle creatures —the Italians were very kind to them. They were all thin for want of food.'

And to Humphry he wrote: 'The best stunt I had in the battle was the day the Austrians retired over the big bridge at Ponte di Piave. I went to the Italian end of it and we were told there were six Austrian wounded in a dug-out in the bank some way along the actual river side, who had been lying there without any care or anything to eat for several days, forgotten by their Austrian comrades, but now the Italians had come they were being kind to them. But the Italians were too tired and too busy fighting to carry them out along the mile of slippery mud-bank under fire. So to save their lives four of us[7] went to carry the Austrians to our ambulances, and when we turned up on the river bank the Italians holding the line were so pleased at our coming there and so sorry for the Austrian wounded that the good fellows helped us to carry them all the long mile along the river bank, up and down mud-banks, though they were dead tired with fighting. Two out of the six died on the way but we saved the others.'

From the end of June to the end of October there was little fighting while the Italians prepared for the final advance. Before the end of the Piave battle, on 22 June, George wrote to Elinor Young: 'GWY has come up to the front and his presence has delighted and astonished the Italians. The Italians are fighting splendidly, better than 1916–17 and more *cheerful*. It is a great national and moral recovery of immense historic promise and import. We are proud indeed to be among them at this moment of all others in the War.'

[6] 'I want to go with the British Red Cross.'
[7] G.M.T. was one of the four, Phil Baker another.

This great improvement in 'morale' was in part due to the presence of British, French and now American troops at the front. Of the Americans, George wrote to me: 'The Americans have set up a canteen next to our cars on the Piave, and it is run by two nice bright Americans. We are great friends, but we laugh at them sometimes. For instance the other day, as there weren't enough infantry men passing to eat all the chocolate they had to get rid of, they asked the soldiers of the Sanità section to have each a stick. There were thirty soldiers of the section, but they got 150 sticks, for they came round and round like a stage army five or six times each. Their doctor officers told us next day that many of them had been ill in the night from too much chocolate"

The pause after the Piave battle and the more hopeful general outlook for the Allies on the Western front now (the end of July) enabled him to turn his thoughts once more to writing. While in England in August 1918 he wrote to Geoffrey Young that he was arranging with his Italian friend, Colonel Filippo de' Filippi to 'write a book about the Italian war with his criticism to safeguard.' De' Filippi was the most remarkable of all the Italian friends George Trevelyan made during the war. Doctor, writer, explorer and mountaineer, he had before the war been created a KCIE for his geographical exploits in the Himalayas, and he had played a leading part in preventing any further outbreaks of cholera in the Italian army after the terrible disaster of November 1915.

To him, 'true son of Italy, true friend of England', George dedicated his book. In his villa at Settignano, an ancient place looking out and down to Florence from the olive-clad hill-side, he was more than once the host of George and Janet Trevelyan in the years after the war. He exhibited to perfection that combination of complete cynicism about all political matters with warm and generous human feelings and activities which is often the mark of the Italian character at its best. The book which George now planned to write under his guidance was published in the spring of the following year 1919 with the title *Scenes from Italy's War*. But he began it now, in the pause before the final victorious campaign, writing it partly during his leave in August at Robin Ghyll, partly at Villa Trieste. The unexpected speed with which the war ended that autumn meant, however, that the bulk of it was written after his final return to England.[8]

Having arranged things satisfactorily with the Government and the Red Cross about the future of the Unit he returned to Italy in mid-September. From Paris he wrote to us bidding us to 'solemnly say good-bye' for him to all the Langdale scenes—the oak trees on the fell, and the ghyll below. His letters for the next month, while waiting for the final Italian offensive to begin, are full of relief and delight at the way the war was now going on its widely-scattered fronts. Most of all he rejoiced over the Serbian advance from Greece and the defeat of Ferdinand of Bulgaria who had put his money on the wrong horse.' 'I jump for joy,' he wrote to Humphry, 'at my poor dear Serbians going soon to get back to their country.' Most of all he said he would have liked to have taken part in the 'gallop over Palestine', when General Allenby rounded up the Turks. 'Don't you wish you were a cavalryman there now?" he asked, 'and aren't you glad Mummy taught you lots of Old and New Testament so that you can think of all the wonderful old places we are conquering there?' But he wanted us to feel the deeper meaning of what was happening. He turned as so often to the Bible to express his feelings. 'The beginning of Revelation XXI I liked best of all,' he wrote, 'about the new heaven and the new earth. We have now to do that. But God in us must do it, the godlike in us must do it, he will not do it *for* us from outside as the old Jews thought and many since then. We must have 'new Hearts to believe that war can and shall be abolished for ever by the League of Nations, and then it will be. If we go about saying like some silly people " O there will always be wars "—then there will be. But there need not be, people are so horrified of war now.'

Two days after this letter was written, on 24 October, the Italian offensive began. There was a fierce struggle in the north, on Monte Grappa, for two or three days, until the Alpini and the French, pushing up the Piave gorge on the east, forced the Austrians to give way. Then on the night of 26–27 October came the crossing of the middle Piave by the British and Italian infantry under Lord Cavan, where the river was a mile and a half broad, a system of low limestone islands divided by channels of the river, which, if it were to rain heavily as it often did at this time of year, would rise in spate and make the crossing impossible.

[8] See further pp. 188 and 196 below.

The rain did indeed begin in the night but it stopped just as the attack began, 'and it never rained again anywhere I was,' wrote George afterwards, ''till I had been a fortnight in Trieste. The weather-god, like every one else, had begun to *Wilsoneggiare* ('Wilsonise') as the Italian papers called the prevailing political tendency in Europe.'[9]

The bridges over the Piave were not yet strong enough to take wheeled traffic—another day passed before the 'genio' could complete new and stronger ones so that artillery, ambulances and lorries could cross. George meanwhile, with Herbert Dyne, had crossed on foot and entered a village two miles further on, called San Polo. Returning, they found the 'genio' just finishing the last bridge, and, quick as thought, Phil Baker fetched up two small Ford ambulances to the bridge head, and so it came about that Unit cars were the first wheeled vehicles over the Piave. They were soon followed by British artillery. The Unit ambulances took over a ruined castle in San Polo, but the Italian infantry had raced so far ahead in pursuit of the Austrians that it was difficult to keep up with them, especially as the Austrians in their flight had not neglected to blow up the bridges. But in fact the fighting was virtually over, and very large sections of the Austrian forces, especially the Czechs and Croats, were surrendering wholesale. 'Every day,' wrote George afterwards, 'as we advanced, we met ever longer columns of weary prisoners, shepherded in thousands at a time by two or three cheerful Tommies, or two or three majestic mounted Carabinieri. Many, I think, had "bowed the head for bread", rather than remain with a starving army or return to a starving land.' The roadsides were littered with 'Boche' helmets thrown away as being no longer of any use. And there were grim sights too. The Austrians had deserted even their own wounded in the hospitals, leaving them 'doctorless, foodless and in the last stage of human misery', just as they had, George remembered, at Kragujevatz in November 1914 when the Serbs drove them out. The English captain who was attempting to cope with this dreadful situation in an Austrian hospital, said he had never seen such a shocking sight in all his war experience. Yet even here, Italian women of the locality, untrained but filled with compassion, were doing what they could to relieve their suffering enemies.

[9] *Scenes,* p. 222.

The countryside had of course been stripped of all supplies, and the inhabitants subjected to a good deal of ill-treatment; the worst tyranny coming from the German officers from Germany proper, and from Magyar troops, as previously in Serbia. For the first time since he had been in Italy George Trevelyan now heard that Austrian prisoners had been insulted by some of the liberated population, but fortunately this was of short duration.

'On the night of November 2nd,' he wrote afterwards, 'it chanced that I had a long way to walk back beyond the Piave, not wishing to take the car back over the bridge. I was walking under the stars through the scenes of our June battle, ghostly in the starlight. As I went, I became aware of a singing and cheering all around for miles away. I was quite alone, and could only guess its significance; but when at last I struck our old Treviso main road, I asked the first group of soldiers I met what was the meaning of the still-continued, universal shout. They told me that the Austrians had sent a general to the Commando Supremo to ask for an armistice. I shall never forget the distant and continuous noise of a whole army scattered over the plain, shouting all night in its joy under the glistening winter stars because their warfare was accomplished, and Europe at last was free.'[10]

Among his letters to us is this pencilled note: 'Nov. 4. 1918 dawn. Somewhere Half way between the two great rivers.[11] Dear Mary and Humphry, We're *trying* to catch the Austrians but can't. They go off so fast. So last night no wounded passed thro' this town; all the better. Phil Baker and John Yates are ahead on the great river we crossed in rain and misery last year.[12] Now it's fine, and anything but misery. I'm so happy. So's everyone. The soldiers sing and carry flowers in their rifle muzzles. The liberated inhabitants cheer us as English. They've had enough of Austrians and Germans! Daddy.' And on the back is a note to Janet: 'I've just heard for certain that the armistice is signed and "*cessa il fuoco al quindici oggi.*" (Cease fire at three o'clock to-day). It is past laughter, past tears, "deeper than flower and than fruit." '

One little episode in these tremendous days was not past laughter. '*The* event,' he wrote to us on 8 November, 'besides the dissolution of the Austrian army and Empire, was my tumbling into the Tagliamento! The night before last, as we were coming

10 *Scenes*, p. 228.
11 The Piave and the Tagliamento.
12 The Tagliamento.

back across a pontoon bridge a little below S. Vito, I ran on in front of the car to see if the bridge was clear for it to pass, and a mule cart came dashing down the slope of the bridge at me, and to avoid it I stepped aside onto what looked in the darkness like the solid side of the wooden bridge but which was really a bundle of faggots. Next moment I was falling ten feet down into the river, I went splash under into the strong deep current just there and lost my cap and electric torch but scrambled out quite jolly!'

The next ten days took the Unit back through its old haunts and into the long-coveted city—Trieste. They visited Villa Trento, and found it filthy, gutted and derelict, but they parked their cars on the front drive, and for a short time used it as an out-station. 'The peasants at Villa Trento,' he wrote to us, 'tell me that the Austrians when they came a year ago were so hungry that they ate the pigs we had fattened for ourselves so fast and so greedily that a lot of them died! So they held an enquiry to see if the pigs had been poisoned by us before we went and found they hadn't been . . . There's a warning to be careful at Christmas time!!'

'The pleasure and romance of the final rush to Trieste,' wrote my father in the *Record*, 'was much enhanced by the fact that we were going in fine weather and with light hearts, over the very roads we had fled over so disconsolately in the rain just a year before. The climax of the Caporetto retreat had been the wet "Beresina" scenes on the narrow bridge over the Tagliamento, then a foaming flood . . . Now the winter sun was gaily shining on the distant circle of the Alps and Monte Nero's ledge of snow; the river bed was stone dry, white shingle a mile broad; the bridge that had borne the weight of so much misery a year ago had disappeared, burnt to the ground; and cheerful American "doughboys" who knew not the tragic meanings the place had for us Europeans, were marching over dry-shod to help garner the fruits of Austria's "Caporetto".'

On 9 November he, with Geoffrey Young and two other Unit members entered Trieste. They were given a handsome modern villa on the outskirts as their headquarters; their ambulances came up—the first to enter and work in the city—and there was plenty of work to do. Down on the docks there was an enormous camp containing 60,000 returned prisoners of war. They were starving and many of them were sick. From 10 November until the end of the month the Unit cars in Trieste carried 6,775 cases from the camp to the hospitals in the town, or from the hospitals to the ships and trains. Food was at first a terrible problem, but, George told Humphry on 20 November, 'a very good, clever British officer bought 200 horses and got a lot of dixies for cooking, and cooks 50 horses a night for them on the docks and they all have hot horse once in twenty-four hours and like it ever so much, poor dears, as it's their only hot meal and only meat meal. In Austria you can't even get hot horse. We must *feed* the enemy now we've beaten him.'

By the beginning of December it was clear that the Unit's work for Italy was over.[13] Leaving Geoffrey Young, Phil Baker, Dyne, Marriage and the adjutant Braithwaite in charge of the final arrangements, George left Italy on 7 December, but he did not go directly home. He went to Paris, where meetings and conversations were already in progress between Italians, Yugoslavs, and Americans on the subject of Italy's claims to Dalmatia. In these he felt he could usefully take part. 'I have spent about six hours,' he wrote to Geoffrey Young on 11 December, 'talking to the Americans, and to the *thin* borghese of the Gorizia bridge.'[14] Once more he was acting as unofficial middleman, as he had done in 1915, between 'the Jones's' (his code-name for the Italians), and 'the Jugs'. He had besides an hour with 'Colonello Casa' (Colonel House, President Wilson's political adviser). It was, he told Geoffrey Young, 'the most interesting perhaps I have ever spent, he telling me his doings during the war for half an hour and then turning me on to expound my views on the "row" (between Italians and Yugoslavs).'

In England the friends of Yugoslavia were conducting a heated anti-Italian press campaign in the *Manchester Guardian,* led by the archaeologist Sir Arthur Evans. George felt it necessary to intervene in this paper war, which might easily prejudice the chances of a good peace, and wrote a letter to the *Guardian* rebuking Sir Arthur's violence. He was supported by McClure, the

[13] During the three years and four months of their service in Italy, the Unit cars carried 177,522 wounded and sick, of whom over 40,000 were stretcher cases. The Unit members received eight Silver and nine Bronze medals 'for Military Valour', twenty-eight 'crosses for merit in war', and three of the special silver medals of the Italian Red Cross.
[14] Wickham Steed, the journalist with strong Yugoslav sympathies whom George had unexpectedly met at the moment of Gorizia's fall, in 1916. George described him as 'the evil genius of the House of Habsburg and the avenging angel of the races oppressed by the Dual Monarchy.' *Scenes,* p. 99.

British correspondent in Rome, as well as by several Italian political writers, such as Mario Borsa of *Il Secolo* and Guglielmo Emanuel of the *Corriere della Sera,* who feared and distrusted the new and strident Italian imperialism which a year later led to D'Annunzio's raid on Fiume, and ultimately to the triumph of Mussolini and his fascisti.

George was home for Christmas—the first 'peace Christmas' celebrated at Stocks with an immense children's dance. Earlier, before returning to Italy in September, he had gone from Robin Ghyll to Wallington to greet his parents. He walked from Hexham to the house, and his father, now eighty years old, knowing that he was going to do this, walked to the top of the hill beyond Wallington Bridge at the appropriate time to meet him. 'And there,' said the old statesman to me afterwards, 'I did what Laertes did to his son Ulysses, I began to weep on his breast.'

His first task after his return was to finish *Scenes from Italy's War,* in which he intended not only to give the Unit its due publicity by telling the story of its labours, but to 'smooth down a few of Jones's very ruffled feathers.' 'Having said my say on the Jones question in the proper quarters' (namely in Paris), he wrote that he would now 'engage in "smoothing business"' by showing from his own knowledge how Italy had first thrown off the Teutonic influences on her economic and cultural life, and then, in spite of persistent and ingenious propaganda against the Allies, had sacrificed almost half a million dead and almost a million wounded of her ten million males between eighteen and sixty-five years old, and had proved how she still retained her old friendship for England by the support and goodwill she gave to the representatives of England who came to her aid in the war, whether they were troops or Red Cross units. 'Filippi, dear little great man,' he wrote to Geoffrey Young on 8 January, 'is hopping with delight at what he has seen of the book from the "smoothing" point of view.' 'What days we have seen and what a story it makes!' he exclaimed. 'I realise that now, as I work eight hours a day at conjuring up the scenes and transferring glimpses of them to paper. The Retreat, since it has been followed by recovery, makes such a wonderful "interest" just when a filip is needed, and S. Gabriele seems a climax that cannot be better.' The book was published in February 1919 by T. C. and E. C. Jack. It would catch the market before other books on Italy.

To Charles he wrote on the last day of the old year that he

would finish *Lord Grey of the Reform Bill,* and 'beyond that I have no intentions except to think out what I really want to settle down to for life—a book I mean. You can help me choose perhaps. I don't think my life or occupations will have been much changed by the war, though I hope I have been personally freshened up a little and am less of an old gentleman . . . The seismic character of change nowadays has altered our standards about all such matters. We each dree our ain weird, and so, by heaven, does the world!'

At the end of his chapter on 'The Work of the Unit' in the *Record,* George wrote: 'And so, after all, things came out at the end as nearly perfectly for us as human affairs ever do. The only thing not perfect was that the hospital could not go on to the end. . . . The end was indeed like a day-dream. We got back to Villa Trento, we had one month in long-desired Trieste—the only well-fed people there because Perceval fed us[15]; I even visited still vexed Fiume. . . . Apart from the public objects achieved the fellowship of our Unit was a good thing in itself. It was a "Unit" with a soul of its own, not a mere aggregation of individuals . . . a fellowship which was an end in itself, over and above the work it accomplished, but which would cease to have that quality if it did not do its work superlatively. Now the work is over and the fellowship remains.'

That the Unit was such a fellowship was due to the spirit of all its members, but above all to its Commandant. He had used his great gift for friendship to be the friend of all the members whatever their jobs and whatever their backgrounds; whether they were artists and intellectuals like Tonks and Ashby, accustomed rather to give than to submit to rules and orders; or the drivers who bore the burden of the heaviest work, often in danger; the mechanics ceaselessly repairing and renovating damaged ambulances; or the youngest VAD nurses far from their homes in a strange land. Every year after the War the Unit held a dinner for its members, which in simplified form still continues for those who yet remain. George always attended, and always made a speech. 'Sometimes,' writes Philip Baker, 'he would be hesitant and obscure. Sometimes he would be gay, as he had so often been in our Italian days. Sometimes there would be a burst of quite stupendous eloquence when he was moved by what he had to

[15] Deane Perceval, the steward and caterer of the Unit.

say.' But, whatever his mood, he was still 'Trevvy, the same loyal, understanding friend who had led us, made us a fraternal unit, and helped us through the War.'

The new year saw George Trevelyan moving rapidly about England, Scotland and Wales, giving lectures about Italy and her part in the War. Manchester, Liverpool, Sheffield, Bangor and Edinburgh were thus visited in one strenuous week at the beginning of March 1919, with one day's walking in Snowdonia by way of refreshment half-way through. He also gave in the same year the Creighton Lecture at London University on 'The War and the European Revolution in Relation to History', in which he discussed 'a few, a very few of the unnumbered historical causes' of that war and that revolution, as his great knowledge of the past and his recent experiences had enabled him to see them.

In that sickly spring of 1919 we had formed a joint household with two families of friends from London in a furnished house at Berkhamsted belonging to my mother's uncle Dr Frank Arnold; the whole household contracted 'Spanish 'flu', fortunately not very badly, and Humphry was an exile for six weeks with scarlet fever. But after that came a most wonderful Easter holiday in Cornwall at Gorran Haven, George making friends once more in enormous walks with the coast he had learnt to love in his Cambridge days. 'I shall never forget,' he wrote afterward in his *Autobiography*, 'the exhilaration of (that) Cornish holiday when all the world seemed young again and the sands and rocky headlands rejoiced. Even when joy is based in part on ignorance of the future, and in part it nearly always is, it is none the less joy, the breath of life that carries the poor human race forward along its chequered path.'

Then in May we made the final move from London to the pleasant house which George, helped by his father, had bought on the southern edge of the little town. We re-named it 'Pen Rose', partly after my mother, and there we lived for eight years until the final move to Cambridge in 1927.

The house had an excellent and well-stocked garden stretching up the hill behind; in front it looked onto the hockey-field of the girls' school which was now my place of education, only three minutes' walk away. There was a jobbing gardener who came twice a week—he was an excellent gardener though he irritated

Nannie and our maids by his over-religious conversation. He was in fact a 'Plymouth Brother', and sang lustily to the Lord while he worked. My father did not object to this—it was a link with Cromwellian Puritanism. In the garden there was a weeping wych-elm whose branches came down to the ground and made a perfect tent. Under it he would often sit writing on warm days in summer.

The garden, besides producing plentiful roses, vegetables and apples, was also frequented in our first years there by a pair of noisy wrynecks—a bird now so rare as to be practically extinct. They inhabited a dead tree-trunk in the opposite field but often came across to us and uttered their piercing, rather distressing cries.

Inside the house his study was the dining-room. This was an arrangement scarcely worthy of the work he was to do there, but I do not think it ever occurred to him to question it. The room upstairs which should have been his was given up to me and Humphry as our school-room.

All around lay pleasant country; on the other side of the town were large commons of bracken and gorse where we often rode on ponies hired from a riding-school in the town, and beyond them were the beech-woods of Ashridge, familiar to us from earliest days at Stocks (which was only five miles away), leading out at last to the splendid bare downs of Ivinghoe Beacon looking north over the midland plain. These woods and commons soon became of special concern to George Trevelyan because of the danger of building exploitation, and it was his energetic labours which eventually saved them for the nation.[16]

It was a happy time of the renewal and strengthening of old friendships and the creation of some new ones. The spare room was in great favour for week-end guests. John and Susie Buchan, Ralph Vaughan-Williams—who 'sat in my big chair which he filled completely and talked about music in the Elizabethan theatre and lots of jolly old things'—Laurence and Barbara Hammond, Geoffrey and Elinor Young, Maurice and Lucy Amos and many others. Once George and Ruth Mallory came—not long before his last and fatal Everest expedition, and once old Mr George Haven Putnam, who had fought for the North in the American Civil War. His publishing firm was bringing out my

[16] See below, pp. 207–8.

mother's book, at last finished—*A Short History of the Italian People.* He was a tiny little man with a beard and plentiful graying hair. His presence and his stories about his war made us children feel important. Unit members came, of course—'Daddy' Dyne, Phil Baker and his wife Irene who owned a great estate in Euboea and was descended from an Indian princess; Rupert Thompson and Dr Brock. Once too, we had a very precious visit from George's mother and Booa—an event indeed as 'Mama' had long ceased to pay visits away from Welcombe and Wallington. Unfortunately it was marred by Booa having a serious fall in the steep part of our garden and having to be put to bed with a cut over her eye. I shall never forget the look upon my father's face as he lifted her up.

George's interest in English politics continued in a lower key. His brother Charles and other friends had joined the Labour Party in the middle of the war and though Charles and many of his friends who had followed a more or less pacifist line during the war lost their seats in Lloyd George's 'coupon election' in November 1918, they all regained them with large majorities at the next one in 1922. George was not at any time in much sympathy with doctrinal socialism, so he could not follow them into the Labour Party; but the Liberal Party was now sadly divided between 'Liberals', under Asquith, and 'Lloyd George Liberals' who with the Conservatives supported Lloyd George's government from 1919 to 1922. George had a considerable admiration for the Prime Minister, without whose energy and genius he believed the war would never have been won, but he disliked his methods of granting honours and administering his 'political fund' as much as King George V did himself.

At Berkhamsted he accepted the presidency of the local Liberal Association, for it pleased him to feel that Liberal politics were still a reality in spite of Lloyd George, and when Stanley Baldwin, the Conservative Prime Minister, suddenly sprung an election on the country in the late autumn of 1923, unwisely making 'Protection' a leading issue when there was scarcely any section of British industry which needed to be protected, George became quite excited, for a very intelligent, though not well-known man was standing as Liberal candidate for West Herts. George took the chair at an eve-of-poll meeting, made a speech and was gratified to see a large audience containing many of our friends. To everyone's surprise the Liberal candidate was returned. The

Tories were enraged and ascribed their defeat to fog on the line which delayed the evening train from London on which many of them were returning, so that the poll closed before it arrived. But then, as the Liberals said, why didn't they vote before leaving in the morning?

His chief friend among politicians at this time was Herbert Fisher, Minister of Education in Lloyd George's Government and later Warden of New College. One day, soon after Lloyd George's defeat by the Conservatives in the autumn of 1922, Fisher took him to call on Lloyd George in his new house at Churt. They found him there with his 'henchmen', Mr Geoffrey Shakespeare, whom George liked, and Lord Riddell, whose looks he liked a good deal less. Lloyd George was in very good form in spite of his recent defeat. 'The little man took us all out; he wrapped himself up in a big old cloak and looked like a little wizard. He led us to the top of Kettlebury hill . . . and for twenty minutes stood or walked round its summit, talking and chaffing about everything and everybody in politics in the gayest manner, seeing the joke of it all, *acting* with his big stick the 'fencing' that he said he had had to do with his 'sword' in the election, lamenting that Grey[17] would make Liberal reunion difficult by abusing him worse than the Tories, and finally discussing with us all the methods and possibilities of Liberal reunion and of future relations with the moderates of the Labour Party if they would drop their taxation programme. He asked us all our opinions on these big subjects and seemed interested in them all. His wit, *joie de vivre* and humorous good nature with everyone and everything was astonishing within a few days of so mighty a *débacle*. I expect it was in part the intense relief of the moving of the load of responsibility . . . The little man has *méchanceté* but no permanent malice, no brooding ill nature. He hits out hard and forgets. He sees the fun of everything. It was a memorable morning.'

The most striking result of the 1922 election was not so much the defeat of Lloyd George as the return of a hundred and forty Labour members to Parliament in a very militant mood. George Trevelyan saw and felt the nation's dangers and difficulties at this

---

[17] Lord Grey of Fallodon, formerly Sir Edward Grey, Foreign Secretary 1906–1916, now retired from active political life, but a very severe critic of Lloyd George. Later, George Trevelyan became his biographer. See below pp. 222–3.

time quite as much as he had felt them in his historian's mind for the seventeenth or nineteenth centuries. 'The serious thing is,' he wrote to me, 'as I realise better after a talk today with dear Charles,[18] that there is such a division between the industrial north and the south of this island: 140 Labour members are coming down south with immense majorities, with a sense of having rolled Tories and Liberals out flat and having a mandate to do all sorts of things for the unemployed—and down south we all think Labour is rolled out flat. The trouble is that the amount of unemployment in the industrial north is terrible. You can't have $1\frac{1}{2}$ millions unemployed and not be in danger of a revolutionary turmoil of some sort, if unemployment continues for years and years as this is likely to do owing to the non-recovery of our markets in Europe. . . . We shall be lucky if we get nothing worse than the return of 140 Labour members! The *buffer* of a strong Liberal party no longer mediates between capital and labour, between North and South Britain. But,' he added, 'we must hope for the best and try and understand each other.'

The Treaty of Versailles, Charles had said, was the chief reason for the defeat of the government, because, by heaping German reparations on France, it had destroyed our own European markets. George felt very bitterly about France, and sorrowfully also about America when after all she would not join the League of Nations.

In 1920 George was asked to take part in an important piece of public work. He was appointed a member of the Royal Commission on the Universities of Oxford and Cambridge. The Commission made many recommendations in its report which were afterwards embodied in legislation. For George personally it was an opportunity for gaining and strengthening friendships among his colleagues. One of these was Hugh Anderson, the Master of Caius. He had, as Master, a house on the east coast at Hunstanton, where George used to stay, working with him and others on the Report of the Commission. While there he was thrilled by a visit to Castle Rising, built in the reign of William Rufus and scarcely altered or even damaged since. 'We were all alone,' he wrote, 'with Puck and Norman knights and ladies and

---

[18] Charles was now Labour member for Central Newcastle.

Saxon thralls. . . . You walk up a magnificent staircase into a room which is all carved round in Norman arches, doors and windows, and then wander on through room after room and passage after passage, upstairs and downstairs, like the knights and ladies did long before the first policeman King!'[19]

Another colleague on the Commission who became a close friend was Albert Mansbridge, that great son of the people who founded the Workers' Educational Association, the Seafarers' Education Service and the National Library for Students. He and his wife often visited us and he brought into our life something of the prophetic spirit, the forward-looking power of Christian faith and hope.

The Commission was chaired by Mr Asquith, now ageing somewhat. He used not infrequently to drop off to sleep and when this happened George would be quietly asked to take his place. About the Commission itself, George wrote to me before it started: 'If I can help to reform Oxford and Cambridge I shall do a great deal of good, for they are tremendously important places, and I am very fond of the one I was at and should be of the other if I had been at it.'

The Commission's work laid the foundations of modern University finance and practice. Hitherto the Colleges had provided almost all the teaching work of the University. But now the University itself was to take the full burden, for increased salaries, greatly increased staff for research and extra-mural work, and a uniform pension scheme—involving expenses far beyond the means of the Colleges. Large grants from the Treasury would in fact be necessary, and a Statutory Commission would have to be set up to carry out the changes in University and College Statutes. So, after the Commission had reported, the recommendations had to go to Parliament, and as a result the University Grants Committee was established, with ample funds to supply the new needs. In those days there were still University members in the House of Commons, and when at the 1924 election J. R. M. ('Jim') Butler, a son of the old Master of Trinity and a young member of the Cambridge History School, was unexpectedly elected for Cambridge, George rejoiced greatly, for 'Jim' would certainly support the Commission's findings. Another friend, the well-loved John Buchan, became

[19] Our nickname for Henry II.

in 1927 MP for the Scottish Universities. He was a Conservative but with a truly liberal mind, so George and his Commission friends could feel their work was in good parliamentary hands.

As has been seen, George returned with fervour to writing as soon as the war was over. *Scenes from Italy's War* appeared in February 1919, and was followed by *Lord Grey of the Reform Bill*, of which only three of the eventual sixteen chapters had been completed before the outbreak of war. On taking up the story once more he wrote, at the end of chapter three: 'Since the above was written another great war has been fought and won. It has been fought on behalf of the principles of Fox and Grey, in alliance with Republican France and America and free Italy, against the despotic principle represented by Prussia and Austria, the powers of darkness whom the posthumous victory of Burke and Pitt made masters of the Continent for a hundred years . . . Even if we regard the war against Republican France as having been forced upon us by the French Jacobins, we must feel that it has indeed proved the tragedy that Fox, Grey and Wordsworth then believed it to be.' Then, in rapid succession he wrote two books: one which for many years and even to this day has been the friend and guide of Sixth forms, undergraduates and 'general readers' alike—*British History in the Nineteenth Century*. The other was the last and final volume of his Risorgimento series—*Manin and the Venetian Revolution of 1848*.

The preface to *British History* opened with a statement of his aims in writing it: 'The object of this book is to enable the student or general reader to obtain, in the compass of one volume, a picture of change and development during the hundred and twenty years when things certainly, and probably men and women with them, were undergoing a more rapid change of character than in any previous epoch of our annals.' And he explained that he had called it 'British History' because, 'though it cannot claim to be a History of the Empire, it is more than a History of Britain.' It covered events in Ireland, India, Canada, Australia and Africa from the beginning of Pitt's ministry in 1782 down to the death of Queen Victoria. A more useful book, for its purpose, can seldom have been written, and it is anything but dry-as-dust in language and style. It was published in the spring of 1922 and in two years had sold 13,000 copies.

He was amused when the Tory press praised him for his 'impartiality'—he being classed as a 'Whig'. He felt he must be like the man who 'was so upright that he fell over backwards'. 'But,' he added, 'the Church papers restore my self-respect by their disapproval.' A foolish disapproval one feels it must have been, for the Church's affairs, her problems and the changes in the character of her clergy, are handled with singular sympathy and understanding by this 'puritan atheist'.

The Manin book which, he said, he wrote for his own pleasure entirely, meant visits to Italy once more, to delve in the archives of Venice and Vicenza. But in the previous year, 1921, he had written an article for the *Times Napoleonic Supplement* (published at the centenary of Napoleon's death), which reads almost like an introduction to the story of 1848. 'Napoleon and Italy' showed how the young General Bonaparte, the Corsican who lapsed into Italian when excited, when in 1797 he set up his 'Cisalpine Republic' in Lombardy and Venetia as the protégée of revolutionary France, was really creating not only the first of the Napoleonic Kingdoms but the first state to fly the Italian tri-color. He did not give it 'free institutions' but he did destroy the old and corrupt feudal jurisdictions both there and in Naples, and he did 'train the Italians in administration, justice and war'. When he departed and Austrian tyranny took the place of his Republic, the new generation of educated men in North Italy could not endure the reaction. The first leaders and martyrs of the Risorgimento in the 'twenties and 'thirties were men who looked back to Napoleon as their inspiration, for in Italy his rule, though by no means liberal, had created national feeling. Manin's great enterprise in 1848 would not have been possible without Napoleon's foundations, although Manin himself was no lover of Napoleon.

So in May and June 1922 George was in Venice and then Vicenza, where he settled for a few weeks to work, 'in the foot-hills of the Alps all ablaze with roses, cooled with cypress, acacia woods and vines running linked between ripening corn strips and melodious nightingales', scenes that he had known so well in 1918. Then in 1923 he went again—and this time Janet and I went with him—on a long visit lasting from February to May, and including Florence and Rome. I was left for three weeks in Florence to learn Italian while my parents went on to Vicenza and Venice. By this time I was beginning to take an interest in pictures as well as poetry, so George could share with me his love of Browning, especially 'Old Pictures in Florence' and 'Fra Lippo Lippi', and give guidance in his letters about their difficulties for a young reader. He had finished his research for Manin, and so was amusing himself with reading Vicenza's early history, and also Fra Paolo Sarpi's great *History of the Council of Trent*—'really a history of the Reformation as seen by a Liberal Catholic—very anti-Papal . . . Macaulay thought him one of the world's great historians. The edition I saw in the Library to-day was printed in England in 1619 and dedicated to James I—the learned umpire of such controversies. I expect Sarpi had difficulty in getting it printed in Italy.'

For lighter reading, 'I am reading *Hamlet,* the blue Shelley, Ward's *Poets* last vol, Macaulay's Life, *Diana of the Crossways* and enjoying them all as if I had never read them before.' And then he gave a judgment on what the 'love of good books if once you have it', can do for you. 'It lasts for *certain* longer than anything else in life, much longer than things dependent on one's athletic powers, longer than some (at any rate) of one's hopes for mankind if they are disappointed, and can outlive the people one loves too, if and when they die.'

He was also reading Maitland's *Constitutional History,* and this set him thinking about the Middle Ages in England, and the history of England that he seriously wanted now to write. 'I'm beginning to see "in my mind's eye",' he wrote to me, 'a vision of the evolution of English society and character and habit "down the ages"—if I could get it on paper it might help some unlearned people to have it too.' Characteristically he was thinking of 'the people' as his readers rather than the specialists. 'On that theme,' he went on, 'so much has been found out by scholars in the last thirty years, mostly out of apparently very dull material. But the net result is perhaps the most important thing in the world—one feels that, the more one sees of foreigners, if one prefers one's own country . . . Their differences from us interest me largely because they *are* differences, making one feel the value—or the curiosity—of English institutions one always before took for granted. E.g. Fascismo, thank God, is neither necessary nor possible in England. Why? History alone can give the *complicated* answer.' For, six months before, in the autumn of 1922, Mussolini and his blackshirts had marched on Rome, taken over the government, put down by force the violent socialist reign of terror which the ordinary parliamentary government failed to control, and were engaged in arresting their opponents, murdering some of them and administering lethal doses of castor oil to others.

Our friend Lina Waterfield—formerly Lina Duff-Gordon[20]—was the Italian correspondent of the *Observer*. She lived outside Florence at Ponte à Mensola, near de' Filippi, at Settignano, and was immensely kind to me while my parents were away. She was a sharp critic of the new régime, but she had to be careful how she spoke of them. So she always referred to the Fascists as 'the Bundleists' ('fascio' meaning 'a bundle') so as to be able to discuss their doings fairly freely in conversation.

In Venice my mother completed her biography of her mother Mrs Humphry Ward, who had died three years before. Then at last they were able to have a real holiday together, renewing their friendships with several old friends, Italian and English. From Venice they went to Gorizia where they hired a car and spent a day visiting George's old battlefields on the Isonzo front. He was glad to find the devastated villages well rebuilt even in remote Slav hamlets, and the Slav masters kept on in the village schools. They drove up onto the Bainsizza plateau by the Sella di Dol road where Geoffrey Young and the others had been wounded, and finally made their way on foot to the top of Monte Kuk, 'a wilderness of nature,' wrote George to Geoffrey; 'mixed with primrose and bramble and white limestone were all relics of war —shells exploded and unexploded, clothes and litter—and on the summit, raised on this altar of white rock to the blue heaven, pure and dry in wind and sun, the complete skeleton of a "milite ignoto" [unknown soldier]—Austrian or Italian none will ever know. Perhaps no one will ever find him again.'

After that strange experience they paid a visit to Villa Trento, now once more inhabited by its real owner, the Conte Trento, and then, turning south to Tuscany and Umbria, we all together paid our first visit to Assisi.

The Fascist régime was about as distasteful as anything could have been to George and Janet Trevelyan, closely involved as

---

[20] She is the Lady in Furse's famous picture 'The Return from the Ride'. Her formidable aunt, Mrs Janet Ross, lived in a castle at the top of the hill above Ponte à Mensola, where she was visited by many and enjoyed being rude to most people, particularly to Lina's charming artist-husband, Aubrey Waterfield.

they had now been for many years in the cultural relationships of England and Italy, as well as in her war. Fortunately, thanks to the enthusiasm and wisdom of some of Italy's English friends and lovers—particularly Mrs Waterfield and Sir Rennell Rodd, who had been for eleven eventful years British Ambassador in Rome—something had been established before the Fascists came into power, which proved a bulwark of Anglo-Italian relations at the deepest level. The British Institute of Florence came into being in 1918, 'a British intellectual centre in the heart of Italy' as my mother called it, providing courses for Italian students in English language and literature and conversely for British students studying Italian. George and Janet had both been closely involved in its creation, and Janet even drew up at Berkhamsted one Sunday morning in 1919, a draft for its Royal Charter, unaided and with no model except the Charter of the British School at Rome! The Fascisti were proving the enemies of free speech and would brook no opposition to their rule. But George and Janet were soon convinced that open and violent hostility to 'the Bundleists' would do no good: the British Institute of Florence would almost certainly be closed down unless it could preserve the approval of the Italian government. So they made no attempt either to dislodge or to rebuke the Director, Harold Goad, who was a passionate supporter of the régime. The Institute flourishes yet; it even survived the Second World War and the German occupation, besides the floods of 1962, in which parts of its library suffered severely.

In the autumn of 1923 George was invited to give the Sidney Ball lecture at Oxford. He undertook to speak on the 'Historical Causes of the Present State of Affairs in Italy'. This gave him the opportunity to describe the very different ways in which England and Italy had, all through their histories, approached their constitutional problems—England through the gradual growth of representative institutions—the partnership or rivalry of Crown and Parliament; Italy, a land of self-governing and often rival cities with no central government until 1870, and no tradition of orderly change in the city governments either, only that of a less or more violent 'row in the piazza', a demonstration of popular feeling by the citizens of Florence or Milan or Pisa. Fascism had come to the rescue when the government was weak and indolent, by methods such as those which were of immemorial Italian tradition. But George made clear his fears; the Fascisti

200

were much too ready to condemn all criticism and all opposition and to employ violent methods against their opponents. His prayer for Mussolini—whom he called in the lecture a 'man of genius', was that he would not destroy freedom but restore it along with order and discipline. As the years went on of course it became clear that this was not to be and that the 'Duce' was becoming more and more of a dictator with militarist and imperialist aims.

Manin was his last venture in Italian history. In the early spring of 1924 he went on his second visit to America, lecturing on English history. To Geoffrey Young he wrote: 'I am getting launched on a one-vol history of England "down the ages", of which these American lectures are a preliminary canter. I think I have finished with the dagos for now. I shall think of nothing else (than the *History of England*) for the next three years.'[21]

Actually the book was finished in April 1926 and published in June. George was a very rapid worker, but even so he could scarcely have completed the *History of England* in under two years unless he had already been deeply familiar through his earlier work with some of the periods, particularly the Stuarts, the nineteenth century and the age of Wycliffe. There had been much written recently about the earlier periods—Roman, Saxon and Norman—and his new studies had been mainly in these. In 1924 he wrote to me (then at Oxford) as I struggled with Vinogradoff's *Growth of the Manor*: 'V. is stiff, but there is brain, not dulness. And he has somehow got to interest me, "romantic" as I am; that sort of work is the straight and narrow pathway to romance—that is, to realising the actuality of our distant forefathers. I am trying to put all that sort of thing briefly and interestingly now in the first part of my history.'

Other new contributions to the historical knowledge of periods with which he was already familiar were appearing at the time. When Keith Feiling of Oxford produced in 1924 his *History of the Tory Party from 1640 to 1714,* no one welcomed it more gladly than George Trevelyan. It, and the sixth volume of Holdsworth's *History of English Law* (another Oxford production) helped him in the revision of his early book *England under the Stuarts,* in 1925. In this revised edition it has continued

---

[21] The lectures were the Lowell Lectures given at Harvard. He dedicated the *History of England* to President Lowell.

in print ever since, appearing as a 'University Paper Back' in 1965.

In the summer of 1922 George Trevelyan for the first and only time in his life wrote for the stage. Berkhamsted possesses the remains of a fine castle, built first by Saxons to guard the valley where now the railway and canal run side by side, and kept in a good state by all the Norman and Plantagenet kings down to the time of Henry VIII. The masonry is all but gone now except for some sections of flint walls, but it has a large mound and spacious bailey, with a double ring of moats; great trees had grown up on these old fortifications so that it was a lovely place of 'beechen green'; the bailey was still a clear open space. Here it was decided to hold a historical pageant. George Trevelyan was enlisted as chief writer. He wrote five scenes and an epilogue, beginning with King Offa of Mercia firmly but not rudely refusing his Archbishop's request to do away with Monday, Tuesday etcetera, the pagan days of the week, and 'baptise the week to Christ and God'. Then came a glorious scene—it was really historical too—of William the Conqueror, fresh from Hastings, being asked at Berkhamsted by the Saxon thegns and bishops to receive the Crown of England at Westminster Abbey. Horses ridden by most splendid Norman knights came charging in at a gallop from beneath the trees, led by Duke William who promised to be a 'good lord' to all his obedient subjects of whatever race. Later came a charming monologue by George himself in the person of Geoffrey Chaucer, who had been 'clerk of the works' to the castle. His Chaucerian soliloquy was a sort of prophecy linking medieval Berkhamsted to the days of the Reformation, when, as depicted in another scene, Incent, Dean of St Paul's, founded the boys' grammar school there. Next, he wrote of the Princess Elizabeth's dangerous sojourn at nearby Ashridge in the days of her sister Mary, and finally a short epilogue about the poet William Cowper, who was born at Berkhamsted rectory, brought the pageant to an end.

Music, song and dancing by children of all the schools filled the intervals, but two things tried the patience of us all. A main railway line—then called the London and North-Western—ran immediately alongside the castle grounds; the frequent trains that thundered past or stopped at the station drowned the voices of the actors and singers. The other was the weather. The pageant went on for a week, and it rained at every performance except one. George enjoyed the whole thing greatly. 'My Saxon, Norman, Henry VIII and Elizabeth scenes all came off very well,' he wrote to Geoffrey Young; 'for the first and last time in my life I had the pleasure of seeing my words and ideas *acted*, and quite well too.'

IX

Historian of England

The nearness of Berkhamsted to London meant that both George and Janet could pursue their interests and meet their friends there without difficulty. For Janet it was, at times, almost a case of 'commuting', for she was both Chairman of the Evening Play Centres for Children (her mother's creation) and Secretary of the British-Italian League, which tried to foster cultural relations between England and Italy in the difficult atmosphere created in Italy by the Fascist regime. 'I feel the breach widening month by month,' George wrote in October 1923, when he was about to give the Sidney Ball lecture in Oxford about Italy, 'between the fascists and the liberal friends of Italy in England. There is less than no use preaching to the Italians but there is the question of English opinion about political affairs. I fear some of the Italians will not like my lecture or me for it. But it can't be helped.' Three years later he wrote: 'Mussolini is becoming a *European* nuisance. He has to do something hysterical once a month to feed the appetite of the party's nerves. . . Nasty little spit-fires, lie down and sleep!—drink poppy, mandragora, aspirin, anything, and be at rest!' But neither the Fascist party nor Mussolini wanted rest.

A very enjoyable and entirely non-political social activity in which he now took part in London was 'The Club'—Dr Johnson's dining club which still met, gathering together for conversation, not debate, the most distinguished people of the political, literary and scientific worlds. The numbers at each meeting were small so that conversation could be general. After a meeting in November 1924 he wrote: 'It was a dinner of six—two of us were Kipling and Haldane who are hardly on speaking terms as Kipling has views on Haldane of the most ignorant and violent *Morning Post* type. Yet they are both *gentlemen* and Haldane a peculiarly clever and urbane one. So we had general conversation the whole time, about the war much of it, and no flashes or contretemps. Later on I had talk apart with Kipling, who rather likes me; we argued about France and Germany. Two things were more than ever clear to me—what a nice, kind "real gentleman" Kipling is in himself, and how utterly crude his intellect is in dealing with all public questions. And yet he is a man of high genius. How much one has to distinguish in saying a person is "clever" or "stupid". Which is Kipling? Both in a high degree.'

Another great pleasure in these years was the Old Vic and its constant repertory of Shakespeare played by the best young actors of the day. In the autumn of 1923 he saw *Troilus and Cressida, Love's Labour's Lost* and *Two Gentlemen of Verona* in succession, and commented 'I am getting to recognise and admire each of half a dozen actors now I have seen three plays running.' *Troilus* he particularly enjoyed—it acted far better than it read. Ion Swinley's Hamlet he said was the best he had ever seen, 'not excluding Forbes Robertson's.'

Then there were the great productions of Shaw's *St Joan* at the New Theatre and of *The Beggar's Opera* at the Lyric, Hammersmith. *St Joan* he felt sure was 'absolutely the true historical interpretation of Joan and her times in spite of the conscious anachronisms. It'll do people a lot of good. All the nobility and fire, and none of the sentimentality and Popery.' *The Beggar's Opera* was produced by his old Cambridge acquaintance Nigel Playfair, who made it beautiful as well as uproariously funny. Soon the drawing-room at Pen Rose re-echoed to its songs; for hearing Frederick Ranalow as MacHeath in fact first drew Humphry to discover his own voice, which later developed into a fine baritone.

Troilus set George thinking and marvelling again about Shakespeare. 'They acted it in Elizabethan not ancient Greek dress, which was quite right. You felt it was not Troy, not "the great Achilles whom we knew", but W.S. in a peculiarly bitter mood talking to us about the treachery and lechery he had found even in Elizabethan England. The triumph of mean, horrible, brainless creatures like Achilles and Ajax and Diomed over splendid people like Hector and Troilus, and the cruelty of the fact that a man like Troilus can fall wholly in love with a light "black" lady of the Cressida type—these are terrible facts of life that Shakespeare insists upon. He is not of the same experience as the psalmist—he *has* seen the righteous forsaken. Yet, yet—*yet* even at his bitterest he feels life grand and noble for the sake of noble creatures like Hector and Troilus.'

The first Labour Government of 1924 was of some personal interest to us because Charles was in it as Minister of Education —a post he had long hoped for. It was also of great historical significance. George wrote on 21 January: 'As an historian and an Englishman it delights me to see the flexible old machine of the constitution swallowing and assimilating yet another "bloodless revolution"—we have had such dozens of them. The long row of new Privy Councillors (from mine, factory and Harrow-on-the-Hill) all kneeling to take the oath (to the King) had both its humorous and its impressive side as described by Charles . . . A sense of relief predominates,' he went on; 'people think the Cabinet well chosen.' There was of course a good deal of old Liberal blood in it. 'It is good,' said George, 'that Buxtons and Trevelyans should be in the first Labour Cabinet. It carries on the "continuity" of English political life.'

At Berkhamsted he had, as has been seen, accepted the presidency of the local Liberal Association. He kept it until midsummer 1926, when he said he was 'so disgusted with Asquith' that he could keep it no longer. In May of 1926 the General Strike took place and lasted for eight days. Asquith took the severe line about it but Lloyd George pressed for negotiations with the strikers and ridiculed the idea that the trade unions were revolutionary. Here George agreed more with Lloyd George, though his feeling about the strike was that it was high tragedy in which both sides were in the wrong. 'Baldwin's and Thomas's speeches in the House made that clear to me,' he wrote. 'Each made out a clear case against the other side and neither contradicted the other. If it had been left to those two there would have been no lock-out and no strike. But owners, miners, TUC have all behaved evilly and the Cabinet unwisely.' He thought the event so terrible that 'we must each summon up the resources of his or her *character* and *religion*, if either are worth anything. You seem to be doing so.' (I was at Oxford, on the eve of Schools, but managed to do a little work for the Archbishop of Canterbury's compromise proposals.)

On 12 May, the day on which the General Strike was called off, he gave the Romanes Lecture at Oxford, in the Sheldonian Theatre. 'I shall bicycle,' he wrote, 'if there are no trains.' His

206

actual mode of transport has passed out of memory, but he may have secured some conveyance by car. The Lecture was on 'The Two-Party System in English Political History'—a theme in which he was well at home. Its opening sentences made his Oxford audience smile. 'I have long,' he said, 'had many strong and personal reasons for an affectionate familiarity with your streets and Colleges. And yet I confess that in the Sheldonian Theatre I have never felt at home. . . I still gaze up at its always surprising outward shape, or down into its interior depth, mystery, and colour—so strikingly different to the clear mathematical lines and white lights of our Senate House on the banks of Granta—with misgivings such as a tribesman from the far north may have felt as he lifted the curtain on the inner threshold of Jupiter Capitolinus.'

During 1925 and 1926 George, when not working at the *History of England*, was engaged in his first big task of 'saving the countryside'. The Ashridge estate which included all the great beech woods and commons stretching for miles to the north of Berkhamsted, and which had been familiar to us children all our lives, beside Ashridge Park itself and the Ivinghoe downs, came onto the market. A business 'Syndicate' of faceless men from London were after it for commercial purposes; the Trustees had heavy death-duties to pay; it would be necessary to raise a large sum from the public if it was to be preserved from spoliation. In October 1925 there was a great Town Hall meeting at Berkhamsted at which the Secretary of the National Trust, George Trevelyan, and a fine collection of local notables were present and at least eight speeches made with enthusiastic approval of the plan—which was that as much as possible of the estate should be purchased and vested in the National Trust. A public appeal was needed; the Prime Minister (Stanley Baldwin) was approached by my grandfather, Mr Humphry Ward, and together with other Ministers signed a letter to Lord Brownlow (one of the Trustees), asking him to allow the sale to be held up for a month so as to give time for a national appeal to be made. Best of all an 'Anonymous Donor' had come forward with a most generous offer. She was in fact a local lady, Miss Renée Courtauld, one of those quiet and retiring people with a horror of publicity but a great wish to use her wealth for the public good. George meanwhile had been asked to act as the National Trust's adviser on the beauty-value of each strip of land, and was engaged in 'hectic negotiations' in London between the Trust, the Syndicate and the Trustees. 'We were near ship-wrecked,' he wrote afterwards, 'but saved by (I think) skilful steering,' by the chairman of the National Trust, his friend John Bailey, the man of letters and critic. Before the end of the first week of November they had got an agreement from the Trustees for the sale to the National Trust of the most essential parts of the estate. The total cost would be £50,000, of which £36,000 was already available, including the gift of Miss Courtauld. To raise the remainder a public appeal was launched in *The Times* by means of a letter from George in November. The properties passed safely into the hands of the National Trust in June 1926. George was a member of the local Committee for the care of it all and greatly enjoyed the work of preserving, fencing and protecting which this entailed. He also did missionary-work among the numerous visitors who made their way every week-end to Ivinghoe Beacon and other favourite spots, courteously requesting them to leave no litter. He even carried a box of matches with him to burn up unsightly rubbish. The problem of litter-bins was indeed a serious one, as those at first provided proved too small.

On an autumn day in 1926 he went through the woods with the forestry expert of the Trust, and Marks the forester. 'We settled a big policy of thinning and replanting which will be gradually carried out.' They also arranged to sell a lot of the fallen and dead timber 'to supply the fire-wood market in this fuel-less winter'—for the long miners' strike was still going on and the poor were suffering. 'The villagers of Ivinghoe and Aldbury are helping themselves very freely,' he wrote. 'One cannot stop them when one knows they have not got enough to burn in these cold days and nights.' And the historian in him added: 'The conditions for them and many other English villages are nearly as bad as what obtained in most of rural South England before the canals began to make the general distribution of coal possible in the inland parts.'[1]

The years 1927 and 1928 were once more years of change in the spheres both of work and home-life. In June 1927, Professor

---

[1] The villagers of Aldbury had always had fuelling rights on those parts of the estate which were accounted 'common'. There was one occasion early in the century when the landlord had attempted to enclose these 'commons' but the fences were removed by night by a party of local patriots.

Bury died at Cambridge and in July Mr Baldwin, the Prime Minister, not unexpectedly appointed George to succeed him as Regius Professor of Modern History. So the pleasant days at Berkhamsted came to an end, a house was bought in West Road, Cambridge, plain but with a garden which had associations with Tennyson's *Gardener's Daughter*; in October he was re-elected to a Trinity Fellowship and settled down to write first his Inaugural Lecture on 'The Present Position of History', and then a series of eight lectures on Constitutional History, which he delivered in the following spring term. 'Everyone is being very kind to me in Cambridge,' he wrote, 'the *Tories* (as Pickthorn at Corpus) are being particularly nice.' Some resentment still lingered among the dons over some of the changes made by the Royal Commission for which he was largely responsible. 'But,' he said, '*the fact is* they are so many of them *so much better off* as a direct result of that Commission's work that the feeling has no *punch* in it and is gradually subsiding.' He himself became more than ever convinced that the Commission had been right on the larger issues.

Fortunately, before these new labours descended upon him, he was able to take, in the spring of 1927 a long and exciting holiday in Greece. Janet and Humphry went also, and after a sea-voyage from Venice, they came to Athens, and eventually to Delphi. 'In the cool of the evening up there,' he wrote to me, '3,500 feet above the near seashore, we saw Parnassus top (8,000) crowned in snow, and pine clad slopes beneath its snow cap coming down gradually to where we stood.' At their feet grew yellow and white irises, and the ruins enshrined 'some of the greatest memories in the history of human imagination.' They visited Phil and Irene Baker in Euboea, and from there he wrote: 'At present I am still in the feeling that Greece at this time of year is the most beautiful country in the world, but I know well that in another ten days I shall be panting for England in May like the hart for the water-brooks.'

The most adventurous part of the expedition was their invasion of the Peloponnese, 'wading deeper and deeper through the Peloponnese, by "bummelzug" trains, motors, horse carriages, mules and feet, far from letters or news of the world.' 'The remoteness and inaccessibility of it all is extraordinary and very fascinating. It is like travelling centuries ago, both as regards the simple peasant life of the people, quite innocent of anything modern, and the absence of roads where you would expect them. Our arrival in this great valley of old Messenia from the corresponding great valley of old Sparta . . . could only be effected by the roughest of mule tracks under and along the top of steep precipices over the famous Lampada pass. M. and H. half rode mules and half walked and I walked all the way as of course did the two mule-teers who led their mules and drove the mule carrying all our baggage.' There were ruins of all ages around them, 'and old Frankish castles frown finely from the precipices out of which they seem to grow.' At the end he wrote: 'I feel much fresher and better than perhaps I have done for some time. Our days are so full of beauty and interest and we are out of doors so long that I have hardly read anything at all for ten days—nothing but one Shakespeare play to be exact.'

He gave his Inaugural on 26 October to an audience of over 1,000 people. There was some irony in the occasion, for it was his predecessor Professor Bury's Inaugural of 1902, in which he had called history 'a science, no more and no less', that had in-spired George to proclaim that Clio was a Muse as well as a scientist.[2] Now he looked back with thankfulness to the Cam-bridge of his youth, and the great historians, Seeley, Acton, Maitland, Cunningham and Bury himself, from whom he had learnt the nature of his studies, their difficulty and complexity, and the rich stores of knowledge and enjoyment which they brought to the student. Acton, with his immense weight of learn-ing in foreign fields, his passion for toleration and truth, his moral and philosophic power, was the greatest name. But F. W. Mait-land had unlocked the problems and treasures of English con-stitutional history, had shown us also our great ignorance of 'the real thoughts and motives of men in those far-off days—our English ancestors who walked the lanes we tread'. This sense of the mystery of the past had always been dear to George. 'To peer into that magic mirror,' he now said, 'and see fresh figures there every day is a burning desire that consumes and satisfies the historian all his life, that carries him each morning, eager as a lover, to the library and the muniment room. It haunts him like a passion of almost terrible potency, because it is poetic. The dead were and are not. Their place knows them no more and is ours today. Yet they were once as real as we and we shall tomorrow be

[2] See above p. 80.

shadows like them. In men's first astonishment over that un-changing mystery lie the origins of poetry, philosophy and religion.' The study and teaching of History which now was to such a large extent centred in the Universities with their great libraries and opportunities for research, was indeed itself a form of imaginative life, but it could not be satisfied save by facts. 'It is the fact about the past that is poetic; just because it really happened it gathers round it all the inscrutable mystery of life and death and time.' 'Therefore,' said he, 'let the science and research of the historian find the fact, and let his imagination and art make clear its significance.'

The Professorship, and the work which it brought, meant for George Trevelyan a closer acquaintance with his fellow-historians than would have been possible had he remained at Berkhamsted. Chief among these was John Clapham of King's, who was just now writing his great *Economic History of Modern Britain.* George had known him for many years, but now they formed a close personal friendship, for John Clapham's rugged north-country nature enclosed a knowledge and love of the Bible and of poetry which endeared him to George, while he was also a passionate mountaineer, loving, as George did, 'the harsh, delight-ful contact with nature at her roughest and grandest.' Clapham, said George afterwards, 'put Economic History in its true place in human history, and prevented it from becoming an arid and theoretical study apart.' It was, he believed, 'probably the greatest economic history ever written', based as it was 'on the ultimate criterion of statistical fact', but 'connected with the thought and literature of each successive period'. Clapham's *Economic History* and George Trevelyan's *England under Queen Anne,* each in three volumes, were written and published almost simul-taneously in the years following George's appointment to the Professorship. It was a great historical companionship.

As Professor he took immense trouble about his history students. Sometimes he had them to the house for coachings and discussions; sometimes he took them for walks. And once he made a man whose Tripos papers for his special subject had been illegible, come to the house and read the papers to him, although the examination in this form took up the whole morning.

He was now hard at work preparing for his next book, which

was to be the history of the reign of Queen Anne. To continue where Macaulay had been obliged, by death, to stop, was a challenge he gladly took up and carried through in six years—four years less than the ten he had set himself in 1926. He began collecting books as soon as the *History of England* was published, and was delighted at being able to purchase, for £2 10s., the five great folio volumes of Rapin's *History of England,* 'with the great maps of all the fortresses besieged and actions fought in Anne's reign'. He had one disappointment about manuscript material. He could not use the papers at Blenheim, because Winston Churchill was at that time engaged on the life of Marlborough. It was not a fatal prohibition because Archdeacon Coxe had transcribed and printed most of them nearly two hundred years before—but it was a disappointment, as a sentence in the Preface to his first volume discreetly shows. But he bore no grudge about it, and twenty years later he was able to do Churchill a good turn. He had lent Churchill an autograph letter of the year 1680 which he had in his possession, from John Churchill, afterwards Duke of Marlborough, to Prince William of Orange, afterwards William III, to be reproduced as an illustration in the first volume of Churchill's book. In 1946 he gave the letter to Churchill, who accepted it with delight and hung it among his most precious trophies of the great Duke.

The East Anglian countryside into which we had now migrated, though it lacked the great beech-woods of Ashridge and Aldbury, had plenty of interest and was made very accessible because George had now invested in a second-hand car and a chauffeur to drive it. My father was pleased that his first chauffeur, Arthur Hallworth, was studying for the Baptist ministry. It was in a way a link with Bunyan. Every now and then George would take a 'long day off' and visit some distant place of beauty and old time. Once he went to Tattershall, which was 'utterly unlike any other place I know. A great noble's Palace of 1440 in the form of an immense red brick keep, ostensibly for war but really for grandeur and delight. Its beauty is amazing.' And on the same day he walked for two hours 'in a lovely valley bottom in South Lincs which used to belong to Hereward the Wake', and saw there Edenham church, 'of amazing beauty and interest, where I was lucky enough to find the parson, a Sidney Sussex man, with whom I made great friends, who showed me all the treasures. What wondrous things there are stowed away in this island! He and the sexton had spent six months cleaning the oak roof and its angels with their own four hands.'

Meanwhile he and my mother also explored the country on their bicycles, especially the Fleam Dyke—an ancient earthwork to the south of Cambridge, where she found eleven nests (exclusive of blackbirds and thrushes) in forty minutes one day in May 1928—or the Mare Way, to the west, where rare flowers grew. Best of all, for my mother, was the discovery that there were nightingales in and around Cambridge; sometimes one could be heard (in those happy days) from the windows of our house. This was a great consolation to her, as she had feared she was leaving them behind when we moved to what she called 'the mud-flats'.

Visits to scenes connected with the histories he was writing had always been one of George's chief pleasures. In the spring of 1928 he went to Spain—to see Madrid, Cadiz, Vigo Bay and above all Gibraltar, which had been besieged and captured by British sailors in 1704. In Gibraltar he stayed with Hubert Young, the Governor, worked in the Library there and explored the Rock from every coign of vantage. 'I have found out finely,' he wrote, 'about my siege and defence of 1704–5', partly in the Library in the town, partly in the little market-town of San Rocque inland whither the municipal and parish archives had been moved after the end of the siege. He enjoyed this visit greatly—'the little town of the hills fresh and white and grass-grown and lovely with bow windows, a feature of South Spanish architecture.' They were received in state by the Alcalde and Mayor in the Municipal Room, and then in the parish church they were shown the parish register for Gibraltar for 1702–4, 'with hurried notes by the parish priest Don Romero to say the English had taken the town and were sacking the famous shrine overlooking the straits, Our Lady of Europe, where many women of the town had taken refuge, and had beheaded Our Lady's Image and Holy Child and had thrown them out on to the stones outside.' The sailors however were not blood-thirsty; the only casualties in this sacking of the shrine were their own through the explosion of a magazine. 'It was curious,' wrote George, 'to see and copy down the poor priest's last notes that he made in his register before the final exile of his flock and records to San Rocque in the hills—actually written while the bombs were flying and the houses crashing and the women shrieking—and finished when the town had surrendered and our jolly sailor-boys were rushing about making themselves at home on the Rock for the first time in history.' The 'Englishness' of Gibraltar impressed and amused him, as it does all who visit it. There was even a Gibraltar fox-hunt, 'in Spain of course, as the Rock itself is less huntable than Bow Fell.' At the great naval and military ball he went to, 'half the garrison were in red tail-coats of the Hunt—the rest in the red Eton jacket of the army and the fleet officers in naval dark blue and gold. It was a gallant show.'

After a visit to Cadiz, he went north by a night train to Madrid. Rudyard Kipling occupied the next compartment; George shared his sleeper with Lord Fitzwilliam of Whig and Irish descent. 'We three,' wrote George, 'had a great yarn and crack before turning in.' In the morning they woke in the midst of the great plain, 'flat, arid, treeless, hedgeless, in large parts houseless, but all of it cultivated by peasants living in great villages far apart.' Far away could be discerned the snow peaks of the Guadarrama range. There in the middle of the flatness stood Madrid, 'uninteresting, fairly prosperous cosmopolitanism'—the creation of the Bourbon kings. But the Prado picture gallery was thrilling. 'Here only can you see Goya, *very great,* and Velasquez, *infinitely greater.* The Velasquez room of thirty mere masterpieces is perhaps the greatest room in Europe.'

The character of the greatest man in that prolonged and complicated drama—the War of the Spanish succession which filled so much of the new volumes—John Churchill, Duke of Marlborough, had long attracted and fascinated George Trevelyan, so that he was eager and ready to become the historian of his wars. Writing to me when I was in Holland in 1927, enjoying the sights of The Hague, he said: 'I have just been reading how in 1701 when William III sent Marlborough over to the Hague to make the Grand Alliance (which he did most successfully) the Dutch put Marlborough up in the Mauritz House,[3] and there he received, charmed and persuaded the various 'Hoogende Moogende' ('High and Mightys') of Northern and Central Europe ... I shall always think of 1701, of the departing William and the incoming Marlborough, when I see or think of the Mauritz House again. I am getting very fond of Marlborough for all his faults. He was *humane,* he was wise, he was not passion's slave,

[3] Now the exquisite picture-gallery of The Hague.

or party's, or fanaticism's, and he served his country and his age with all his incomparable armoury of genius and temper till he had completed William's work and ushered in the age of toleration and reason—he himself being the most tolerant and reasonable of men.'

As he drew near the end of his story, it became necessary to go to Paris to search in the archives of the French Foreign Office for documents about the Peace of Utrecht and the secret negotiations carried on between Louis XIV's government and the English Tories, Bolingbroke and Oxford, who were now in power and bent on peace—and bent also on being reconciled with James III, the 'Old Pretender' when Queen Anne should die. The English ministers' messages on that subject which he unearthed were 'pretty hot stuff', which could have cost them their heads if the Whigs had got hold of them, when they returned to power in 1714 and were faced with a Jacobite rising in Scotland. This was the kind of research and discovery which George loved, especially as it did not, after all, end in executions, except of some of the Jacobite rebels. While in Paris, he saw Molière's *Misanthrope* wonderfully done—'we have no such performance of anything in England for it needs tradition as well as natural ability.'

In August 1928 old Sir George Trevelyan died at Wallington, having just passed his ninetieth birthday. In the previous January Caroline, his wife, had also died. In death they were not long divided: to live without each other was, as their son said in his memoir of his father, 'an impossible experiment'. By his mother's will George inherited a considerable part of the old Philips fortune—the house and estate of Welcombe being left to Robert—and by his father's, besides a handsome legacy, the control of Sir George's personal papers which included Macaulay's diaries and the Fox papers given to Sir George by Lady Agatha Russell.[4] There were also a number of books, pictures, some pieces of furniture and ornaments which were just now extremely useful and acceptable in the furnishing of Hallington. For in the previous year Dr Cacciola had died and George had become the owner of the Hallington estate.

George's new wealth enabled him to launch out into further activities for the preservation of historic and beautiful places in

---

[4] These are now in the Library of Trinity College, Cambridge.

the threatened landscape of England.[5] To his great pleasure, the first of these was his purchase of Housesteads farm, beside which lay the Roman camp of Borcovicum on the Roman Wall a few miles south-west of Hallington. The Clayton estate, whose owner had lived at Chesters, another great camp beside the North Tyne at Chollerford, was breaking up and the actual camp of Borcovicum was given by the owner to the National Trust in 1929. George then bought the farm and land adjoining it so that the camp should be protected from any form of unsightly building development. A little later he built a small museum within the walls of the camp to house the various altars, statues and relics of the Roman days which were found at the site. Thenceforward visits to Housesteads became a regular pilgrimage for all his friends who stayed at Hallington, with himself as commentator and guide.

Hallington Hall, where henceforward he spent his Christmas, Easter and summer vacations, was a small eighteenth-century country house which had been enlarged by Mrs Spencer Trevelyan, the mother of Florence Cacciola. The house had no particular beauty, but its grounds were delightful. Through the deep 'dene' or glen in front of the house flowed a stream which had been dammed to form a pond; it was the haunt of dippers and kingfishers; tall trees, beech and oak, overshadowed it, and George took pleasure in planting the Osmunda Regalis fern on its banks. On summer mornings for many years to come he bathed there before breakfast. It was a more commodious bath than the stony pool in the ghyll at Robin Ghyll! Near the house to the west were the Hallington Reservoirs, part of the water-supply system for Newcastle; here there was much bird-life, especially in winter. The estate included a farm, and George soon added another; and over these grassy uplands (for it was all pasture), with their small streams draining to the North Tyne, and views to west and south stretching as far as Cross Fell, and northwards to the Great Cheviot, George Trevelyan loved to walk, in winter

[5] In 1931 George gave the Rickman Godlee Lecture at London University, calling it 'The Call and Claims of Natural Beauty.' In it he traced the changing relation between the natural world and the imagination of man—from distrust of the wild and the untamed to the modern passion for mountains, rocks and moors which he said, is 'one of the sacraments prepared for man or discovered by man.' The lecture is one of the most poetic of his writings.

216

and summer, alone or with some chosen friend, year after year until he could walk no more.

He did what he could to clothe the rather bare landscape of his little estate by making plantations of hardwood trees in suitable places; there was a little shooting, and he employed a woodman to look after the trees and such game as there was. Close to the house there was a fine old walled garden with fruit trees and a greenhouse, where grew a vine and peaches. In his later years he used to walk, looking up at the tall beech trees which over-shadowed one corner of the garden, lovingly murmuring snatches of poetry. My mother, with the advice of Miss Marjorie Taylor of Chipchase Castle on the North Tyne, stocked the flower-beds near the house and turned a rather dull conservatory into a pleasant 'sun-room', where people could sit, play at ping-pong, have tea and generally 'fleet the time carelessly'.

As he was not in residence at Hallington all the year round he did not develop close relations with many of its neighbouring squires. But Wallington was only eight miles distant and between it and Hallington there was much happy coming and going, for Charles had now come into his long-awaited inheritance, and was busy planting trees, repairing cottages, entertaining con-stituents and political colleagues and generally behaving as a good landlord who was also a socialist should, until in 1936 he handed over the entire estate to the National Trust, though re-maining himself life-tenant and manager until his death in 1958. In all the arrangements for the transfer of the estate George was consulted and was able, in his usual way of reconciliation, to calm the fears and soothe the disappointments of such members of the family as did not wholly approve of Charles's doings.

Although now a landowner in his own Northumberland, the Lakes still held his heart and seemed to demand his protection. Shortly after buying Housesteads he had made some very im-portant purchases at the head of Langdale—nothing less than the farms of Stool End, Wall End and High Dungeon Ghyll. He was determined to prevent any dangerous developments in that beloved valley. All these he gave directly to the National Trust, and three years later, in 1932, he bought Mill Beck, the farm at the foot of the great waterfall that issues from Stickle Tarn. This he kept for the present, placing it under covenant with the Trust so that its lands, which extended onto the other side of the Lang-dale Beck, could not be built on, and finally he bought Harry

H   217

Place, the farm next door to Robin Ghyll, very vulnerable because its fields extended almost into the village of Chapel Stile. Robin Ghyll itself he placed under covenants. These Langdale gifts may be said to have been completed after his death, when in 1965 with money bequeathed by him to her, and with a gift from Trinity College, the last remaining farm in Upper Langdale, Side House, opposite High Dungeon Ghyll, was bought by the author of this memoir and handed to the Trust. A gathering of old friends in the farm-yard witnessed that ceremony, on a day when, only just after it was completed, a great storm crashed down from the Crinkle Crags above, as though the mountains too were bearing witness to the covenant.

At the New Year in 1933 he went roaming on foot and by car through the Lake District, visiting his farms. From the New Dungeon Ghyll hotel he went 'after tea up the valley to Stool End, the moon throwing my shadow on those well-known fields, and the Crinkles clear against the sky.' He made friends with his own farmer Mounsey at Millbeck. 'I talk to him while he milks by lantern light, and turns his bright melancholy Ancient Briton's eyes at me. If Martindale [the old farmer at Stool End] was the Norseman, he is the aboriginal.'

The next episode in the Lake District campaign was more complicated. It involved prolonged negotiations with the Forestry Commission, which was buying land in and around the Lake District and planting it with conifers. George was now chairman of the Estates Committee of the National Trust, and in that capacity he opened private negotiations with Sir Roy Robinson, the chairman of the Forestry Commission, at the beginning of 1935, in the hope of getting a sort of treaty made by which the Forestry Commission would refrain from planting within the 'central' Lake District—the great holiday and sheep-farming area which included Borrowdale, the Langdales, Rydal, Grasmere and Ullswater. By a very unwise and thoughtless decision, the Government had instructed the Forestry Commission to proceed with afforestation 'in and within fifteen miles' of the areas on the coast of Cumberland where unemployment among miners was now very bad, regardless of the fact that only a fraction of the unemployed could be helped in this way. The effect of this policy was to place the whole of the Lake District within the Commission's field of action. 'Never,' wrote George later in a letter to *The Times* after a satisfactory agreement had been

218

reached, 'was the Lake District in such danger.' Fortunately the Forestry Commission agreed to the appointment of a Joint Informal Committee with the Council for the Preservation of Rural England (C.P.R.E.). After more than a year of negotiation it produced a report which, while not satisfying entirely either the C.P.R.E. representative or many Lake District preservationists, nevertheless embodied some very substantial concessions by the Commission, chief of which was an undertaking not to acquire land for afforestation 'within a central Lake District Area of approximately 300 square miles' and to co-operate with the C.P.R.E. in giving 'special consideration' to areas on the frontiers of this central district, such as the fields round Esthwaite and the valley bottoms of Duddon and Esk. George Trevelyan had been co-opted onto the Joint Committee 'for Lake District purposes only', and he worked on it as a practical, not a fanatical idealist, realising the great importance and difficulty of winning concessions from the Forestry Commission, backed up as it was by Government and Government money. He believed that the C.P.R.E. could not, under the circumstances, have obtained more concessions, and that further co-operation between it and the Forestry Commission would in fact result in further valuable agreements about land which already belonged to the Commission on the southern frontiers of the '300 square miles'.

Meanwhile he had been making on his own account a very important purchase on the north-western borders of the Lake District. In 1935 he bought Gatesgarth farm and its great sheep-runs at the head of Buttermere, and put it under covenant with the National Trust, as part of a scheme negotiated with the other landlords in the Buttermere valley. It was a splendid mountain world—'3,000 acres of sheep farm including the top of Haystacks, Brandreth, Fleetwith, Honister and the ridge of Dale Head and Robinson, with the valley head below including two sides of Buttermere Lake.' He was still young enough at fifty-nine to spend two days 'scrambling about in its inmost recesses. There is a wonderful high lonely tarn called Bleaberry Tarn in the arms of the crags of High Style, where I bathed. I never saw it before. It's a great land.' Mr Richardson of Gatesgarth with his three sons managed the farm with its thousand head of sheep—it was one of the most famous sheep-farms in the Lake District.

At the same time the road from Borrowdale to Buttermere over the Honister Pass had been widened to take motor-coaches, and many conservationists resented this. 'I am in hot water,' wrote George, 'with extremists both about that and about coming to terms with the Forestry Commission. Personally I think Buttermere was made for man and not man for Buttermere, and as we can now preserve Buttermere valley intact, I am rather glad than not that many folk should come there.'

This work for preservation in the Lake District was not interrupted by the war. On the contrary, in 1943 he was appointed by the Forestry Commission—who had learnt to trust him—to be chairman of a small committee to advise and report on the use of the important area of fell, called Hardknott Forest, belonging to the Commissioners, between the valley-heads of Esk and Duddon. With him on the committee was his cousin Morgan Philips Price, who was MP for the Forest of Dean, and his old friend James Cropper of Burneside, a Westmorland landowner and business man. By this time the Forestry Commission had, thanks largely to George Trevelyan's persistent representations, advanced greatly in its attitude to public amenity and access to its land; and also had agreed to the creation of a National Forest Park in the Lake District, which would include all this area of Commission land, and would give access to the public. The committee had mainly to report on such matters as the character and extent of planting on the open fell country, especially at the head of Duddon, particularly the avoidance of 'hard outline edges' to the plantations (always a matter of special concern to George); access by foot through planted areas; the careful siting of camps or hostels, and the preservation of the Roman Road and the various sets of ancient stepping stones in the area. The main recommendation throughout their report was—constant co-operation between the Forestry Commission, the C.P.R.E., the National Trust and, where necessary, the Ministry of Works. All this took place at the same time that John Dower, who had married George's niece Pauline Trevelyan, was producing his historic report on National Parks—a work undertaken when he was already a sick man and which in fact a few years later cost him his life. 'Poor England!' exclaimed George, when in 1947 John Dower died.

George desired not only the preservation of the English countryside, but the lessening of the awful barrier between the urban and rural communities so as to reveal to the 'townees' their national heritage threatened by the urban way of life. From the early 'thirties he was President of the Youth Hostels Association and loved to go about opening new hostels in various parts of the country. It was always his faith that the countryside was made for man, if only man would learn to love and respect it.

While George was 'saving the Lake District', Janet was engaged from 1929 onwards on the even more difficult task of saving nine acres of open land in Bloomsbury from being built over, and turning it into a permanent play-ground for London's children. This was the old site of Captain Coram's Foundling Hospital—now called, after him, 'Coram's Fields'. The story of the long and complicated negotiations about this project which she undertook with Lord Rothermere, the London County Council, the Board of Education, and the Governors of the Foundling Hospital; the launching of a great public appeal for £425,000 (in the midst of the 'slump' of the early 1930s) by the Appeal Committee of which Janet was the Honorary Secretary with Lord Crewe as the chairman; the support of Queen Mary in visiting the site before the Appeal was finished and the grounds only kept open by Lord Rothermere's 'option'; the staunchness of the Committee in refusing to accept defeat in face of much discouragement; and the final victory and handing-over to the LCC in 1936 of this wonderful oasis—all make a moving tale which Janet many years afterwards was able to tell in her own words.[6] She was victorious, though the long seven-years' strain told on her health. 'The Foundling' (as we called this campaign) was, besides, an additional burden to the heavy one she was already carrying, for since Mrs Ward's death in 1920 Janet had been Chairman of the London Evening Play Centres Committee—a work she really loved and did not relinquish until 1941 when the Centres were finally taken over by the LCC. She often went forth visiting Centres (sometimes in remote and rather un-get-atable parts of London like the Isle of Dogs), by taxi or even on her bicycle, finding real refreshment in the happiness and gaiety of the children and the devoted work of the Superintendents. Underneath all her work for London children lay the inspiration of Theo's memory. When the 'Foundling' was finally saved, Lord Rothermere caused a small pavilion to be built in that part of the grounds which he had purchased as a memorial to his two sons killed in the war. Round the interior of the dome George and Janet put

[6] See below p. 239.

an inscription commemorating the little boy who had been their playmate for nearly five years of unbroken joy.

George and Janet were so close to each other at the deepest levels that they could work in widely different fields without losing touch, and without making unfair demands on each other. When they were apart they wrote to each other every day. However absorbed she was in her London activities, Janet never grumbled at having to break off to furnish Hallington or, later, the Lodge, look after visitors and evacuees, or welcome old friends. Though she undoubtedly loved London and could never adapt herself to social work of any kind in Cambridge, she never demanded a domestic foot-hold in the metropolis. And though she did not really love Northumberland—the Southern Lake District was the place of her heart—she realised how much Hallington and its surroundings meant to George.

England under Queen Anne had been finished and published between 1931 and 1934 in three volumes—a labour of love which had taken him not only to France and Spain but to the great houses of some of the English nobility, to Althorp and Chevening, where Earls Spencer and Stanhope had opened their family papers to him, and to the Duke of Buccleuch's house, Boughton near Kettering. Of the visit to Althorp he wrote: 'There are about forty Sir Joshua's and Gainsboroughs of the family and friends, all in one long drawing-room, the most splendid room I have seen since I saw the thirty Velasquez in one room in the Prado at Madrid. There is also another still bigger room with fifty Sir Peter Lelys and Knellers, crowned at one end by a most glorious Van Dyke. One can study the family physiognomy of the Spencers and the Churchills through four centuries in the portraits.' He was delighted to find that the young Lord Althorp (aged eight) was 'the image of the Reform Bill Lord Althorp at the same age as depicted by Sir Joshua.'

Besides *Queen Anne*, George wrote in 1931 a short personal memoir of his father, who was a type that flourished most in the Victorian age—'the literary man who was also a politician, the politician and literary man who was also an historian.' *Sir George Otto Trevelyan. A Memoir* tells, with George's characteristic vigour and charm, the story of a brilliant and highly individual personality whom he loved and understood.

In September 1933 Lord Grey of Fallodon died after years of blindness and failing health. Since becoming the owner of Hall-

222

ington, George had seen much of him, their houses being only thirty miles apart, and so it was fitting that he should be asked to be his biographer. 'It is the most tragic story I have ever undertaken to write,' he said, 'for we are still involved in his failure to appease the world; but it is a very noble tragedy—his life I mean —and tragedy suits me just now.' Grey had united in himself two of George's most cherished loves—poetry (especially Wordsworth) and the natural world. He was besides a Northumbrian and a kinsman of the Greys of Howick, at whose request George had, twenty years before, written the life of Lord Grey of the Reform Bill.

During these years, the early thirties, both Humphry and I got married. I married in 1930 John Moorman, the son of Frederic Moorman, editor of Herrick and poet of the Yorkshire Dales. At that time John was curate of a Leeds parish, and eventually in 1959 (to George's great delight!) he became Bishop of Ripon. As his son-in-law became the leading historian of the Franciscans in the Middle Ages, he and George had a great deal in common. And Humphry married in 1936 Molly Bennett, whose parents lived at New Haven, Connecticut—an American connection of the kind that gave George the keenest pleasure. Another pleasing event, in 1932, was his being made a member of the Order of Merit, as his father had been before him.

The middle thirties saw some public events which alternately delighted and distressed the British people. In the first of them George Trevelyan played an important though unobtrusive part. In May 1935 King George V and Queen Mary celebrated the Silver Jubilee of their reign. Among the events was the reception of the King by his Houses of Parliament at a ceremony in Westminster Hall. There had never been such a ceremony before; it was decided to keep it simple and dignified without pomp, so, except for the Speaker and the Lord Chancellor, who made the loyal addresses, everyone wore morning dress. The King, standing on the steps leading to St Stephen's chapel, replied in a speech recalling the historic relationship of Crown and Parliament. I was walking along the beflagged Mall, listening to the speech relayed by loud-speakers, when I was suddenly startled by hearing His Majesty quote two lines of verse: —

> While thought to wisdom wins the gay,
> While strength upholds the free.

I recognised them as lines from one of Edward Bowen's Harrow

223

songs, 'When Raleigh rose', which we had often sung at home in old days; not many other listeners, probably, would have known them. A few days later George told me, in confidence, that he had written the King's speech.

Only seven months afterwards the King died and in a few more the nation was plunged into the uncertainties and dangers attendant on the new monarch's desire to marry 'Mrs Simpson'. Immediately after the abdication and the King's departure, George wrote to me: 'Getting G. (VI) instead of the nervous and unreliable E. is a great gain in more ways than the marital. My Cabinet Minister friends, two of them, tell me they had doubted whether he (Edward) would take the Kingship on at all, he disliked it so. If he had not disliked the office he would not have given it up for Mrs S.'

One of his 'Cabinet Minister friends' at this time was the Prime Minister, Stanley Baldwin, who was also Chancellor of Cambridge University and a lover of the things George most loved—poetry and the English countryside. On 27 April 1937 Baldwin unveiled a memorial plaque to Lord Grey of Fallodon 'out in the Horse Guards under the Foreign Office wall, beneath sun and blue sky' and in the presence of 'a small but very noble company' which included the Archbishop of Canterbury (Lang), Neville Chamberlain and 'all Grey's surviving friends and colleagues.' 'I am particularly glad,' added George 'that it is out of doors.' Baldwin, he said, 'was *perfect* in the speech he made . . I never heard a more artistic performance, and if he had not been in love with his subject he would never have found time to compose it (out of my book of course, but transmuted into a new form) in these heavily loaded last days of his burden'.

On 12 May 1937 King George VI and Queen Elizabeth were crowned in Westminster Abbey. George received an invitation, and found himself high up above the Poets' Corner, in 'a strange eyrie among the gothic arches', looking down on the 'ermine and bald heads of the massed Peers below. Next to him was his fellow O.M. and old friend Ralph Vaughan-Williams and together they watched 'the greatest "occasion" in the world'. 'The scale of beauty,' he wrote, 'was so immense and it was all history. The monuments had all disappeared under the scaffolding and tapestry. It was Henry III's church again for the nonce. No ceremony on earth could equal it for splendour, history, religion and Englishry, all blent into a unique thing . . . The King in golden robes and a large crown holding the two sceptres was like a mediaeval king. The Queen was the most moving thing in it all, and Queen Mary next—and the King the finest.'

So England was able to enter into the new reign in peace, while the war-clouds darkened and the dreadful conviction was gradually borne in on the nation that we should probably have to fight Germany for the second time as more and more of Central Europe succumbed to Hitler's violence and greed. In March 1938, after Hitler annexed Austria, it became clear to George and his friends that the end of all hope for a free Europe was now at hand. Geoffrey Young came up to Trinity 'Commem.' in March, having just returned from Germany where he had witnessed the failure of 'the last decent element' there 'to warn and combine with us'. General conversation on public affairs was impossible, but 'on the second evening,' Geoffrey wrote, 'George and I frankly sat down and faced it, talking it all out in its grim possibilities. Next morning, before I left, he walked round the table and said in his most thoughtful tones: "I must discipline myself again . . . I have been living too much for pleasure. . . You have always had yourself in hand since you lost your leg. But not so myself . . . We must look now for little happiness in the future . . . and I must recover discipline." Strange,' commented Geoffrey, 'in his forceful, puritanical temperament, the few relaxations he had allowed himself in later years had *helped* his humanity . . . smoking an occasional cigarette or drinking a glass of wine or taking a shooting . . . They had given him a certain serenity and almost suavity which his youth had lacked and had fitted well with his immense personal position in the country. But I record what he said—as characteristic.'

A year later, at the end of March 1939, George and Janet went for a fortnight to Italy—to look once more on Rome and say farewell to the British Institute of Florence. It was an anxious visit, for Mussolini had committed himself to Hitler and meant 'to march the people into war whether they liked it or not when Hitler gives the signal.' Coming back through Switzerland they found the Swiss expecting soon to be attacked, 'the spirit of William Tell rising in them'. 'It is very difficult,' George wrote to Charles, 'to adjust one's mind and spirit to living (personally) amid all one most cares for, all a human being could ask for, of

I

what is best in a fine and still flourishing civilization (as civiliza-
tions go) and to think it more likely than not that it will shortly be
knocked to smithereens and that one will live to see it.'

They stayed with their old friend Filippo de' Filippi in his
villa at Settignano in the hills above Florence where George learnt
to know him more intimately. Long before, de' Filippi had had a
few perfect years of happiness with his American wife, who was
a poet, and who gave him the 'detachment and realism of outlook
on a world he sees through'. 'He is so *anti-septic*,' said George,
'but not bitter or rodent, because there is love behind.' 'Nothing,'
said de' Filippi, 'can ever destroy the friendship between us',
whatever tragedy the politicians might insist upon.

George was to a certain extent reassured by 'the sight and
sense of Italy's vast ancient peasant life, so much more solid and
natural than anything in England.' But terrible preparation for
war was in progress. Mussolini was in a dangerous mood; having
won his Abyssinian campaign he was now aiming at turning us
out of the Mediterranean with the aid of Franco's Spain. The
Italian people were still friendly but the press, on Mussolini's
orders, was violently hostile to England.

Before the situation became entirely hopeless, George had
begun, in the autumn of 1937, to write another book. This was a
source of blessing to him throughout the next agonising year of
1938. It was a volume written for the Home University Library
series of which his friends Gilbert Murray, H. A. L. Fisher and
Julian Huxley were now the editors. He called it *The English
Revolution, 1688–9*, and started it in August 1937. 'Reading it
all up in the original authorities again has been delighful. It is
one of the most amazing stories in the world and never grows old
to me.' By September 1938 it was ready for publication, but that
September was the month of gloom and terror in England, when
slit-trenches were hastily dug in parks and gardens and gas-masks
distributed to children. For Hitler was threatening Czecho-Slo-
vakia in insolent terms about her frontiers and war seemed un-
avoidable. Neville Chamberlain's missions, first to Berchtesgaden
and finally to Munich at the end of the month, won not (as he vainly
hoped) safety, but a breathing-space, which lasted for a year. Some-
time during that month of September 1938, George sent an advance copy of his new book to George Kitson Clark, the History
tutor at Trinity, with this inscription: 'G. Kitson Clark from G.
M. Trevelyan—A book that may or may not come out on Oct. 6,

1938. At present this is the only copy extant except one in possession of the author, so its rarity value will be considerable in case
unfortunate public events prevent publication on Oct. 6!' The
little book, which achieved its publication safely, thanks to Mr
Chamberlain, besides giving a clear and vivid narrative of the
complicated events, pressed home to the readers their immense
importance in laying the foundations of modern England, tolerant
in religion, moderate in political partisanship, powerful not
through huge standing armies but through commercial and mari-
time enterprise. The Revolution, he said, ushered in 'the great
religious and party truce' which not only made us the most prosperous and influential nation in the world, but also the most
peaceful and on the whole the most humane in our domestic life.

When war eventually came, George Trevelyan was sixty-three
years old, still physically vigorous and almost as swift a walker
over moors and fields as in earlier years. As Cambridge gradually
emptied of young men, his trade as a professor of history there
diminished somewhat. He took an assistant post in the Regional
Commissioner's office, though as invasion never in fact material-
ised it never demanded much of his time. What was to become of
Hallington? Evacuee children from Newcastle were in occupation
of Wallington, although Charles and Molly continued to live
there in reduced quarters, with visits from their family in the
school holidays. Nothing happened at Hallington until the summer of 1940, when the RAF took the house, leaving the garden
and dene still in George's hands; the furniture was stored in some
empty rooms at the farm; the garden was dug up for vegetables.
The RAF officers were considerate and careful and grateful for
permission to 'sport over the manor' occasionally. George was
really glad to have them there, for, as he wrote, 'I feel rather that
I am doing nothing real for the country in this war, as I did in
the last, so I should like my house to do it for me.' When he
finally went south on an October morning he wrote: 'Getting up
at 5.30 I saw a wondrous autumn dawn over hoar fields and woods
as my farewell to Hallington that I shall never forget.' He felt that
it might be farewell for ever.

With Charles he was in perfect agreement about the war—
there was no painful difference of principle as there had been in
1914, though George was amused to perceive Charles's unshake-
able conviction that *only* 'the Tories' were to blame for the mess
we were in. They shot together at Wallington and Hallington

during the Christmas holidays of 1940, while Charles's eldest son and younger daughters got engaged, Humphry fought blitz-fires in London, and John and I, with Janet who happened to be staying with us, safely survived the great air-raids on Manchester of 22 and 23 December.

In a post-script to a letter to Charles written in March 1939, he said: 'You and I have never been good at discussing politics. But I should like you to know, once and for all, that, much as I disagree on some things, I think you have been at least as right as I have on the policies of the last forty years that have ended in this pass.'

As for his thoughts and feelings about the war, though having no doubts that 'the other side is the side of the Devil', he always believed that 'we and France and America in different ways have had our share in *raising* the Devil from 1919 onwards.' For the ordinary person, 'character is what we have each to live on now—it is rather like living on one's capital—which also we shall presently be doing.' He took refuge in literature and history with greater zest than ever, for 'the *past* at least cannot be destroyed and is as real as present and future.' To him indeed it was much more real, for 'the present nightmare *seems* to have so little to do with the world in which I was brought up, though actually it is its natural child.' Ever since the fall of France, he said, his dreams had been of evil, and he now expected nothing else when he lay down to sleep. 'By day,' he added, 'I maintain a sober interest in all things and a decently cheerful demeanour as we are all most strongly bound to do.'

By far the most tragic event, for him and Janet and for many of their friends, in this first year of the war, was Italy's entry into it, on 10 June 1940, at the orders of Hitler. But it had been for some time a foregone conclusion. The folly of British 'sanctions' policy against Italy at the time of the Ethiopian war had made the Italian people despise us, had angered Mussolini, and had been totally ineffective in saving Ethiopia. In an article in the *Spectator* of 14 June 1940, called 'Italy, June 10th', George plainly declared that the 'old diplomacy' had never devised a method of proceeding at once so weak and so provocative. Mussolini rode roughshod over it and appealed to the tradition of Imperial Rome. But he made one great and ultimately fatal miscalculation. The Imperial Rome of the New Europe was not Rome, but Berlin.

On 19 May, at the request of Lord Halifax, the Foreign Secretary, George had spoken over the radio to the Italian people, who were still free to 'listen in' if they wished. He spoke of course in Italian, the translation being made by an Italian Jewish ex-professor in the BBC, who also coached George in pronunciation. It was a last appeal, before the guns silenced speech. 'We, and the world with us,' he wrote to me on that day, 'are being punished, this time with terrible severity for the old incorrigible English fault of not adapting policy to armaments, or armaments to policy. *All* parties are to blame for it.' As for Italy herself, he knew, from his visits there in the last three years, that there was no popular wish there to have a war with us and that it was the Germans, not the British, who were hated and feared.

So, in his broadcast appeal to the Italian people, he recalled first the old, happy days—'the happiest part of my life'—when he travelled through Italy, collecting materials for the Life of Garibaldi, and 'following on foot the marches of your national hero, who so greatly loved England and whom England so greatly loved'; and then his three and a half years of service on the Italian front in the war, 'carrying your wounded in ambulances of the Croce Rossa Britannica'. During that war Italy had fought, with England and France, to prevent a German hegemony in Europe and had rejected all Germany's attempts to win her over. Now the broad outlines were the same, but, if Germany won, 'the pride and cruelty with which she will use her dominance will be even more odious than if Kaiser Wilhelm had won the war in 1915. . . We have this time seen the cruel murder of Denmark, Norway and Holland . . . and the treatment of the Poles shows how all other races are to be treated when Germans covet their lands.' Would Germany, he asked the Italians, be a safe partner with whom to share Europe and Africa after everyone else had been destroyed? Italy, he admitted, had some valid grievances against us, and England had been much too slow to perceive Europe's danger. But she was awake at last and America too was awakening, and if Germany did not win this summer (1940) she would never win at all. Italy and England, he said, 'are joint inheritors of a more civilised and noble culture, deriving largely from old Rome and mediaeval Italy, and a more subtle and broad psychology than these Germans who understand nothing but the material might of Germany and her right to crush and trample on everyone else.'

His appeal was made just before the German advance into

229

Belgium and France, and their speedy overthrow, but it came too late, and the Italians had to pay for Mussolini's mistakes through the appalling experience in 1943 of being themselves invaded and held down by German troops until the British slowly released them, aided by the heroism of their own peasants and guerrillas whom Fascism could not terrorise or destroy.

He felt deeply also the invasion and conquest of Holland—that little country which had led Europe in religious toleration, good government and civilised living when most other states were torn by religious and civil strife and with which over the last three hundred years we had often had such close ties in peace and in war. Churchill had just become Prime Minister, and on May 11th 1940, before Holland was finally overwhelmed, George wrote to *The Times*, recalling, as his historical learning well enabled him to do, the importance of the Dutch military record in resisting tyranny and preserving the freedom of Europe. He reminded his readers how the great Dutch army built up by William III, 'was one of the two or three decisive factors in the wars that our new Prime Minister has told so well—wars named after his great ancestor, Holland's greatest ally (John Churchill, Duke of Marlborough). The courage and skill of the Dutch in defending their country has in the past been proved on land as well as on water, in the open field as well as on dykes and behind the walls of starving towns.

'This war is full of bitterness. The thought of Norwegian mountains in the power of the dog is scarcely more bitter than the thought of the lovely old brick streets of Holland, full of art, civilization and history, crumbling under bombs. But if freedom died in Europe, what would even they any longer be worth?'

Most fortunately for him, before this terrible year, 1940, was over he had been offered and had accepted a post which fully occupied his mind and all his practical faculties for the rest of his working life. On 27 September Winston Churchill, now Prime Minister, asked him to be Master of Trinity. When the old Master, Sir Joseph Thomson, died, the Trinity dons had felt inclined to ask to have the mastership left in abeyance 'for the duration', as the Vice-Master, Winstanley, was perfectly acceptable to them as acting Master and Winston's choice might not be so. George agreed with this view, but 'wisest Fate said No'. Churchill absolutely refused to postpone an appointment, and after consulting with Baldwin offered it to George. The dons urged him to accept and he himself felt that it would be ungracious and even 'cowardly and lazy' to refuse. His war job at the Regional Commissioner's had faded out; Hallington was shut to him; and he could no longer feel that writing books was 'good enough' by itself in this awful crisis. So he accepted, and what he called 'the struggle for the occupation and beautification of the Lodge before the bomb comes', began, and continued for many months, though they began living in parts of it from early January 1941. 'Perhaps,' he said with a wry smile, 'I shall be "buried in the ruins of my palace" like the Bishop of Bath and Wells in the great storm of 1703.' This disaster did not occur—though the wife of one of his greatest friends in Cambridge, Donald Robertson the Professor of Greek, was killed while fire-watching in Jesus Lane near by. They were able to maintain a domestic staff sufficient to allow of receiving visitors and 'evacuees' including Dorothy Ward, who was bombed out of her London home. Janet instituted Saturday afternoon tea-parties—a sort of open house—and a Christmas party for the choristers. She also managed to give occasional bucketsful of coal-dust to freezing undergraduates in the fierce winter of 1946-47! Vegetables and fruit were supplied largely from Hallington, but also from the garden of the Lodge in which grew some wonderful apple trees. In the autumn of 1941 these were loaded with apples, and George, said my mother, 'climbed up a tall ladder like a steeple-jack and got them all off in about an hour.'

Hallington meanwhile from 1942 onwards had become a small hospital for convalescent soldiers, and George and Janet fitted up and furnished the cottage which he had built there for a married gardener and which at present was not needed for that purpose, so that he was no longer cut off from his little estate and from Housesteads, and was able to go there for occasional shoots in winter. George was pleased when in 1944 some wounded from the Normandy beaches were sent there, and the men liked its peace and quiet.

One of his tasks during the war, and one in which he took great pleasure, was that of conducting parties of American servicemen and other visitors round the College. Their appreciation of these expeditions encouraged him to write a small book—*Trinity College, an Historical Sketch*—which was published in 1943. In the Preface he said that it was 'meant primarily for Trinity men, old or young, who know as little about Trinity now as I did when I came up in 1893 and, looking round the Great Court and the Cloisters, wished that someone would tell me something about them.' Ten years after his death it was reprinted, with some additional material, by Dr Robson the Senior Tutor.

George Trevelyan while he was Master habitually attended Chapel on Sunday evenings, and once, in 1945, he preached. His sermon, or rather his address, was by request on 'Religion and Poetry'—and dealt, as might have been expected, less with religious poetry as such, than with the essential message of all great poetry—that there is in the spiritual and imaginative power of man something which 'forbids him to take a purely material view of the world, and gives him glimpses of something divine, either external to, or immanent in, nature and humankind.' Three English poets especially, he said, had felt the presence of the spirit in nature and in man with overwheming intensity—Wordsworth, Shelley and Meredith. Shakespeare did not think in religious terms, but in King Lear—set in a heathen world—he dealt with the power of evil—cruelty and sin doing their worst against goodness and love. But it is goodness that triumphs, in 'the goodness of good people, the all-enduring love of Cordelia, the loyalty of Kent, the power of Edgar to "bear free and patient thoughts"'. The message of Lear is that 'virtue is its own reward', which, however difficult a saying, 'lies at the base of religion and of morality.' In the same way Milton, though he became blind, was able to master his affliction and even to make it the inspiration of his greatest poetry, in the sonnet on his blindness, *Samson Agonistes* and the opening of Book III of *Paradise Lost*. This last he quoted at the end of his address, calling it 'the closest identification of religious feeling and personal experience with pure poetry.'

Soon after becoming Master of Trinity, George had completed his last major work—*English Social History*. He wanted, he told us some time previously, to write a history of England 'without any battles in it'. What he really meant to do, as he said in the Introduction, was 'to imagine the life of our ancestors in such partial light as modern research can afford'—a life that did not depend on 'the well-known names of Kings, Parliaments and wars', but which moved 'like an underground river, obeying its own laws or those of economic change, rather than following the direction of political happenings that move on the surface of life.' His lifetime of study and examinations of the past had shown him

232

that there was in the story of the people 'no clear cut'; 'in everything the old overlaps with the new—in religion, in thought, in family custom.' He had meant to begin at Roman times, but left to the last the part he would find most difficult—the centuries preceding the fourteenth, and started with the age of Chaucer.[7] Then came the war, after he had written most of the six centuries since Chaucer's time, and further research was impossible. In fact, the mid fourteenth century made a very good starting-point, for by that time England had become a nation with one language in which a fine literature was developing; her kings were English, no longer Norman-French, and she was creating her own legal and parliamentary systems. So he tried to tell the story rather like scenes in a play, where the actors and the scenery are partly the same and partly new in each scene. He carried it down in eighteen chapters to the end of Victoria's reign and the 'railway age'.

The book could not be published in England because of shortage of paper and manpower. But Longman's arranged for it to be published in the United States in 1942. The first English edition came out in 1944. The sales were enormous, but the profits, owing to taxation on royalties, were negligible. He was astonished at its popularity. After seven years it had sold nearly four hundred thousand copies.

Lord Briggs, in his Inroduction to the illustrated edition of the *Social History* (Longman, 1978), has revealed that the suggestion of such a work was first made to George Trevelyan by his publisher, Robert Longman. George was at first hesitant at the idea of 'isolating' social history from the political narrative, but when assured that this was the history greatly desired by the public as a sort of companion volume to the *History of England*, he agreed. He had always been at heart a 'social' historian; his first book had been on the Peasants' Revolt. For he had always 'loved the people' since he was a boy at Harrow, and in the *Social History* he showed his love for the English and Scottish people of earlier

[7] It should be noted that a very fine essay entitled 'Social Life in Roman Britain' is included in his *An Autobiography and Other Essays.* From a list at the end of it of 'Books for Further Reading', it looks as though it was intended as the first chapter of the *Social History*, as a similar list is provided at the end of each chapter of that work. It is possible that the succeeding essay: 'The Coming of the Anglo-Saxons', would also have been used in the *Social History*. 'Roman Britain' was given as a lecture over the BBC Third Programme.

times in a manner far more intimate and sympathetic than Macaulay had done a hundred years before in his 'Third Chapter'. Macaulay had been chiefly attracted by the contrasts in all aspects of social life between the Stuart and the Victorian ages; the immense material advance in national wealth and prosperity which he regarded as unmitigated 'progress'. But George loved the past for its poetic quality—both its reality and its mystery. 'Here,' he wrote, 'long before us, dwelt folk as real as we are today, now utterly vanished as we in our turn shall vanish. History can miraculously restore them to our vision and understanding, can tell us a little of what were their hopes and fears, their words and works.'[8] He was not concerned so much with 'progress', being only too well aware that great wealth had brought evil as well as good to his country. What did concern and indeed enthral him was the character and genius of each succeeding epoch as it unfolded itself from the last and gave birth in turn to the next.

The invasion of Italy in 1944, by a British Army, to fight, not Mussolini whose armies had been defeated in Africa and who had by now been deposed, but large forces of very determined Germans, was a time of dreadful apprehension to the historian of Garibaldi's campaigns. In June 1944 he wrote to me: 'I walked so often and with such happiness over all those wooded Alban heights where this terrific battle is now going on. It makes it all the more interesting to me—but—ay de mi!' Would the Germans and the Americans between them destroy Rome, was a question of most anxious import. Early in June the BBC put out a programme, on its European Service, on the value of Rome to Europe and the world. George led off with a short talk on Rome as the capital of Italy, and was followed by the Archbishop of Westminster (Cardinal Hinsley) on Catholic Rome, and the Duke of Wellington on its monuments and art treasures. In the event, Rome was not badly damaged, and the long battle began up central Italy against the slowly retreating Germans. 'By the way,' wrote George, with boyish enthusiasm, 'what fun it was reading of the capture of one place after another in the Lays (of Ancient Rome)—Cora, Velletri, Lanuviana, Ardea etc.' He could still enjoy the news of victories, but he had been well aware, since it became clear that the war in the West would ultimately be won

[8] 'Stray Thoughts on History' (1948) in *Autobiography*, p. 82.

by Britain and America, of the appalling difficulties that would arise, before the war was over, in every liberated country desiring to return to democracy by means of general elections as Churchill had promised. He was sometimes able, during the war, to serve the cause of history and of freedom at the same time. On 12 July 1941 he spoke on the Overseas Programme of the BBC on 'The Nature and Function of History'. 'History,' he said, 'is the entrance to all knowledge of the great achievements of mankind, including the literature and art of past times and distant countries', and of the scientific and mechanical power over nature which has been achieved. To drop history would be to abjure all knowledge of our own past; to falsify it or suppress the real study of it, to teach only what the party in power wishes should be taught, creates the Nazi and Fascist mentality that has brought disaster on the world. History is indeed a study easily abused, and no historian can see more than a very little of the immense field— but provided that historians of different outlooks are free to write and publish, and are conscientious in their search for true facts, the abuse of history in newspapers and by politicians will be held in check, and 'the knowledge of past transactions, coolly viewed from the distance of later years, will provide the best education in life and in politics, broadening the thought and moderating the judgement of men', and so will help to build up the Commonwealth of Man. Such was George Trevelyan's faith, then and always; such the definition of his beloved study which he would fain bequeath to a dark and violent world.

War, as is well known, makes strange bed-fellows. On 30 October 1941 the Master of Trinity presided over an enormous meeting in the Guildhall at Cambridge to support and welcome the Russian alliance. It was called by all the four political clubs in the University from Conservative to Communist, and the Union Jack and Red Flag were both displayed on the platform. 'I took a lot of trouble,' he wrote, 'about the arrangements beforehand and everyone behaved perfectly, both audience and speakers, the lion lying down with the lamb (or tiger). Not a ripple of a row.' He always fervently believed that without Russia we could not possibly have won the war, and at that time the worst of the 'tiger's' misdeeds were still in the womb of time.

Trinity itself played a silent though important part in the preparations for 'D Day' in 1944. A conference of British officers

235

was held there in the last days of March, the Great Court being given up to them, and the front rooms of the master's Lodge forming their headquarters. There General Bucknill coached them for their respective parts, and wrote from the Normandy beaches on 10 June to the Master how he hoped soon to be able to explain to him 'how the plans laid in Trinity helped to mould the course of history'.

In 1946 George reached the age of seventy which, under the new Statutes he had helped to create, was now the retiring age for heads of houses unless they were requested to remain for another five years. In his case the request was made and accepted, so that he was able to enjoy in July 1947, from that position, the fourth centenary of the College's foundation, to which King George VI and Queen Elizabeth came as guests of honour. It was a happy and enjoyable occasion—everyone, wrote Geoffrey Young afterwards 'glowing with enjoyment of it all and in the fashion of celebrating it with such decorum, dignity and good taste.' He also recalled one or two 'moving moments'—as when 'the King and George successively stood before the Henry VIII portrait,[9] each with his "ghosts" behind him, and gave the tremendous sense of historical continuity and of the Trinity inheritance of dignity and service to mankind.' At the lunch the King made an entirely impromptu speech without notes or hesitations.

In the next year, 1948, the University chose General Smuts to succeed Stanley Baldwin as its Chancellor. Again, Trinity was called into action; the lunch, at which Churchill was also present, was held in its halls, and the Master proposed a toast of 'the greatest Cambridge man now living'. For Smuts was not only a great soldier and statesman, but a man of learning as well, a writer on philosophy. In his speech, George reminded his audience of days half a century before, when Smuts's early career 'conducting what the newspapers used to call "British mishaps", had in it a touch of Garibaldi, while his subsequent statesmanship has had in it more than a touch of Cavour and Lincoln—though never of Bismarck.' Through all the dreadful years of the twentieth century, 'of which the keynote has been hatred, strife and tyranny, he has stood for the opposite of those things, under circumstances of great difficulty on his side of the globe.' And in all his

[9] The great portrait in the Hall.

doings in world affairs, the new Chancellor had used his influence 'for peace where possible, for freedom always'.

It was always a matter of delight to George Trevelyan that Trinity had been the home of Sir Isaac Newton in his earlier years, and had fostered and promoted his genius and that of his first pupils. So, when the Royal Society met at Cambridge in 1946, he the historian welcomed the men of science to Trinity, reminding them how 'the acceptance of Newtonian studies as the chief part of the Cambridge curriculum in the eighteenth century was largely due to the lead given by Trinity College.'

In the spring of 1947 he and Janet at length paid their last visit to Italy—as she emerged from her long enslavement to Fascism. They went to Rome, empty of visitors because travel restrictions made it difficult for the English to come, and the Germans—who had been everywhere when they were last there in 1939—had not yet re-arrived. 'It is to-day Roma degli Italiani,' he wrote . . . 'The Piazza di Spagna, where Macaulay in 1838 saw forty coaches of the English nobility . . . has nothing English about it now . . . It is pleasant to see, in place of fascist and *duce* symbols and monuments, electoral appeals to people to vote for the "blocco popolare" with Garibaldi's picture on the posters and marble monuments—quite a lot—to the martyrs of the Resistance.' In Florence they met many Resistance movement people, Italian and English. 'It was a very fine affair,' he said, 'in the true Garibaldian spirit, and supported by the universal loyalty (to death) of the contadini [peasants] just like those who saved Garibaldi in 1849.'

He had not been forgotten by the Italians. Ten years later he was made an honorary member of the 'Institute for the History of the Risorgimento' whose President, Alberto Ghisalberti, he had met at Villa Trento forty years before. Old now and beginning to go blind, George wrote to him, saying he could no longer hope to see again 'my dear Italy. But I have always in my mind and heart those scenes so dearly loved' which he had traversed on foot or bicycle in youth from Marsala to Venice and the Alps, searching out things Garibaldian with an enthusiasm which, he said, 'still remains'.[10]

---

[10] I am grateful to the Instituto per la Storia del Risorgimento for a copy of this letter, which he wrote in Italian in his own hand.

X

Last Words

The post-war world, towards which George had looked with so much doubt and foreboding, reassured him somewhat as far as England was concerned. Churchill was dismissed by the general election of July 1945, and George was not altogether sorry. 'I should as soon see Labour win as not,' George had written in May . . . 'I think if we are to go on getting coal the mines must be nationalized: the miners won't work during the Jap. war under a Conservative government.' It was a different matter of course in Eastern Europe dominated by Stalin's Russia, and he thought we and America had blundered badly 'to undertake responsibilities in Berlin without control of communications. It was midsummer madness.' Meanwhile in Cambridge he laboured to get the civil servants out of New Court at Trinity in time to put the flood of new undergraduates in—nine tenths of them were veterans. It was 'a neck and neck thing,' he said, but was accomplished just in time. When term began all the freshmen were welcomed to the Lodge with an address by the Master about the College and its buildings, and 'light refreshments' provided by the indefatigable hostess. And by Christmas 1945 the hospital had left Hallington which was thus ready to receive back its stored furniture and be opened once more to friends, cousins and now grandchildren. The *Social History* was also ready, in its tens of thousands, for publication in England and the great cheque for £27,000 arrived from Longman's in May, 1947. But of this sum, £25,000 was at once put aside into a special account for paying the taxes which the Labour Chancellor would exact!

All indeed seemed set for a happy old age, when the blow of Janet's illness fell early in 1949. It proved to be a kind of arterial sclerosis which gradually completely crippled her powers of walking, besides affecting her memory of recent, though not of long-

238

past events. From that time onwards George seldom left her, but she was just able to manage the journey by road to Hallington in the summer, and in fact she died there in September 1956. Those who watched that long-drawn tragedy said that they had never seen anything quite like George's devotion, his total self-giving to her needs and wishes.

But in the earlier stages of her illness, before it became too acute for concentrated thought, she accomplished, on George's suggestion and with his help and Dorothy's, a remarkable piece of work. Long before, in the two years that followed Theo's death, she had written in loving detail the story of his little life. It was privately printed and given as a memorial of him to those who had known him. Writing was in her blood as it was in George's, and besides a memoir of her mother, Mrs Humphry Ward, she wrote *A Short History of the Italian People*—a task which took her many years, as it had to be fitted in with her public activities and with home and family life. It was published in 1920. And now in these years of weakness she was able to set down the story of the saving of the 'Foundling Site',[1] with all its frustrations and anxieties, and its final success. It was published in 1954, by Longman's, with the title *Two Stories*, the first story being Theo's life.

In 1951 the Mastership finally ended and they returned to their former house, Garden Corner. A total change of abode would by that time have been unwelcome to George; familiar scenes and familiar faces became more and more dear. But he was not inactive. In 1951 he became Chancellor of Durham University which at that time included King's College, Newcastle. Nearly forty years before, in 1912, when he was but a young historian, Durham had given him an honorary doctorate—the first of many he was to receive. Now as Chancellor, he was allowed to choose the honorary graduates in his first year of office. He made it an occasion for honouring some old friends—Claude Elliott the Provost of Eton; Professor Adrian who would soon succeed him as Master of Trinity; Professor Dover Wilson whose Shakespearian studies were after his own heart; and his fellow-historian G. N. Clark, the Provost of Oriel. He also conferred one on Dorothy Sayers whose detective fiction had given him great pleasure and amusement.

At Durham he was lodged in the Judges' quarters of the Castle.

[1] See above p. 221.

'To go to my bathroom,' he said, 'I pass through five feet of passage cut in the ancient Norman wall. The amount of ancient masonry on this acropolis is wonderful indeed. Those Normans!'

He was as mentally vigorous as ever and before he left Trinity he had begun writing again. First came a very short autobiography—undertaken, he said, 'to record those circumstances that affected the production of my books.'[2] It was published, with several other essays, in 1949 by Longman and is eminently readable. And in this first year of his retirement he produced a delightful picture-book. He had always loved the political cartoons of 'H.B.'—John Doyle, the father of 'Dickie' Doyle the great illustrator and creator of the original cover of *Punch*. John Doyle's was an entirely new style of political cartoon, not savage and coarse like those of Gillray and Cruickshank, but kindly, humorous and not in the least partisan. His portraits of politicians were not caricatures but sensitive and accurate likenesses. Out of the great number of his drawings George chose sixty-two which illustrated the era of the Reform Bill of 1832—the premierships of Grey and Melbourne. He called it *The Seven Years of William IV*, writing a general introduction on the political events, and also a detailed description of each cartoon. These descriptions reveal his remarkable knowledge of all the political figures portrayed, even those of minor importance, and also the zest and pleasure he still took in his old age in the story of the victory of the Whig aristocracy and its alliance both with radicals and the conservative-minded middle class, which he had chronicled so lovingly thirty years before in *Lord Grey of the Reform Bill*.[3]

Then in 1952 his mind turned to the loves of his youth—Carlyle and Meredith. Both had fallen out of fashion and he wondered whether he could rekindle, for the younger generation, by means of selections from their writings, a sense of their genius and art. *Carlyle: An Anthology* appeared in 1953. In it he was able, by the selections from *Past and Present*, from *Cromwell*, and above all *The French Revolution*, to show how Carlyle had taught him that history is not statistics or constitutional documents, though these have their part in it, but a living scene, 'pulsing with life', full of the passions and faiths and fears of men. The passages

[2] *An Autobiography and Other Essays*, Longman, 1949.
[3] *The Seven Years* was published by the Avalon Press, in association with William Heinemann. The fine collotype plates were printed in Holland by L. van Leer and Co.

he chose are long enough to give a good idea both of Carlyle's narrative methods and of his extraordinary insight into the way men's passions work and break forth in terrible or memorable events. Carlyle, George believed, had indeed a most wonderful understanding of the 'psychology of the mob'—for example in the critical days of the French Revolution—and of the psychology too of one great leader of men, Oliver Cromwell, and of the passions and beliefs of the people he led, in the greatest conflict of their history. George showed Carlyle besides as a great writer of poetic prose—he was an imaginative artist with poetic qualities like a great Hebrew prophet. He did not take sides politically; his *French Revolution* (the event not fifty years old when it was written) is, said George, 'a striking example of the value of history written with the least possible amount of prejudice.' And it reads 'like the reports of a very unusual type of journalist analysing the emotions of Paris from day to day.'

The Meredith selections[4] are likewise on a generous scale. The 'deplorable state of things' which had allowed Meredith's poems to fall out of print except for a recent edition of *Modern Love* edited by Cecil Day Lewis, prompted him to bring out about a third of the total of the poet's writings, in the hope, as he said, of enabling other lovers of poetry to judge if Meredith, who had meant so much to him, could mean anything to them. Although primarily a poet of Nature and Man like Wordsworth, Meredith was also, like Wordsworth, a severe and discerning critic of his own country. He, who knew Germany before 1870, realised how dangerous a rival she would be to the island kingdom off her shores and how formidable would be the task of preserving British independence and freedom. Like Carlyle, Meredith saw deep into historical reality. Unlike him, he did not, in his later years, fall into the error of thinking that only despots like Frederick the Great could save the world.

In 1953 George gave the Clark Lectures in Cambridge, being invited to do so by the Council of Trinity College, which had founded them. He chose for his theme one in which he could feel perfectly free and at home, and he gave the six lectures the title of 'A Layman's Love of Letters'. 'For this purpose,' he said at the beginning, 'I am only a layman—a "lewd man" as Chaucer

---

[4] *Selected Poetical Works of George Meredith, compiled with some Notes by G. M. Trevelyan, O.M.,* 1958. He had previously, in 1912, edited a complete edition of the poems.

would call me—not a professional scholar and critic at all.' As the Clark lectures were usually given by some authoritative scholar in English literature, Trinity's invitation had surprised and moved him. He certainly enjoyed himself in writing them,[5] and intended through them to help his hearers to find in literature, both prose and poetry, the highest form of enjoyment. He did this partly by plenteous quotation, from Shelley, Keats and Byron, from Scott and the Border Ballads, from Meredith and Housman, and from his two poet-friends, Geoffrey Young and Margaret Cropper, but also by well-directed argument and disagreement with some critics on the merits of some of his poet-heroes, particularly Matthew Arnold on Shelley and Keats, Raymond Mortimer on Kipling, and E. M. Forster on Scott. By quoting from their criticisms he could give point to his own admirations. 'Yes,' he wrote to me after the first lecture, 'I shall have two controversies against debunking, but not quarrels. I must defend the better parts of Kipling from the complete condemnation by Raymond Mortimer, but fortunately R.M. has written well against the debunkers of Browning, so I have said as much for him as against him and foresee no quarrel. In the case of E. M. Forster's total condemnation of Scott—especially of the Scottish novels— I shall avoid a quarrel by extreme politeness and by praising (quite honestly) the parts of E.M.F.'s own works which I have always liked.'

He achieved these objects very successfully, especially by his defence of Scott, which consisted chiefly of quotations from *The Antiquary* and *Guy Mannering*. Scott had not only created the historical novel—he had shown it alive with flesh and blood human beings—'a fair field full of *folk*', and so had 'written social history in his novels', and opened the door to 'two young men, both of Scottish origin', Macaulay and Carlyle, who because of what Scott had done were able in their own work to make social history a proper part of the historian's task. Perhaps the most fascinating and original of the lectures was the one he called 'The Uses of Geography in Poetry', where he discusses Satan's flight from Hell to Earth in *Paradise Lost*, the wonderful use of Latin and Italian place-names in Macaulay's *Lays of Ancient Rome*, and in Tennyson's *The Daisy*, and shows how Germanic names can be equally effective in prose, by quoting a speech of Uncle

[5] They were published by Longman, as *A Layman's Love of Letters*, in 1954.

Toby's in *Tristram Shandy* on Marlborough's march across Germany to the battlefields of Blenheim.

At the end he spoke out on what he believed to be the essential nature of great literature. 'It is not a set of intellectual conundrums to be solved by certain rules. It is joy, joy in our inmost heart. It is a passion like love or it is nothing.' And to the young people gathered round him he appealed to open the gates of joy and enter. 'While you are young and all the poets are around you waiting to be read, find out what you can love, seeking joy in the springtime, and love it . . . What an immense and variegated landscape is stretched around you for your delight. It is all free for you to search, of infinite variety in its appeal, from comic prose to the highest poetry, all the ages of England and all the moods of her most remarkable men set down in words inspired. It is all your heritage.'

As old age drew on, he looked at it calmly and without regret. 'Now that I am getting really old,' he wrote from Hallington in 1951, 'I walk much less; and my pleasure in the walled garden, the dene and above all the terrace is a much greater element in my happiness here. And I spend much more time simply looking at the view south, which satisfies me so completely.' Inwardly also he was at peace, in spite of his horror at what men's evil passions had brought on the world during his lifetime. 'I think,' he wrote to me in this same year 1951, 'what matters most is not what people *believe* but what they love and admire, and there I think you and I come together very much—even apart from our common feelings about W.W.' (Wordsworth). Like Wordsworth, he lived 'by admiration, hope and love.' Besides Hallington and Northumberland, Cambridge, and especially Trinity, ministered to his recognition of these needs of his soul. One day he was showing a friend of mine round Trinity. He took her up to the altar in the chapel and made her look back at Newton's statue from there, with the light shining down on the upturned face. Afterwards she wrote: 'He looked at it for a moment and then said gruffly: "That always seems to me to mean something —the unity of science and religion perhaps"—and then he stumped off down the aisle as if he had said too much.'

After the Meredith *Selections* he wrote no more for publication. From about the time of Janet's death his eyesight began seriously to fail, so that the library of beloved books at Hallington, to which he looked for companionship in old age, gradually became almost useless to him. His friends marvelled at his patience—serenity almost—under his affliction.

Hallington was more beloved than ever, and he spent more time there, sometimes four or five summer months at a stretch. He wanted it to be the chief home of his old age, but Cambridge too was dear, and when there he continued to dine in Hall on Sundays and to walk in the Fellows' Garden with some chosen companion who could guide his steps when he became too blind to see where he was going. From the end of the war onwards Humphry and his family lived at Trumpington; he had become Reader in German and a Fellow of King's, greatly to George's pleasure, for he had always had many friends in King's. For John and myself life was centred on Chichester, where from 1946 onwards John ran the Theological College and wrote his *History of the Church in England,* which is almost a companion volume to George's own *History of England.* This pleased his father-in-law greatly. I meanwhile had started writing a biography of William Wordsworth, which gave him great and lasting interest. The first volume, published in 1957, he could read to himself with the help of a magnifying glass; the second I read aloud to him as it was written, each time I came to Cambridge, and just succeeded in finishing it before he died. On these last visits I usually found him lying on the sofa, taking comfort from the many poems he knew by heart and did not need to read. Friends from Trinity, King's and other colleges came regularly to see him and to read aloud to him. It was a wonderful ministry. From Trinity came Jim Butler and George Kitson Clark, both historians, to read history, including his own *English Social History;* Noël Annan and George Rylands from King's read poetry and especially Shakespeare; Sidney Roberts, the great Johnsonian, read Boswell; J. H. Plumb from Christ's, again history. His nurse-companion, Elizabeth Thomas, read to him indefatigably during six years from the Bible, *The Pilgrim's Progress,* and from his favourite novelists—Scott, Dickens, Trollope, Wilkie Collins and John Buchan. She also read Winston Churchill's *History of the English-Speaking Peoples,* the whole of Macaulay's works and his own *England in the Reign of Anne.* One day a niece asked him whether he still thought *Anne* just as good as when he first wrote it. 'Yes,' he replied, 'just.'

There was no definable illness at the end; he grew gradually weaker, but his mind never failed. His well-beloved cousin, Phil

Price, came to see him only a week before he died. Phil was well into his seventies, but still hunted—a fact which impressed George deeply with admiration and surprise. They spoke then of the last volume of the *Cambridge Modern History,* just out, with the ominous title 'The Age of Violence'. 'Yes,' said George, 'the last sixty years have been an age of violence. It began with the Boer War, when the Tory Imperialists still thought it possible to expand the Empire and step-up British immigration into South Africa till there was an English-speaking majority. But it did not come off. The age of Imperialism was ending. Social reform at home—old age pensions and unemployment insurance—begun by the Liberals and accepted by the Conservatives, had made it unnecessary for people to seek their fortunes overseas. Imperialism was dying but before it died it brought on in its death struggles two terrible World Wars. It has been indeed an age of violence.' 'It was the last time I heard him speak,' wrote Phil, 'and it was a perfect example of his great power of looking into the heart of historical events and penetrating into their causes with long-sighted vision.'

George Kitson Clark, his fellow-historian of the younger generation in nineteenth century history, saw him for the last time about three weeks before he died. 'He was,' he wrote afterwards to Humphry, 'very much more himself than he had been for a long time. His simplicity and candour, always some of his most attractive characteristics, shone out: so did his boyish cheerfulness which somehow had mysteriously returned to him.' Elinor Winthrop Young—now a widow (for Geoffrey had died in 1958)—came and they talked of old times. '*What* good times they have been!' said George slowly as she went away. And indeed he had had a happy life, in his work, in his achievement, above all in his friends and family. Even its one supreme sorrow, Theo's death, had lost its bitterness, for Theo's life, he said, had been 'something given'.

He died on 21 July 1962. On the day before he died Elizabeth Thomas read to him some of Macaulay's Third Chapter. Perhaps as she did so, his memory went back to that time when his mother first read it to him as he lay, a little boy of eight, on the hearth-rug in the Library at Wallington. The love from which his life's work had sprung was with him at the end.

His ashes were buried beside Janet's in Theo's grave in Langdale churchyard, as he had always wished, 'beneath the bracken and the rocks'. And high on the wall of the barn at Side House in Upper Langdale, where his friends had gathered to dedicate the little farm to his memory on that stormy afternoon in 1965[6] a slab of Westmorland greenslate was inserted, with an inscription telling how he had loved Langdale 'above all other places.' And indeed it was, as he had said long ago, 'the place of his heart.'

[6] See p. 218 above.

For George Trevelyan's 80th Birthday

The Fells speaking:
>   We remember this man, there's scarcely one amongst us
>   That hasn't felt his quick step running in youth,
>   Yet he was most our own as his age drew on,
>   And our spacious wisdom became bone of his bone.
>   He was of our kind, there was rock and fern in his being,
>   Tenderness too, like the little treasures we harbour.
>   Snow capped is he at last? but the sky that blesses
>   The white topped hill is the blue of our kindest hope.
>   We remember this man.

The Farms speaking:
>   We remember this man, he was welcome when he came,
>   And sat down famishing for a giant's supper.
>   He wasn't a stranger to shippon and cobbled yard,
>   Or the dignity of solid walls and beams;
>   He felt them in his heart, like one of our own:
>   We remember this man.

The Streams speaking:
>   We remember this man, we leaping turbulent singers,
>   We'd make him a lullaby as the dusk drew on,
>   And all was hidden but the last white flash
>   In the ghyll, and at last all sounds were still but our voices,
>   That will never be still, though we shrink from the fierce glory
>   Of foam and speed to the softest of soft whispers.
>   We've quenched his thirst and cooled his tired head,
>   He knew the chill of us over the naked limbs.
>   We remember this man.

The Creatures speaking:
> We remember this man, I the wide-winged buzzard
> Swinging from peak to peak, and I the herdwick
> Making my way up the sheep track that he followed;
> And I, the wild fell pony, and I, the calf
> In the dusky hull; and I, the curlew
> Crying my broken note with its throbbing fall;
> And I, the lamb by the hearth in the flagged kitchen:
> He was our friend; he saw us with watchful eyes.
>   We remember this man.

> We remember this man, though many springs have gone by,
> And the years that bring their griefs and their sudden glories;
> We think that he often comes and goes amongst us,
> And in his spirit's hoard we have our place:
>   He remembers us all.

Margaret Cropper. 1956

Index

250

252